# Learning and Awareness

# The Educational Psychology Series

## Robert J. Sternberg, Series Editor

**Marton/Booth** • *Learning and Awareness*

# Learning and Awareness

**Ference Marton**
*Göteborg University*
**Shirley Booth**
*Chalmers University of Technology*

**LEA** LAWRENCE ERLBAUM ASSOCIATES, PUBLISHERS
1997  Mahwah, New Jersey

Cover design by Kathryn Houghtaling

*About the cover:* The painting is "Mukati Dreaming," by
Dorothy Napangardi, partially reproduced here in black and
white. It is owned by Birgitta Marton and was photographed
for use on the cover by Otto Prohászka. Permission to use
the art was granted on behalf of the artist by the Gallery
Gondwana, Alice Springs.

Lawrence Erlbaum Associates, Inc., Publishers
10 Industrial Avenue
Mahwah, New Jersey 07430


**Library of Congress Cataloging-in-Publication Data**


Marton, Ference.
Learning and awareness/Ference Marton, Shirley Booth.
p.    cm.
Includes bibliographical references and index.
ISBN 0-8058-2454-5 (cloth : alk. paper). — ISBN
0-8058-2455-3 (pbk. : alk. paper)
1.Learning, Psychology of.  2. Awareness.  Teaching.
I. Booth, Shirley (Shirley A.)   II. Title.
LB1060.M338  1997
370.15'23—dc20                              96-46002
                                                            CIP

Printed in the United States of America
10  9  8  7  6  5  4  3

# Contents

# Prologue

Welcome. We hope that you are about to read the book that we, as we write these words, are on the point of completing. Maybe you are standing in a library, browsing in a book shop, sitting in front of the fire, or in your air-conditioned office. Wherever, you seem to have been moved to open the book, presumably curious as to what might be in it. Let us set the scene.

The book is about learning, not learning in all its shapes and forms, but learning in a particular sense—learning as coming to experience the world, or aspects of the world, in particular ways. We give priority to the notion of experience, a notion that we develop successively throughout the book. The research that is described actually seeks the variation in ways in which people experience situations and phenomena in their worlds, generally studied with an educational research interest. Ways of experiencing things are described in terms of the structure of awareness, a word used synonymously with consciousness. But beware that in our research specialization, which we call *phenomenography*, awareness or consciousness does not carry the same connotations it does in certain other fields. These ideas are also developed in the course of the book.

In all modesty, it was never our aim to write a modest book. Indeed, we make a couple of claims that might be seen as bold. We claim, for instance, to have identified what for two millennia has been the major obstacle to man[1] gaining important insights into the nature of learning of the kind we are interested in. In so doing, we claim to have arrived at a better understanding of learning, and hope that you will do so too.

---

[1]We have also been quite bold in our use of gender-specific words. Here "man" is used in its sense of "all persons over time"; elsewhere we have referred to individuals with male or female pronouns as we felt appropriate. We feel quite comfortable with this, because in Swedish the word for "man" is also the indefinite pronoun "one," whereas the word for "person" (människa") takes the otherwise largely obsolete feminine pronoun. We hope that our readers are also comfortable with it.

Let us offer a taste of what is to come. Learning—in the sense of gaining knowledge about the world—is frequently seen as a progression that starts with acquiring some basic facts (where facts are seen as pieces of valid, elementary knowledge) and goes on through building ever more complex and advanced forms of knowledge out of, or on the grounds of, simpler forms. Although learning does work like this in some cases, and can be forced to work like it in others, we do not believe it to be the prototypical path to learning. In our view, learning proceeds, as a rule, from an undifferentiated and poorly integrated understanding of the whole to an increased differentiation and integration of the whole and its parts. Thus, learning does not proceed as much from parts to wholes as from wholes to parts, and from wholes to wholes. To put it very simply, in order to learn about something you have to have some idea of what it is you are learning about.

The initial undifferentiated and unintegrated wholes that the learner grasps when embarking on learning something are likely to appear confused and erroneous when judged against the criteria of received wisdom. But on closer examination—and such closer examination will be going on throughout this book—these wholes, the learner's initial ideas, turn out to be partial rather than wrong. They are the seeds from which valid knowledge can grow. If we apply that message to the reading of this book, it means that all your previous experience of learning is the whole, and yet partial, and your readiness to look at it in an open way is your main resource when it comes to gaining insights into what we have to offer, provided that there are such insights to be found, of course.

We have tried to write this book in agreement with our view of what it takes to learn. We are not opening with a list of definitions of concepts that will be used later on, nor are we identifying all the facts, terms, and conditions of the work from the outset. We prefer to foreshadow concepts by introducing them first in a less than developed form—often through examples—and elaborating on them at appropriate points. We take up other traditions of research into learning (admittedly to a limited extent), not to provide a supporting framework for our arguments, but rather to highlight what differentiates our perspective from the alternatives and hence throw our arguments into relief.

The ideas that you meet in this book, you meet *throughout* this book. No one part can stand alone. In fact, we have developed our own ideas considerably in the course of writing this book, and we hope that the reader will do so too. Structure and meaning are interwoven; principles are related to examples, and these are used to bring out foundations and generalizations. There are progressions in the book that reflect our own way of understanding—from the whole to the parts and back to the whole, from learning to teaching and back again to learning. There are threads to be followed, ideas that are be developed little by little, questions to be asked here, and answers to be sought there. By reading the whole book—maybe focusing more on the things that interest you most, but all the time relating ideas to examples, being open to development of ideas that you already have met earlier—we hope that you will come to experience learning in the way that we do. In other words, we hope you will learn about learning.

In a peculiar way everything is everywhere in this presentation. Such a book is difficult to write, and we are afraid that it will be a bit difficult to read. But it is great fun to have written it, and we hope that it will be great fun to have read it.

So, again, welcome to the book. We leave it to you to judge the extent to which we have achieved our most sincere aim: to bring you to think differently about learning—and to recognize it as a more enlightened and powerful way—than you do as you read these opening words.

*—Ference Marton*
*—Shirley Booth*

# Acknowledgments

It is clear to anyone looking through this book that we have brought together strands in a research program to which many have contributed. We want to start by acknowledging all of those, both named and unnamed, who have participated in the development of the perspective on learning and awareness that we put forward here. It is impossible to distinguish each individual contribution, whether research project, seminar debate, or discussion over lunch, but without them this book would not be written.

Some specific instances of support can, however, be identified. Our home institutions, the Department of Education and Educational Research at Göteborg University and Educational Development at Chalmers University of Technology, have provided the supportive environment needed for any intellectual effort. In particular we thank Kjell Härnqvist whose support was absolutely essential for creating a research environment in which this work could take root and flourish. Thanks also to Agneta Österlund for her indefatigable help and good humor. We wish to thank the Griffith Institute for Higher Education in Brisbane, and particularly Carol Bond and Don Margetson for hosting us while we put together the initial framework for the book; the discussions we had there were stimulating, the view from our office inspiring. Going even further back, the book owes its inception to Andy Hargreaves talking of the need for "a good book on learning"; its subsequent development was not straightforward, but the aim to produce a good book on learning endured.

A number of these people have read parts of the book at various stages and made valuable comments. We wish to thank Anders Berglund, Eva Ekeblad, Márta Fülöp, Dagmar Neuman, Torgny Ottosson, Mike Prosser, Andrew Stephanou, Lennart Svensson and Keith Trigwell for such help. Discussions with colleagues from far and near have offered interesting insights of different kinds, and we thank Roy Booth, Michelle de Courcy, Lars Owe Dahlgren, Noel Entwistle, Lauren Resnick, and Roger Säljö for giving such opportunities. We are most grateful to Christine

Bruce who helped us over the hurdle of forming an index. Richard Snow and an anonymous reviewer have given us yet another opportunity to refine our arguments, and we thank them for their thoughtful and honest appraisals.

We wish to express out gratitude to the Swedish Council for Research in the Humanities and Social Sciences for their financial support at crucial stages in the development of this book.

Last, but of course not least, we wish to thank our respective families for enduring what they did not deserve to endure—late, late nights and many lost weekends—and for offering their peerless help—patience and good cheer.

*—Ference Marton*
*—Shirley Booth*

# 1

# What Does it Take to Learn?

One thing that people have in common is that they are all different. This disturbing sentence—whether considered conceptually or grammatically—boils down to this: People may be created equal, but they do things differently. There are other ways of putting it—for any one of the things people do, some do it better, others do it worse. To the extent they have learned to do that one thing, they must have learned *to do it differently—some better, some worse.* Rather, they have *learned differently—some better, some worse—to do it.* This is the starting point for our book: If one way of doing something can be judged to be better than another way, then some people must have been better at learning to do it—or have learned to do it better—than others.

Now, if we take that as our starting point, can we reasonably hope that by *finding out* what it takes to learn something we can make people dramatically better at learning it or make them learn it dramatically better? In the rest of this book, argue that it is, and point the way to revealing what it takes to learn the multiplicity of things we are expected to learn.

Inasmuch as we can learn different *sorts of things,* the notion of "what it takes to learn" has to be expressed in different forms. The question "What does it take to learn to do something?" is one form, "How do we gain knowledge about the world?" is another. The latter is the question we are going to address explicitly in this chapter. An answer would empower people to gain knowledge, as well as deeper knowledge, about the world, and it is to develop just such an answer, and just such an empowerment that is our goal in writing this book.

## HOW DO WE GAIN KNOWLEDGE ABOUT
## THE WORLD? A STORY OF PARADOXES

"How do we gain knowledge about the world?" can be seen as the epistemological form of the question "What does it take to learn?" Epistemology has to do with the question of gaining knowledge but also with the question of the truth value of the

1

knowledge gained, as, indeed, does education. We are living in an age of relativism, but a fundamental principle we are assuming in this book is that education has norms—norms of what those undergoing education should be learning, and what the outcomes of their learning should be.

## PARADOX THE FIRST: MENO'S PARADOX

We find the most famous formulation of the question "How do we gain knowledge about the world?" in one of Plato's early dialogues, written in 403 or 402 BC, when the author was in his mid-20s, some 3 or 4 years before Socrates calmly drank the cup of poison administered as punishment for his dangerous ideas (Day, 1994, p. 8). The dialogue was between Socrates and Meno, a young Thessalonian visiting Athens, and started with Meno posing the question: "Can one be taught virtue?" Socrates replied that he did not even know what virtue is, and he argued that neither did Meno. Socrates suggested that they embark upon a search for an answer together, but Meno puts forward an objection that has become known as Meno's paradox: "How can you search for something when you do not know what it is? You do not know what to look for, and if you were to come across it you would not recognize it as what you are looking for." Socrates agreed with this objection, and elaborated:

> It's impossible for a person to search either for what he knows or what he doesn't.... He couldn't search for what he knows, for he knows it and no one in that condition needs to search; on the other hand he couldn't search for what he doesn't know, for he won't even know what to search for. (Day, 1994, p. 47)

The surprising answer of Plato—or Socrates— to the question "How do we gain knowledge about the world?" is that we *cannot* gain knowledge about the world. Learning is impossible. The paradox lies in the observation that we certainly do learn!

There is an obvious counterargument to this line of reasoning: Meno's paradox may be valid as far as *searching* for knowledge is concerned, but surely we can learn by being *told*? However, Plato had already ruled out this solution in an earlier dialogue with Protagoras on the grounds that if you do not already know a teacher's assertion when you are told it, then you cannot decide whether it is true or false. Moreover, it is impossible to choose a teacher who knows, on the same grounds as the impossibility of finding knowledge by oneself (Day, 1994, p. 26).

Plato—again using Socrates as mouthpiece—suggested another solution to the apparent paradox, his theory of recollection, which has it that the human soul is immortal even if the human body is not. The soul is reembodied again and again, going repeatedly from one life to the next. All knowledge is laid down in the soul prior to the series of lives. It is then forgotten by its current vessel but is there to be recollected. Learning is such a recollection. Knowledge thus does not originate from the world or, from the outside, but from the immortal soul or, from within. In the course of his dialogue with Meno, Socrates wished to demonstrate that knowledge is innate and called in a young slave boy who was able to count but was ignorant of geometry. Socrates gave him a geometrical problem: to find the length of a side of a square, the area of which is twice the area of a given square. The boy's first answer was wrong, but Socrates managed to act as midwife and draw forth the answer by putting questions that repeatedly showed the inherent contradictions in the boy's way of reasoning. Socrates' method amounts to breaking the problem down into component parts and prompting answers to each part separately, an instance of his famous midwifing, or maieutic, pedagogical method resembling the teaching strategy that in modern educational research has been called *piloting* (Johansson, 1975; Lundgren, 1977). By doing so he claimed to have shown that the knowledge necessary to solve the problem was there in the boy's soul from the beginning, a remnant from some previous embodiment, because the boy did not previously know any geometry.

On hearing what Socrates did we are tempted to rebuff his claim that knowledge comes from within. He did, after all, ask questions, show diagrams, and firmly guide the boy's thinking. But he did not hand over the answers; the boy had to arrive at them using his powers of reason, and in that sense one could argue that knowledge may indeed be gained from within oneself (Day, 1994, p. 23). This does not imply, however, that Socrates presented strong support for the theory of recollection and that he had solved Meno's paradox. As White (1994) convincingly showed, the theory of recollection gives rise to a paradox that is a mirror image of Meno's paradox, which it was supposed to solve. Just as you cannot search for knowledge in the world outside, you cannot recollect knowledge from within. That which is already recollected you do not need to recollect; and that which is not recollected you cannot recollect because you do not know what you are trying to recollect. Indeed, if you were to come upon it, you would not know that it is what you want to recollect.

Thus Plato did not solve the paradox he had formulated. Nor did anyone else (for some fairly recent and less than convincing attempts from the field of education see Bereiter, 1985; Halldén, 1994; Petrie, 1981; Steffe, 1991).

## PARADOX AVOIDED: BEHAVIORAL PSYCHOLOGY

Some 23 centuries after Plato formulated the paradox of learning—Meno's paradox—learning became an object of research in psychology. Let us take, for example, the pioneering work of Herman Ebbinghaus. His aim was to study memory in a "pure" form—"pure" in the sense of being free from meaningful associations; but in order to study memory it was necessary for someone to learn the stuff that would have to be remembered later. Ebbinghaus prepared lists of pairs of meaningless syllables, and submitting himself to the task of being his own experimental subject, he learned to answer with one of the syllables in a pair when the other was given. His main interest was to find out the extent to which he would be able to recall the missing syllables after different intervals of time. This study was published in 1885 (Ebbinghaus, 1885/1964) and can be viewed in part as a study of learning, or at least of one form of learning—becoming increasingly able to recall something as a function of practice—but nobody would claim that Ebbinghaus had studied how we gain knowledge about the world.

Ivan Pavlov, the Russian Nobel laureate in Medicine in 1904, discovered and studied quite another form of learning (Pavlov, 1927). An organism has a repertoire of innate reflexes: Certain stimuli trigger off certain responses. A toddler starts at a sudden sharp sound; one's pupils dilate when a bright light is shone on them; a hungry mammal salivates more when exposed to the smell or sight of food. Concerning such reactions we talk of unconditioned stimuli resulting in unconditioned responses. What Pavlov found was that if another stimulus is repeatedly presented shortly before the unconditioned stimulus, then eventually a reaction very similar to the unconditioned response will be triggered off by this introduced stimulus. For example, a hungry dog salivates more (unconditioned response) when shown food (unconditioned stimulus). If its keeper repeatedly rings a bell before revealing the food, then increased salivation will eventually be brought about by the sound of the bell alone. The sound of the bell is called a conditioned stimulus, and now the salivation is a conditioned response, being brought about, not by natural reflex, but solely by the sound of the bell.

The father of *behaviorism*, John Watson, applied the same principle in a famous study in which he caused a toddler, Albert, to develop a fear of furry animals (Watson, 1924). When Albert heard a loud noise he reacted naturally with fear: The sound was the unconditioned stimulus that brought about the unconditioned response of fear. Now Watson exposed Albert to a loud noise each time he caught sight of a small furry rabbit: The sight of the rabbit became a conditioned stimulus that triggered off a conditioned response of fear. Albert learned fear of the rabbit, which later become generalized to a fear of any furry animals at all. In our search for illumination, *classical conditioning*, as this form of learning is called, offers no solution at all, because it has nothing at all to do with gaining knowledge about the world; what it does deal with is the transposition of physiological reactions from the stimuli to which they have a built-in response to stimuli that can acquire a conditioned response. Even if the set of stimuli to which reactions can be conditioned is unlimited, what can be learned through classical conditioning is limited to reactions that naturally appear as reflexes.

The American psychologist Burrhus F. Skinner studied learning in the sense of the extent to which a certain behavior appeared as a function of what had followed that behavior in the past (Skinner, 1953). If we think of some sort of organism with a set of behaviors, then Skinner's basic principle can be expressed simply enough: A particular behavior is more likely to appear if its appearance is followed by *reinforcement*, a consequence that is desirable from the organism's point of view. For example, if you have a hungry rat in a box and each time it presses a lever a pellet of food emerges, the likelihood of the rat pressing the lever again will increase because the food is a desirable consequence. If pressing the lever were to be followed by an adverse consequence, a punishment, such as an electric shock from the floor of the box, the rat would be less likely to press the lever again. Such *contingency*, or behavior being related to consequence, can be varied endlessly. If we want to eliminate a certain behavior, we can either punish that behavior or reward another incompatible behavior (and we would probably find that the latter is more efficient). The kind of learning Skinner studied is called *operant conditioning* and deals with how the individual is conditioned by reinforcement and punishment to operate on its environment. Maybe we should not call it a *kind* of learning, but an *aspect* of learning, potentially present in each and every instance of learning. Unlike Pavlov's classical conditioning it is not limited by unconditioned stimulus and response patterns to a finite set of behaviors; it is restricted only by what can be used as reinforcement and punishment.

Operant conditioning can possibly account for the fact *that* someone is doing something. The behavior in question has been directly or indirectly related to reinforcement in the past, whereas alternative behavior has been related to punishment. But even if it can suggest an explanation for the fact *that* someone is doing something, it hardly enables us to make sense of *what* she is doing or *how* she is doing it without reference to the *content* (as opposed to the reinforcing or punishing effect) of her previous experiences. We can try to account for the fact that someone is interested in mathematics in terms of her history of reinforcement, but we can understand her ingenious way of solving, say, differential equations only if we happen to know about her previous experience of mathematics (e.g., that she had studied in the former USSR, for instance, where calculus was taught differently than in Scandinavia). To take another example, what sense can we make of an immigrant to Sweden speaking Swedish with a heavy accent? We might be able to account for his willingness to learn and speak Swedish in terms of his history of reinforcement and even punishment. But to understand the nature of his accent and the grammatical errors he is making we would need to know something of the sound structure of his mother tongue, which interferes with his Swedish, and thus yields a characteristic pattern of deviation from Swedish as it is used by native speakers.

Surprising though it may appear, Skinner was not at all sensitive to the distinction between the reinforcing (or punishing) potential of experiences, on the one hand, and the content and structure of experiences on the other. The former has possible implications for whether or not, or to what extent, people do some particular thing, whereas the latter must be taken into account in order to understand *how* they do what they do. Skinner overgeneralized operant conditioning far beyond the limits of its explanatory power when, for one thing, he sought to account for learning language. He attempted to explain not only that which he possibly could explain but also that which he could not possibly explain.

## PARADOX THE SECOND: MENO'S MIRROR

It was largely a result of this overextension that Skinner's entire research program—not only that which was wrong but also that which was right—was in time rejected by a majority of the scientific community. The most devastating criticism of Skinnerian psychology was delivered by the linguist, Noam Chomsky, in his review of Skinner's account of how children learn their mother tongue (Chomsky,

1959). His critique of Skinner's *Verbal Behavior* (Skinner, 1957) has a familiar Platonian ring to it. The main argument is that a grammar cannot be derived from data provided by the environment because the data are simply not always adequate; despite the great variation in richness of the linguistic environment they experience, children nevertheless learn their language. Chomsky concluded that the disposition for a universal grammar, of which the different grammars as realized are a subset, must therefore be innate. But, one ventures to ask, how can a particular grammar be carved out of that preformed, innate, universal grammar when the only tools come from the inadequate data supplied by the environment? Just as Plato's proposed solution to the search for virtue, Chomsky's proposed solution to the problem of learning language runs into a paradox, which this time can be thought of as the mirror image of Meno's paradox: How can that which is innate be formed according to local demands?

The fundamental idea of behaviorism is that it is precisely *behavior* that is the proper subject matter of psychology and related fields. In line with good scientific practice we should stick to that which is observable. This is something that Skinner, Watson, Pavlov, and even Ebbinghaus, whose work predated the behaviorist movement, had in common. With regard to learning it means that change in behavior is studied as a function of practice, contingency of unconditioned and conditioned stimuli, or schedules of reinforcement. Behaviorists studying learning have never encountered Meno's paradox or its mirror image for the very simple reason that they do not ask themselves the question, "How do we gain knowledge about the world?" In fact, they don't even think it is a very good question to ask.

## PARADOX THE THIRD: INDIVIDUAL CONSTRUCTIVISM

Nevertheless, it was just this question that Jean Piaget devoted his long scientific career to exploring. (His first scientific publication appeared when he was 11 years of age in 1907, and the English translation of his last book was printed only in this decade (Piaget & Garcia, 1991). Piaget has never been considered primarily a student of learning, whether by others or himself. Because his main interest was the development of human knowledge, he labeled his field genetic epistemology. For Piaget's sake, then, we perhaps should recast the question "How do we gain knowledge about the world?" as "How do we *develop* knowledge about the world?" But if one is interested in *learning* as gaining knowledge through experience—as we certainly are—and if one is interested in *development* as gaining knowledge through experience as well—as we also are—the distinction between the two is rather slight (Marton & Säljö, 1976c).

Piaget was a *constructivist*. He did not assume that knowledge exists "out there," ready made, and that we somehow "take it in" from the environment, as the empiricists assumed, nor did he assume that knowledge is fundamentally innate as Plato and Chomsky did. According to Piaget, knowledge is constructed by the individual through her acts, through her interaction with the environment, by means of the complementary adaptive mechanisms of accommodation (in which the individual adjusts to the environment) and assimilation (in which the environment is adjusted to suit the individual). In this process progressively more advanced levels of knowledge evolve.

Several questions arise from this view, one of which concerns the locus of development. What gives development its direction? On what grounds can one level of knowledge be replaced by another, more advanced level of knowledge? How can someone select or choose or adopt a more advanced level while still at a less advanced level? This is exactly in line with Meno's paradox: How can we search for (or select) knowledge which we do not yet have? In this case knowledge is supposed to exist within the individual, as in Plato's "solution," but unlike Plato's "solution," it is not present to begin with. Thus the paradox we encounter here is the one we have already identified with Chomsky's solution to language acquisition, which we called the mirror image of Meno's paradox.

A second question has to do with the idea of the individual constructing her world. Because the world as such, the world of Kantian "noumea" (things themselves), is beyond her reach, she is bound in her own subjective, constructed world. Moreover, this world being an individual construction, there is an implication that humans live in their own personal and differing worlds. Where are these worlds and of what do they consist? Or to put our question again: What is the ontological status of the individual's constructed world and the individually constructed worlds? In what sense do they exist at all?

Are these private worlds, isolated solipsistic constructions of individual minds, all that there is? Von Glasersfeld (1990) explained that this is not the case:

[Constructivism] treats both our knowledge of the environment and of the items to which our linguistic expressions refer as subjective constructs of the cognizing agent. This is frequently but quite erroneously interpreted as a denial of a mind-independent ontological reality, but even the most radical form of constructivism does not deny that kind of independent reality. (p. 37)

Thus, there is an independent reality to weigh in with the individual constructions. Now questions flow: What is it like? Does it exist in a certain way, a way beyond all individual constructions, beyond all descriptions? Is it a material reality of particles? Is the independent world a world of things, plants, animals, humans? Now here is the crux: Is it a world with or without meaning? An independent world with meaning implies someone for whom the meaning is there, "meaners." Then can we individuals, "meaners" all, even think of a world devoid of meaning? The very attempt defies its object, so if this independent world is devoid of meaning, we cannot contemplate it at all, and if it is not devoid of meaning, then it cannot be separate from us, the "meaners."

This brings us to another problem implied by the individual constructivist[1] view. It is held that on the one hand there is an individually constructed world and on the

---

[1]We use the term *individual constructivism* and its derivatives to refer to the view of learning described here, which is usually called simply *constructivism*. Our reason is to draw a contrast with the other currently dominant view of learning that we introduce here and refer to as *social constructivism*.

other a real world divorced from this individually constructed world, and that the constructing occurs through interaction between the individual and the environment. Our question is this: How can the individual interact with something she can never reach? Von Glasersfeld suggested that the environment appears in the interaction with the individual in the form of constraints, rather like someone moving around in a dark room: Occasionally she hits a wall and backs away (von Glasersfeld, 1990, p 33). He likens her movements in the room to the acts of construction; the walls are constraints imposed on her acts by the environment, the world. But, we ask, what is the ontological status of the constraints? Are not even these constructed? The picture changes to one of the individual banging her head against walls she has built herself.

This attempt to pursue the logical consequences of the ontological position underlying the individual constructivist view has led us, somewhat unexpectedly, to the Platonian stand on the epistemological question of learning: We cannot gain knowledge about the world *from* the world, and as individual constructivism does not make the Platonian assumption about the recollection of knowledge, this adds yet a third paradox to Meno's original paradox and to its mirror image from which both the Platonian and the individual constructivist "solutions" suffer. We are left asking, if knowledge is not innate and if it does not come from the world, where does it come from?

## PARADOXES FOUR, FIVE, AND SIX:
## THE COGNITIVE PRESENT

At the risk of oversimplifying things greatly, we can point to two main traditions of answering the question, "How do we gain knowledge about the world?" One set of answers has it that knowledge comes form within, from the powers of mind. This is the rationalist tradition of Plato, Descartes, Kant, Piaget, and Chomsky (whose answers certainly differ in other respects). The other set of answers, also differing in other respects, claim that knowledge comes from the outside, from the world around us. This is the empiricist tradition of Bacon and Locke.

As we pointed out, the epistemological question and the very notion of knowledge was alien to the perspective of behaviorism, which heavily dominated the study of learning in the United States during the first half of this century and a bit beyond. Moreover, throughout the century, it was the United States that dominated the international research community engaged in the study of learning.

In the late 1950s what has been referred to as "the cognitive revolution" occurred, embracing strains of both rationalism and empiricism. Questions about the nature, acquisition, and application of knowledge became central to psychology and related fields, with the emergence of computers contributing strongly. The computer became the new metaphor for the mind, and a new research specialization, cognitive science, evolved, mainly from overlapping interests in psychology, computer science, philosophy, and linguistics (Gardner, 1987). It has been argued that cognitive science has shifted from being a field of study seen with a certain theoretical perspective to being a field of study in the more usual sense of the expression, defined in terms of problems and phenomena, which can be examined from *any* scientifically sound theoretical perspective. We must bear in mind, however, that the very idea that the handling of knowledge by humans and by computers could and should be dealt with within the same framework, the very idea that what is going on in the human mind and in the computer are instances of the same phenomenon, is in itself a very strong theoretical statement that imposes severe constraints on potential descriptions and explanatory models. The computer offers a new, precise, language for describing cognitive phenomena and a way of testing hypothetical models of them. At the same time a description that can be programmed in a computer is, of logical necessity, an algorithmic description.

Although the rationalist Chomskian turn in linguistics contributed to the rise of the cognitive revolution (Gardner, 1987, p. 28), it firmly belongs to the empiricist tradition. The object of research is physical symbol systems, each being "...built from a set of elements, called symbols, which may be formed into symbol structures by means of a set of relations" (Vera & Simon, 1993, p. 8). Such a system receives sensory stimuli from the environment and transforms them into internal symbols allied with perceptual processes. On the other hand it can transform internal symbols into muscular responses allied with motor processes, which in turn connect the symbol system with the environment and interact with the internal processes of information that are akin to thinking. The idea that acts have to be explained in terms of an internal representation of an external reality and in terms of processes by which this internal representation is manipulated is the dogma of cognitivism: "the presumption that all psychological explanation must be framed in terms of internal mental representation, and processes (or rules) by which these representations are manipulated and transformed" (Still & Costall, 1987, p. 2).[2]

This dogma leads to our fourth paradox: The internal representation cannot just lie around in the head; it has to be used somehow by something which is other than the representation itself. This something—or someone—has been called the *homunculus*, "the little human in the head," and is the aspect of the cognitive system that operates on internal representations of the external world. The idea of the homunculus follows logically from the idea of internal representation. But what does it take to operate, act on, or handle this inner world? With what does the operative part of the system's homunculus have to be equipped?

Well, if acting in (or on) the world presupposes a representation of the world, then handling the representation, the inner world, reasonably presupposes a representation of the representation, and handling the representation of the representation presupposes a representation of the representation of the representation of the world. The homunculus must have a homunculus within itself, which must have a

---

[2]The reader's attention is drawn to the distinction between cognitive science and cognitivism, the former being a field of study, as mentioned earlier, and the latter being grounded in this particular assumption about the relation between mind and world. Not all cognitive scientists subscribe to the dogma of cognitivism and not all who do subscribe are cognitive scientists.

homunculus, and so on *ad infinitum.* An intriguing notion? A paradox, we venture to claim, challenging even the computer scientists' sense of logic and reason.

This paradox is structurally identical with what is known as Ryle's regress, named after the philosopher Gilbert Ryle who published his passionate attack on mentalism in the book, *The Concept of Mind* (Ryle, 1949). Because it is the overlapping meanings of cognitivism and mentalism that are relevant for our argument, we will treat the two as synonymous. Ryle argued strongly against what he called "the intellectualist legend," according to which doing a task intelligently means being guided by internally represented declarative knowledge about the task. But then the use of internally represented declarative knowledge must be guided by declarative knowledge about *what* knowledge to use, *how* to use it, and so on. The use of *that* declarative knowledge has to be guided by declarative knowledge on a higher level. Again, there is no end: This is Ryle's regress. His line of reasoning originates from the distinction between two forms of knowledge: knowing *that* and knowing *how.* It is the former that translates into propositional knowledge, knowledge about the world; the latter refers to a capability for doing something in a certain way; it is what we mean by having a skill. The force of his own argument—according to which we have dispositions, whether acquired or developed, for doing things in certain ways, and in which "mind" refers to the ways in which we do things and to the way in which those doings are organized—led Ryle to advocate behaviorism.

For Ryle, mind was not the "ghost in the machine," something *behind* our behavior, but it was an aspect of behavior, and believing otherwise meant making "a category mistake." Ryle's famous example of such a mistake concerns the visitor to Oxford, looking for the University. He sees colleges, libraries, playing fields, museums, scientific laboratories, and administrative offices, but still he feels that in addition to all of these there is the University, another entity of a similar kind but different. Not realizing that the University is exactly the way in which its various parts are organized, he insists he has not yet seen it. Following the same argument, Ryle regards the mind as simply the way in which behavior is organized. There are not two worlds, only one—the observable world, the material world, the world of acts, the world of behavior. Ryle escapes the paradoxes associated with the epistemological question "How do we gain knowledge about the world?" simply by refraining from asking the question. Therefore, and not surprisingly, he does not arrive at an answer.

In addition to the paradox resulting from the idea of making use of an internal representation, the very forming of an internal representation is paradoxical. The notion, as we pointed out earlier, is that we receive sensory data from the outside world through our sense organs. The data as such are meaningless but are synthesized into an inner representation of the outer world. The representation does, of course, carry meaning. The question we have to ask is, "How can something meaningful be built out of that which is devoid of meaning?" Does it not presuppose that we already have knowledge of that which is supposed to be synthesized? But the representation is exactly that knowledge. Thus—and this must by now have a familiar if no less paradoxical ring—in order to obtain the knowledge we must have it already.

Finally, we come to the sixth paradox. Let us assume a representation (ignoring for the moment the fifth and the fourth paradoxes arguing against such an assumption). Assume, furthermore, a person encountering some situation. Let us say she has a problem to solve. What happens? According to the cognitivist explanation, to be able to deal with a particular problem and prior to facing it, she must already have acquired a schema, a paradigm or template, for the class of problems to which this particular problem belongs. By using the appropriate schema the problem can be grasped, dealt with, and eventually solved. But how can the appropriate schema be selected? To make a choice, the problem already must have been identified, hence grasped. Here we are again—the very grasping is supposed to be done by using the schema, and to retrieve that particular schema you must have grasped the problem already—a paradox!

*Cognitivism*, which has been the dominant paradigm in psychological and educational research for about three decades, is thus seen to suffer from at least three paradoxes.

## THE PARADOX-FREE FUTURE
## OF THE SITUATED COGNITIVISTS?

Since the mid-1980s a somewhat heterogeneous movement, referred to as "the situated cognition" or "the situated action" movement, has gained strength. It emanates from studies of learning and thinking in everyday situations outside educational institutions (Chaiklin & Lave, 1993; Lave, 1988), from computer scientists looking for alternative models for human–computer interaction (Clancey, 1992), and from the sociocultural or sociohistorical school of psychology developed originally by Vygotsky and his followers (Wertsch, 1985). We prefer to use "social constructivism" as an umbrella term for a rather diverse set of research orientations that have in common an emphasis on what surrounds the individual, focusing on relations between individuals, groups, communities, situations, practices, language, culture, and society. The main question we ask is, "How do the surrounding social or cultural, forces mould or make certain ways of acting and certain ways of thinking possible for the individual?"

Studies with a situated action orientation are characterized by human acts being explained, not in terms of an individuals' or several individuals' mental states, but in terms of what goes on between individuals, and between individuals and situations. The archetypal study is Hutchins' description of how a ship is navigated on leaving San Diego harbor (Hutchins, 1995). What this takes is not capabilities within one individual, but capabilities distributed over several individuals plus the coordinator of those capabilities. Knowledge is also seen as being embedded in the artifacts used, in this case the navigational instruments.

Human acts also can be seen in terms of their social or cultural situatedness. In a study of police interrogation (Jönsson, Linell, & Säljö, 1991) the point is made that the kind of discourse that evolves cannot be understood other than in terms of the legal system of which the situation is a part. Studies of this kind, of course, do not have the epistemological question "How do we gain knowledge about the world?" as their object, and they do not run into any of the paradoxes we have exposed. They deal instead with a world observed or interpreted by the researchers. There is a similarity with the behaviorist position in that "the inner" is not dealt with, and the situation is described only from the researcher's point of view. As diSessa (1993) pointed out, this implies that the participants are assumed to see the situation in the same way the researcher does.

Vygotskian psychology, however, which at least partially inspired the situated action view, does have an interest in "the inner." Cognitivism puts emphasis on explaining "the outer" (acts, behavior) in terms of "the inner" (mental representation). Vygotskian psychology, in contrast, tries to explain "the inner" (consciousness) in terms of "the outer" (society). Thus the thrusts of the explanations proposed by cognitivists and Vygotskian psychologists are in opposite directions. In the Vygotskian explanation "the outer" and "the inner" are linked by means of "internalization." Bereiter quotes Luria's (1979) firsthand account of Vygotsky and his group who had "…recognized this as a problem yet to be solved before there could be an adequate social–cognitive theory" (Bereiter, 1985, p. 204).

Attempts have been made to reconcile the two movements that seem currently to have the most momentum in educational research: social constructivism (Vygotskian psychology, situated cognition, etc.) and what we henceforth refer to as individual constructivism (Cobb, 1994; Driver, Asoko, Leach, Mortimer, & Scott, 1994). The main contribution of individual constructivism is its emphasis on the learner's active role in the acquisition of knowledge. The main contribution made by social constructivism is its emphasis on the importance of cultural practices, language, and other people, in bringing knowledge about.

## OUR WAY FORWARD

Individual constructivism is a form of cognitivism in the sense that it regards the outer (acts, behavior) as being in need of explanation and the inner (mental acts) as explanatory, whereas, as we have pointed out, the reverse is true for *social constructivism*. The two schools are thus mirror images of each other, their focuses being on different sides of the borderline between "the inner" and "the outer." They share the shortcoming of lacking explanatory power with respect to what they claim to account for because they share the separation between "the inner" and "the outer." In order to combine the insights originating from these two camps that relate to our question "How do we gain knowledge about the world?" one has to transcend the person–world dualism imposed by their respective focus on what is within the person and what surrounds her.[3] One should not, and we do not, consider person

---

[3]We must point out again that the terms individual *constructivism* and social *constructivism* are umbrella terms that we use to cover quite a heterogeneous range of research perspectives; we have chosen them as representing the most general and outstanding aspects of large fields of work. However, they differ to varying degrees in other respects; for instance, Barbara Rogoff (1990) took an explicitly nondualistic ontological stance within a generally social constructivist framework.

and world as being separate. One should not resort to hypothetical mental struc
divorced from the world, and we have no intention of doing so. Nor should one
resort to the social, cultural world as seen by the researcher only. People live in a
world which they—and not only the researchers—experience. They are affected by
what affects *them,* and not by what affects the researchers. What this boils down
to—as far as learning of the kind to be dealt with in this book is concerned—is
taking the experiences of people seriously and exploring the physical, the social,
and the cultural world they experience. The world we deal with is the world as
experienced by people, by learners—neither individual constructions nor independent realities; the people, the learners, we deal with are people experiencing
aspects of that world—neither bearers of mental structures nor behaviorist actors.

Thus in this book the dividing line between "the outer" and "the inner" disappears. There are not two things, and one is not held to explain the other. There is
not a real world "out there" and a subjective world "in here." The world is not
constructed by the learner, nor is it imposed upon her; it is *constituted* as an internal
relation between them. There is only one world, but it is a world that we experience,
a world in which we live, a world that is ours.

As we said at the start of this chapter, we are all different, and we do experience
the world differently because our experience is always partial. Gaining the most
fundamental knowledge about the world is tantamount to coming to experience the
world in a different way, and, to rephrase one of our opening statements, if one way
of experiencing the world can be judged to be better than another way, then some
people must have become better at experiencing the world—or have experienced
the world in a better way, or have gained better knowledge—than others, always
with the proviso that we are talking in normative educational terms. The rest of this
book is devoted to the task of learning about how the world appears to all these
different people—how they have come to experience it—following our thesis that
by learning about how the world appears to others, we will learn what the world is
like, and what the world could be like.

# 2

# Qualitative Differences in Learning

At the end of chapter 1, we set ourselves a goal—that of learning about how the world appears to different people, or how they have come to experience it—but we gave no indication of how we might do this, or what form the results of the task might be. In this chapter we start by addressing the question of how people experience learning in one particular respect, namely how they go about the tasks of learning. Thus we begin by considering a fundamental aspect of how people experience the world—learning through the eyes of the learner—while introducing our perspectives on how such questions can be tackled. We leave the somewhat philosophical considerations of the last chapter to ask the question in its simplest form; "Why do some people learn better than others?"

A little history is in order here. In the spring of 1970 a doctoral thesis was presented at the Department of Education and Educational Research at Göteborg University in Sweden, much in the tradition of experimental research on verbal learning, which can be traced back to Ebbinghaus (1885). The external examiner, though finding no fault with the thesis, posed the question of whether or not it told the community anything about how their own students were actually learning, studying, and memorizing the stuff they met in their university courses. That was Ference Marton's (1970) thesis and was something of a turning point for such research in Göteborg, for the examiner's point was taken seriously. It led to the founding of a research group and, eventually, the school of research into learning that has led to this book.

The study comprised 16 separate trials in which participants were given a list of the names of 48 famous people in different random orders. Certain results presented in the thesis did in fact point to the research that was to come. Some of the subjects tried to start by getting an understanding of what different kinds of people were included in the list (film stars, politicians, athletes, and so on). Other subjects tried simply to get hold of as many of the names as possible from the outset. These two

14

groups adopted distinctly different approaches to the rather unrealistic learning task facing them: The former group tried to get a global sense of the list before addressing individual items, by going from the whole list to its parts, whereas the latter group attempted, by accumulating more and more names, to go from the parts to the whole. Initially, the former group used more time and imposed a looser, more flexible structure on the list, but by the end of the series of trials they had found a stable structure and their recall was fast and flawless. The latter group, in contrast, was inferior in the long run with respect to time, structure and performance. As can be seen in the chapters to come, this provides a continuity between research before and after the turn.

If we consider the immediate significance of what happened, we see it as a distinct shift of focus away from measuring the quantity of stuff learned and the psychological means of achieving greater quantity more efficiently to examining the *quality* of what students learned and the educational implications. What eventually happened as a result was another shift, away from viewing the learner from the outside to one that tried to see learning from the learner's point of view.

Let us return to our central question for the chapter: "Why do some people learn better than others?" There are, of course, what might be thought of as straightforward qualitative answers ready at hand: Some people are smarter than others; some are better motivated; some work harder, and so on. Many studies in psychology and educational psychology on intelligence, motivation, and study skills have been carried out with those assumptions, but Entwistle (1984), in summarizing such research and its impact in higher education, said the following:

> This body of research on motivation and study methods has made relatively little impact on higher education. It has provided a rationale for providing advice for students on effective study skills, but the plethora of handbooks on the subject has had little, if any, effect. (p. 12)

He went on to ascribe its failure to its relation of academic performance in terms of success and lack of success, seeking correlations between certain aspects of student profiles (innate ability, motivation, organization, etc.) and high academic performance. Such correlations were not to be found. Entwistle (1984) explained further:

> Not only are such findings too general to be useful and too obvious to provide new insights, but they also remain firmly rooted in an external view of the student—the perspective of the educational psychologists. These researchers continued...implicitly or explicitly to blame the students for low levels of academic attainment. Thus failure is explained away as the result of low ability or lack of organization or application. (p. 12)

Entwistle blamed the impotence of such research on researchers taking an external view of the student, as the teachers do, habitually setting performance against a predetermined scale of achievement and basing highly normative statements on the results: Do this and you will achieve that; work hard and you will do well; waste time and you will do poorly; fear failure and you might do well, or there again you might do badly.

The approach that Marton and his colleagues took to answering their central question specifically eschewed the external research view and attempted to address it from the perspective of the research subjects themselves. But how can researchers do otherwise than take an external view of the students or pupils they are studying? How can their learning or studying be seen from the inside? How can their personal experiences be monitored? One could (and some researchers do) attempt to relate body movements, especially eye movements, to internal learning processes, but that is as uninteresting, for our purposes, as monitoring neuron firing for the same ends. No, the only route we have into the learner's own experience is that experience itself as expressed in words or acts. We have to ask learners what their experiences are like, watch what they do, observe what they learn and what makes them learn, analyse what learning is for them. There is a wealth of important insight to be fetched from those experiences, although research methods differ radically from those that take an external view.

## STUDIES OF LEARNING
## FROM THE LEARNER'S PERSPECTIVE

In this chapter we want to concentrate particularly on the way that learners go about their tasks of learning in an effort to understand why some learners do such a much better job of learning than others. We need to illustrate our arguments from a number of studies of students learning by reading texts, writing essays, and solving problems. Although the questions posed in the various studies might be slightly different, we will be asking: "How do learners gain knowledge about the world, and why do some do it better than others?"

As observed in the previous chapter, there can by now be no doubt that the meaning of "doing it better than others" is far less straightforward than might be thought. If we do not accept "the quantity of stuff learned" as the measure of learning achievement—and we do not—then we have to suggest something else, and in order to do so we will reflect briefly on what "taking the learner's perspective" implies. When we talk about "the quantity of stuff learned," we (whether researchers or teachers) decide what "the stuff" is. For instance, in the case of learning from a text, the text is what *we* understand it to be; *we* can decide what important facts, concepts, or principles there are to be learned, and *we* construct questions aimed at measuring the extent to which the learners have picked them up by reading the text. But are they reading the same text? Is it not the case that even among colleagues there may be different views of what a particular text is really about, what is important, and what is of marginal interest? Is it not the case that when we invite a number of students to read a text, they read somewhat different texts, in the sense that the text that we take to be incontrovertible actually appears different to them and carries different meanings for them? Is it not the case that the extent to which they pick up certain facts, concepts, and principles by reading a text is contingent on what text they have actually been reading? Our first example is exactly about this: How does a text—of which we researchers have a certain understanding—appear to a group of learners with comparatively similar educational backgrounds? By addressing this specific question we want to suggest a way of dealing with the general question of what it means to be better at learning something. Subsequently we deal with the question of why some are better at learning something than others are.

## Example 2.1:  The Outcome of Reading a Text

Our first example concerns a study carried out by Säljö (Marton & Säljö, 1976b; Säljö, 1975) in which 40 female first-term university students were asked to read parts of three chapters from a typical textbook on education, *The World Educational Crisis: A Systems Analysis* (Coombs, 1971, Swedish edition). The basic aim of the third chapter is to give the reader a thorough understanding of the effects of education on individuals and society, the output of educational systems. One point that the author wants to make in this connection can be seen from the following quotation from the third chapter:

> It is impossible to measure with any presently known gauge the full output and eventual impact of an educational system. Some sense of what is involved can be grasped if we imagine a school whose whole output consists of a single student. On the day he graduates, what kind of an output does he embody? The answer is that he embodies a multiplicity of outputs—represented, for instance, in the facts and concepts he has learned, the style of thinking he has acquired, and also such changes as may have occurred in his outlook, values, ambitions and personal conduct. If one then asks how this will affect the future life of this student, his family and society, the difficulty is several times compounded. Such cause and effect relationships are often as indistinct as a line drawn through water. But if these matters are hard to get at in the case of a single student, they are infinitely more elusive when the matter to be judged is the output represented by multiple streams of individuals, flowing through educationally different channels for different lengths of time. (Coombs, 1968, p. 64)

Coombs argued against the simplified notion of the output of educational systems as being equal to the number of people who pass their exams. He stressed the need for a large number of criteria in assessing the real influence of education on society.

The idea of the study was to reveal how the text appeared to the students, what they understood it to be about, so they were asked a range of questions, following from the question, "What is meant by the output of an educational system?" On analyzing the answers it turned out to be the case that there was not a fairly uniform understanding of the issue, nor were there 40 different understandings. Focusing on the meaning revealed by the answers, rather than on the words used to express them, led to the discovery of four distinctively different ways of making sense of the main argument of the text. At one extreme was a global appreciation of the overall effects

A  The effects of education on society and on individuals produced by knowledge and
   attitudes acquired through schooling

"Mm, that's terribly difficult to answer. There was this example about how if you just had one pupil and
wanted to work out the output, it would depend on so many things ... or factors or whatever facts and
concepts it was about ... whether he has completed his education, what his own viewpoint is ... and
everything that is going to influence his life later on and that sort of thing ... and his productivity,
suitability...."

"Mm, it's the knowledge that.. and values ... yes, the knowledge and values that students have acquired.
That is, whatever it is that influences them and makes them read this or that and do this or that."

B  Those who leave the educational system with or without a qualification

"Well, those who have been to school and gone right through the course, and even those who've failed,
they're a sort of output too."

"Well, it's those who pass their final exams, that is, well not necessarily pass, but those who take part in the
course even if they drop out at some point, you know ... those who have taken part and then dropped out."

C  Those who leave the educational system with a completed education

"It's the pupils who have gone right through the system from start to finish."

"It's the trained workforce that the educational system produces. It's well, for example ... well, simply the
trained workforce."

D  What comes out of the educational system
"Something to do with  ... well ... you know, the result of."
"The product ... I think."

FIG. 2.1.  The four distinct ways of understanding the Coombs extract.

of educational measures, supported by detail and example, bringing out the principles involved. At the other extreme was a narrow focus on the title of the text as
such. The four categories are described, with illustrative quotes, in Fig. 2.1.

The four categories represent four qualitatively distinct ways of comprehending
the author's message concerning "output of education." These people had gained
radically different understandings of the author's message. Answers of kind A
imply a full grasp of the author's intended meaning of output of education as the
totality of ways in which education affects society, and answers of kind B indicate
a partial grasp, focusing rather on individuals who pass through the education
system. Responses of kind C, however, indicate an understanding that is quite
contrary to that intended by the author, and those of kind D are focused on nothing
more than the words he used. This sort of result establishes that there are indeed
qualitative differences in the messages that students get from their studies of text;
they are indeed reading different texts. Furthermore, the message can be totally
misunderstood compared with that intended by the author; the reader can quite
simply get it wrong. But we need to elaborate on this point: Is there simply a
gradation from right to wrong as we pass from categories A to D? We wish to argue
that what appears as a misunderstanding or as wrong (and what indeed *is* misunderstanding or wrong if we take the author's intention as the norm) can equally be
seen as *partial* understanding. In fact, all four ways of understanding the text can
be seen as more or less partial understandings of the author's message, each of them
dropping certain essential aspects as we pass from A to D. In Fig. 2.2 we demonstrate this, showing that within a comprehensive statement of the author's meaning
all the four ways of understanding can be isolated.

A    What comes out of the educational system, namely *the effects of education on society and individuals in terms of knowledge and attitudes acquired through schooling* in those who leave the educational system with a completed education or with no qualification at all.

B    What comes out of the educational system, namely the effects of education on society and individuals in terms of knowledge and attitudes acquired through schooling in *those who leave the educational system with a completed education or with no qualification at all*.

C    What comes out of the educational system, namely the effects of education on society and individuals in terms of knowledge and attitudes acquired through schooling in *those who leave the educational system with a completed education* or with no qualification at all.

D    *What comes out of the educational system,* namely the effects of education on society and individuals in terms of knowledge and attitudes acquired through schooling in those who leave the educational system with a completed education or with no qualification at all.

FIG. 2.2.  The four distinct ways of understanding the Coombs extract, expressed as components of a comprehensive whole.

Figure 2.2 shows that the four different understandings of Coombs' text reflect component parts of the most comprehensive grasp of the issue. Furthermore, there are logical relationships between those component parts. D, which expresses no more than what the word "output" means, is tacitly implied by A, B, and C. C is implied by B, is indeed part of it, and B is implied by A in that "acquired through schooling" implies people subject to schooling, (i.e., people coming in and coming out of the educational system). The four different ways of understanding the author's message can now be seen to be ordered in a hierarchy in terms of the logical relationships between them, as Fig. 2.3 illustrates. They represent different degrees of partial understanding of the whole. This does not mean that there is no answer that can be completely wrong or that everything is a partial understanding of everything else; after all, the overwhelming majority of all statements that could be made are completely irrelevant to what the output of the educational system is.

This study did not go into the ways in which the task of learning was tackled—it had another agenda—but it does serve excellently well to show the sort of qualitative differences in outcomes of learning that are to be found when students read their textbooks. We must reiterate that these four categories of understanding are the ways in which the students understood the message offered by the author. We are able to make a normative judgement as to which is best and which is worst, but that does not change the fact that they are indeed ways of understanding it.

A ⟹ B ⟹ C ⟹ D

FIG. 2.3.  The hierarchy of logical relationship between the four ways of understanding Coombs' text.

After reading chapter 1, you will hardly need reminding that we listed no fewer than six paradoxes to which different research and philosophical views of learning could lead. Here students were reading a text on a theme of which they previously knew little, if anything, and reaching a variety of ways of understanding it—gaining some sort of knowledge about it. Apart from the unavoidable question—"How was this possible, given Meno and his heirs?"—the obvious question is: "What accounts for the difference, the variation?"

### Example 2.2: Approaches to Learning from Texts

Let us assume that people read a text for which they all have the necessary prerequisites—linguistic, factual, conceptual—to grasp fully, and which they still understand in a number of qualitatively different ways, just as was the case in the previous example. What is happening while they read the text must vary. How otherwise could the outcome vary? What is it that varies in their way of going about the learning task? As we said at the start of chapter 1, that people learn dramatically different things from their studies goes together with their learning things in dramatically different ways. Studies carried out at the same time as our first example throw light on the nature of this variation.

One such study had 30 university students read another text, this time a closely argued newspaper article written by a professor of education, Urban Dahllöf, criticizing proposed university reforms in Sweden. Marton and Säljö (1976a) described the article this way:

> The newspaper article was 1,400 words long and included three tables. The article was mainly a critique of the approaching curriculum reform in the Swedish universities (UKAS), which aimed at bringing studies more into line with those at the polytechnic institutes through the introduction of set combinations of subjects and stricter regulations as regards duration of studies (termination in the case of unsatisfactory examination results). The reason for the reform, as explained by the authorities, was that the examination pass rate at the universities was considerably lower than that obtained at the polytechnic institutes. The author of the article had, after examining the underlying statistics, divided university students into subcategories and was thereby able to show that, even though the pass rate was very low for certain categories of students, for other categories it was as high as, if not higher than, that achieved by technical students. The author argued that the blanket approach of the university reform, which would affect all equally, was misguided. If the pass rate was to be raised (and this was not considered self-evident by the author) selective measures should be taken by concentrating on those groups that did have a low pass rate. (p. 8)

Having read the rather lengthy article, the subjects were asked in individual interviews, not only to recall the author's main argument, but also to describe how they had gone about studying it. As in the study described above, four distinct ways of understanding it were identified. These are summarized in Fig. 2.4.

Again, we see that we can bring the four different ways of understanding the text together into a "composite understanding," of which they turn out to be parts.

| | |
|---|---|
| A | Selective Measures: Meaning that measures have to be taken only for those groups of students that do not fulfil the necessary requirements. |
| B | Differential Measures: Measures to be taken that allow for differences between the various groups. |
| C | Measures: Measures need to be taken. |
| D | Differences: There are differences between groups. |

FIG. 2.4. Summary of ways of understanding the Dahllöf text on proposals for university reform.

In this case we can state the answer to the question, "What was this article about?" as follows:

*There are differences between groups* (D) such that *measures need to be taken* (C) that *allow for the differences between the various groups* (B) and applied *only for those groups of students that do not fulfil the necessary requirements* (A).

Here A implies B because the former is a special case of the latter, whereas B implies C *and* D because the latter are combined in the former. We can establish a hierarchy between these differing understandings in terms of the logical relations that exist between them. The levels of C and D are indeterminate in relation to each other. We illustrate the complex of relationships between A, B, C, and D in Fig. 2.5.

Svensson (1976, 1977) argued that the critical difference lies between A and B on one hand and C and D on the other. The structure of the text is a presentation of some facts (about differences in pass rates between groups) and a conclusion based on those facts (about selective measures). Whereas A and B focus on that structure, C and D do not.

To account for the differences in understanding of the text, Marton and Säljö (1976a) also looked at what the participating students said about their experience of the situation and how they had gone about the learning task. Two distinctively different ways of relating to the reading of the text were found. Consider these quotes from students talking about how they tackled their reading task:

"Well, I just concentrated on trying to remember as much as possible."

"There were a lot of different lines of thought to follow and to try to memorize."

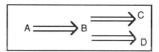

FIG. 2.5. The hierarchy of logical relationships between ways of understanding the Dahllöf text.

Now contrast the previous quotes with these:

"I tried to look for...you know, the principal ideas"

"and what you think about then, well it's you know, what was the point of the article, you know."

"I thought about how he had built up the whole thing."

In the first set of quotes, the readers are concentrating on the text itself or on the discourse itself or on recalling it. They are trying to construe and memorize the text, whereas in the second set the students are looking more at the author's message, what ideas he was trying to convey, what line of argument he was pursuing, and the structure of the argument.

These quotes form examples of a dichotomy that has been widely observed in many contexts between a *surface approach to learning* and a *deep approach to learning.* The essential distinction between them is that a surface approach focuses on what can be called the *sign* (here the text itself), whereas a deep approach focuses on that which is *signified* (here the meaning of the text). The focal awareness of the meaning of the text implies a nonfocal awareness of the text as such, but not vice versa. Hence there is a hierarchical relationship between the two approaches to learning.

In looking at the outcomes of learning and the approaches to learning for individuals in this case, Marton and Säljö (1976a) found that the most advanced outcome, Type A, was achieved only by subjects who also described a deep approach to the task, and that the least meaningful outcomes, Types C and D, came only from students who described surface approaches (see Table 2.1). Thus the qualitative differences in approaches to learning were associated with discernible differences in the outcome of learning: Deep approaches were related to grasping the author's message, and surface approaches were related to miscomprehending or missing the message altogether.

The relationship between qualitative differences in approaches to learning and in outcomes of learning is presented here as an empirical finding based on two kinds

**TABLE 2.1**
Relationship Between Approaches and Level of Outcome

| Outcome of Learning | Approach to Learning | | | |
|---|---|---|---|---|
| | Surface | Not Clear | Deep | Subtotals |
| A | — | — | 5 | 5 |
| B | 1 | 6 | 4 | 11 |
| C | 8 | — | — | 8 |
| D | 5 | 1 | — | 6 |
| Subtotals | 14 | 7 | 9 | 30 |

From Marton and Säljö (1976a).

of data: the participants' account of the experience of the learning situation on the one hand and their account of the text they had read on the other. The two variables are, however, two aspects of learning, and they are functionally related: In order to arrive at a certain outcome you must have approached the learning task in a certain way. The less than perfect relationship between the two aspects reflects our less than perfect data rather than what the relationship between the two is actually like.

Now we are getting closer to the object of our book? people learning in dramatically different ways learning dramatically different things, and so far, no paradoxes!

## Example 2.3: Seeing the Structure of a Text

In Fig. 2.6 there is part of a text that was used in yet a third text-reading study (Säljö, 1982). As you can see the text described a number of perspectives on learning, with principles, research results, examples and applications. You will recognize our second example in which students learned by reading a text about a proposed university reform. Ninety subjects, whose ages varied from 15 to 73 years and whose educational background varied from 6 years in elementary school to completed university degrees, participated in individually run sessions in which the following sequence was followed. First, the participant's view of learning in general was explored in an interview, following which he or she read the text on forms of learning (Fig. 2.6). Thereafter, both the participant's understanding of the text and his or her experience of the learning situation were explored, again in an interview.

When Säljö asked the students in this study, "What is the text about?" he found that there were two principal ways in which the text was understood. One was as a text about forms of learning: Classical conditioning exemplified by a method of torture and Pavlov's dogs, instrumental conditioning exemplified by Skinner's rats, verbal learning exemplified by Ebbinghaus on the one hand and the Göteborg group on the other. The other way of understanding it was as a text about torture *and* classical conditioning *and* Pavlov's dogs *and* instrumental conditioning *and* Skinner's rats *and* verbal learning *and* Ebbinghaus *and* the Göteborg group and so on. For example, when asked about the introductory part, Dave said:

> D  It began with an introduction, a quote.... A Greek who was being tortured by the Greek junta and this was being used as an example of classical conditioning.... This I suppose is an example of classical conditioning which was investigated and discovered by Pavlov.... (Säljö, 1982, p. 97)

In contrast, Suzy listed the bits she recalled:

> S  There was a lot about Skinner, and, for instance, Ivan Pavlov and the psychologist Ebbinghaus and research results. That's always fun to read about.... And then there was something about the torture methods of the Greek junta and you sort of got bad feelings when you read about that kind if thing, even if it's interesting (Säljö, 1982, p. 97)

Thus two radically different understandings of the text were found, a text well within the reach of all the participants in the study. We see these different understandings as being part of the totality of ways in which reading the text was experienced by the subjects, the total situation of sitting and reading for the purpose of being interviewed on it. And the *explanation* for this difference in the ways they understood the text is that they related themselves to (experienced) the situation in different ways—thus *approaching* the task of reading in ways that brought about different understandings.

A particularly telling feature of the study refers to how the students described reading one small extract of the text, which can be found at the end of Fig. 2.6, and which actually describes and exemplifies the deep and surface approaches to reading texts as found in the earlier study related in Example 2.2. None of the subjects who had adopted a surface approach saw that part of the text as being relevant to their own situations, whereas those who adopted a deep approach recognized themselves in what they read there, drawing the text into their own reality, and their own reality into the text. An interesting case is Dora, who in the initial interview had two contradictory views of learning, or in Roger Säljö's (1982) own words, she seemed to illustrate

> through her statements ... two competing realities with rival definitions. One is attending to written or spoken discourses as such and on their own terms as documents ... conveying insights and meanings. The other is attending to them in a way appropriate when factors external to the meaning of the text (e.g., the demands of the assessment system) assume great importance. (p. 86)

After she had read the text, Dora was asked about her experience of reading it, and said:

> Oh, well, first when I read it I sort of thought like this: Right, now I'll try to remember as much as possible ... and then I went on, and the more I read ... when coming to the end of the article I could have burst out laughing 'cause there they described the type of person I'd been myself at first, those who were trying to learn as much as possible ... and then there were certain hints about ... that you should try to find the meaning behind it all, so when I read it once again, I tried to make it make sense in quite a different way. (p. 86)

This is pretty convincing evidence that Dora makes the text part of her own reality, switching from one competing reality to the other, and from her initial surface approach to a deep approach, affected by what she had read. This is without doubt a significant learning experience for Dora, who becomes aware of the possibility of variation in ways of reading a text (i.e., deep and surface) and thereby shifts her own approach from surface to deep.

In learning by reading a text, a surface approach means that the learner focuses on the words of the text, and a deep approach means that the learner focuses on what the text means. A corresponding distinction has been drawn by Svensson (1977, 1984b) between an atomistic and a holistic approach: the former refers to tackling the text in isolated pieces, and the latter refers to maintaining an integrated whole. The difference can be seen even in the two quotes that Säljö included in his text extract (see Fig. 2.6). The second quote, from S, represents reading the text as trying to remember its words in isolation from all else, whereas the first quote, from D, treats reading the text as looking beyond it and setting its whole meaning in a wider reality. We can foreshadow chapter 5 by pointing to the differences examined here: S is shifting focus from one piece of the text to the next in a sequential manner, isolating the parts from one another, whereas D is integrating it part by part into a greater whole. Thus not only do their approaches differ, as well as the outcomes of their learning, but in the dynamics of focus in the act of learning can be glimpsed the functional relationship between approach and outcome hinted at in the previous example.

## Example 2.4: Learning Through Writing Essays

Although reading texts is a common task of learning in almost all disciplines, in many areas the principal task the student undertakes is that of writing essays, described by Hounsell (1984, p. 103) as the Amazon for undergraduates in the arts and social sciences. As he stated, essay writing occupies such a central position in higher education because it is both a tool of coursework assessment and an avenue to learning, and the same is true for many older school students.

Hounsell conducted a study in which students of history were interviewed about an essay they had recently written as part of a module in their degree program. The interviews took up questions similar to those of the Göteborg studies, namely about the content of the essay, how the students had gone about preparing for it, in relation to other essays they had written, and the activity of writing essays, all in an effort to examine the students' experience of essay writing as a learning activity. Thus the goal of the interviews was to reveal the students' intentions in writing an essay and how they actually went about it. Transcripts of the interviews were subsequently analysed for what they said about the students' conceptions of essay writing and their approaches to writing essays in terms of procedure and content. The outcome of the essay writing exercise was also measured in terms of the teacher's grades.

All aspects of the analysis pointed to three qualitatively distinct conceptions of the nature of the essay: argument, viewpoint, and arrangement. Three elements associated with an essay are salient here and serve as indicators of conceptions: they are *data, organization,* and *interpretation.*

The *essay as an argument* is globally characterized as "an ordered presentation of an argument well supported by evidence" (p. 109). The students talk in terms of *interpretation,* of ideas being "moulded" or "crystallized" into a single entity; they talk of *organization,* making a logical and coherent presentation; and they talk of *data,* authenticating the argument with supporting evidence. Of the three indicators, interpretation is superordinate in this conception, with organization and data supporting it. This is the way that history teachers understand essay writing, the way they expect their students to write essays, and the way that they themselves, as historians, write.

The second conception of an essay, *viewpoint,* is characterized as "the ordered presentation of a distinctive viewpoint on a problem or issue" (p. 11). Here interpretation is again the main element of descriptions of writing essays, supported by attention to organization, but reference to data as providing evidence is relatively lacking.

The third conception of an essay, *arrangement,* is defined as "an ordered presentation embracing facts and ideas" (p. 11). Data is present in the shape of discrete ideas, which are not related to any central argument or position. As far as organization is concerned, students speak of using secondary sources for illustration rather than to make a point or support an argument, and they emphasize conscientious coverage of the available sources more than the quality of their usage. Interpretation is lacking.

Comparing these three conceptions of an essay, in the first two, interpretation is the superordinate element, riding on data and organization in the first case and on organization alone in the second, whereas in the third, interpretation is hardly a feature with organization and data carrying equal weight. If we compare these results with those obtained in the original Göteborg studies we see certain similarities. The deep approach to learning from text is associated with a search for meaning (that which is signified by the text), which is akin to the interpretation important to the argument and viewpoint conceptions of essay writing, whereas the surface approach focuses on the discourse contained in the text (the sign), which is clearly akin to the arrangement approach to writing an essay. Hounsell's studies of students learning through writing essays is even more clearly related to the Göteborg work exemplified by Svensson's (1976) analysis in terms of atomistic and holistic approaches. In Svensson's terms, the essay as an argument, and to a possibly lesser extent the essay as a viewpoint, deals with organized *wholes* rather than the *parts* with which the arrangement conception deals.

The conceptions indicated in the interviews were confirmed by a detailed study of actual essays written by the same students, implying a degree of individual consistency. Furthermore, the grades the students obtained for their coursework in history also reflected the differences that the conceptions embodied. To quote Hounsell (1984):

> Taking only the fourteen students who can be ascribed without qualification to one of the three conceptions, four of the five students with an arrangement conception have marks below 60 per cent, while all four students ascribed to the viewpoint conception have marks in the range 60-64 percent. Only two students have marks of 65 percent or more, and both are students assigned to the argument conception. (p. 120)

Again, a relationship is seen between approaches to study—this time through essay writing—and outcomes of study. The act of essay writing in which the intention is to interpret, to seek meaning, is associated with superior results.

Writing an essay as an exercise in learning is seen by the teachers first as an opportunity for the student to review the content already covered, and, more important in the case of these history students, to research their own sources. Second, it is an exercise in presenting a thesis and bringing relevant material to bear on it. The students studied by Hounsell indicated a difference in the structure in their awareness of the task in hand (characterized by the conceptions of an essay as argument, viewpoint, or arrangement) as well as an intertwined structural awareness of the elements of such an essay (interpretation, organization, and data). The outcome of their efforts are essays that focus on different elements and thereby produce a different view of the material. At the same time, their own learning efforts have been focused on different structures of the historical material, leading to a differently structured awareness of its significance in the context under consideration. This is reflected both in the grade awarded for the essay in question, but more tellingly in the final grade for the module.

## Example 2.5: Approaches to Learning to Program by Writing Programs

Quite a different subject of study is learning to program (i.e., to write programs for computers). Students learning to program have a number of different tasks to contend with—listening to lectures, reading textbooks, studying programs that others have produced—but above all they write programs that put into operation the current topics of study. Such programs are initiated as learning tasks in the form of problems that demand some degree of interpretation on the student's part before a model in the form of a program can be devised. Even here, distinctly different approaches have been observed (Booth, 1992a).

The student gets a worded problem, reads it, studies it, and then starts on the task of writing the program. The word "writing" is somewhat misleading in that "writing" in this context does not necessarily involve producing program text (either on paper or at a keyboard) until a late stage, the stage sometimes called "coding." In that sense it is like the writing process rather than the writing act. In its most formal sense, writing a program involves first devising and specifying a solution to the problem in the form of an outline program describing what the program should do and, achieve, and how it should be structured. On the basis of the specification, code (i.e., sets of program commands) can be formulated, some of which will be standard and well-known to the student, and some of which will need a good deal of creativity. Only when the code has been produced is the program in a state to be entered into the computer. In fact, writing a program only rarely follows this formal pattern of interpretation to specification to program, and some bits are treated informally. Nevertheless, the education of potential programming professionals attempts to inculcate the practice of carefully considering a problem prior to thinking about the program that has to be written—in an attempt to counteract the "hacker" approach of the programming hobbyist.

The 14 students involved in this study were just such potential computer professionals, and the educational approach which had been adopted involved introducing programming in the first term of a degree course in computer science and computer engineering through the very high-level language called Standard

Meta-Language (ML; Wikström, 1987). This way of programming has its roots in mathematical structures—in particular the function—and thereby gains a feature of unique importance, namely that programs written in ML lie so close to equivalent mathematical statements formulated as functions (which actually form the specification of the program) that the programs themselves can be handled mathematically. In contrast to most members of other families of programming languages (including Pascal, Fortran, Cobol, etc.), programs written in ML can be proven correct.

While learning programming in this way, students were asked to write programs that solved particular problems of current interest in the course. They were asked to read the worded problem and tell the researcher what the problem was about before trying to produce a program. Four distinctly different ways of handling the problem were observed across two different problems that fall into two pairs—again the surface–deep dichotomy.

The surface approach is indicated in what have been called *opportunistic* approaches in the context of writing programs. On the one hand, the *expedient approach* is typified by the student, who on reading the problem, immediately alights on a potential ready-made program that fits the bill. It might be one she wrote last week that just needs tinkering with (generally a mistaken belief), or a standard program that is indicated because of some similarity in nomenclature. In no event observed was it followed by a successful outcome; students either gave up the attempt totally or went back to the problem and thought again. On the other hand, the *constructual approach* is typified by the student who does not assume a complete solution from the start, but who rather selects constructs from the repertoire studied so far that might be relevant to constructing a program for this problem. In both approaches, the student is not interpreting the problem as such but focusing on the program that has to be written, with neither a formal nor an informal specification in mind.

Deep approaches in this study, here called *interpretative approaches*, focus more on the meaning of the problem as it stands. There is the *operational approach*, on the one hand, in which the student interprets the problem in terms of what the program is going to have to do, what operations it will have to accomplish to satisfy the problem. This is very like formulating an informal specification for the program to be written. On the other hand, there is a *structural approach*, in which the student's reaction to the problem is to interpret it in its own domain, referring to the problem's own features and constraints rather than what the program will be like in any respect. Both of these approaches focus at the outset on formulating a framework for the developing program: the operational framework in terms of the program's way of working, and the structural framework in terms of the problem's own structure.

The process of devising a program is often analyzed into three phases: problem, specification and program. The problem, not surprising, is the situation that the programmer is given, experiences, or sets out to solve, and dealing with it involves studying it, and coming to terms with its structure in such a way that it is possible to write a program for it. Eventually this leads to a specification, which is a more

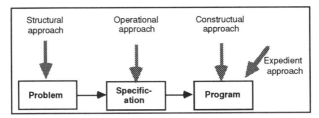

FIG. 2.9. The approaches focus initially on different phases of the program-writing process.

or less formal statement of the program's requirements in terms of data structures, algorithms, internal relations such as routine inter-connectivity and external relations such as programming environment and input/output devices. On the basis of the specification, the actual program can be written, after ensuring that all its aspects are feasible in the computer to hand. Now, as shown in Fig. 2.9, the approaches identified in this study point clearly to one or the other of these phases: the structural approach points to the "problem" phase the operational to the "specification" phase, and the constructual approach to the "program" phase (as does, in some sense, the expedient approach).

Although the phases are not rigid requirements for writing a program, and any program-writing will cycle through them back and forth, several times refining the whole program, it is clearly seen that a direct constructual or expedient approach is hardly conducive to considered programming. This is one, normative, datalogical criticism that can be leveled at the opportunistic approaches.

These programs, however, are being written, not to produce programs of any significant value, but to bring about significant learning. On the one hand, we can call on the by now well-established functional relationship between deep-like approaches and superior learning, and note that structural approaches and operational approaches are therefore both to be preferred and encouraged. We can also refer to the very nature of programming and learning to program and how these are experienced by students (Booth, 1992a) to see that the expedient approaches are closely related to experiencing programming as making use of the computer in an unspecified way (i.e., hacking) and to experiencing to programming as learning the codes of the languages rather thoroughly. Both of these views are what the sort of programming exercise was intended to eradicate, and another learning outcome is seen. While the student who deliberately considers the structure and the principles of the problem is learning that lesson, the student who tries to expedite a quick fix or runs through the current repertoire of constructs is merely avoiding the lesson.

Two distinct differences between this study and those described earlier in the chapter should be mentioned. First, the term *approach* has apparently different usages. In the studies of reading texts, "approach" refers to the overall strategy (consciously adopted or not) that a student reports to have employed when the text was read. In this study, "approach" refers more to the initial response to getting the problem, which set the scene for the development of a program. It is in keeping with the fact that the approaches to reading text were found in students' descriptions of how they had gone about the whole task, whereas the approaches to writing programs have been observed and discussed in the very act of writing the program.

Second, it is less easy to identify the outcome of learning for these isolated tasks within the overall task of learning to program. The typical student will tackle several hundred such problems during the course. However, the lesson pointed out above, developing a principled way of writing programs, is clearly linked with certain approaches and not with others. Again, foreshadowing chapter 5, further implications can be drawn from this when thematic and peripheral awareness during the program-writing process is considered.

## DESCRIBING QUALITATIVE DIFFERENCES
## IN LEARNING

In Examples 1, 2, and 3 we have described qualitative differences in the outcome of learning and in Examples 2, 3, 4, and 5 we have described qualitative differences in approaches to learning. In every case studied, a limited number of distinctively different ways of understanding the content of learning and/or a limited number of distinctively different ways of approaching the learning task were found. When approaches to learning are mentioned, we think of both the way in which the learning situation is experienced and the way in which it is handled. Furthermore, we have argued that outcomes of learning are functionally related to approaches to learning in the sense that both are aspects of the very same experience of learning. To account for differences in outcome in terms of differences in approaches, we explain one aspect with another aspect of the same whole.

The qualitatively different ways of understanding the content of a learning task are logically related to each other because they represent a more or less partial grasp of the same complex of constituent parts. The differing understandings can thus, as a rule, be hierarchically ordered, as can to some extent the different approaches to learning.

# 3

## The Experience of Learning

In the first two chapters of this book we attempted to open up the questions: "What does it take to learn?" and "How do we gain knowledge about the world?" In this chapter we pursue our search for answers or partial answers or answers to parts of the questions.

We have taken pains to point out the difficulties that certain research approaches meet when tackling this or related questions, difficulties that we have suggested arise from their inherent epistemological assumptions and that manifest themselves in a series of apparent paradoxes. We prefer to describe learning in terms of the experience of learning, or learning as coming to experience the world in one way or another. Such learning inevitably and inextricably involves a way of going about learning (learning's *how* aspect) and an object of learning (learning's *what* aspect).[1] The previous chapter described research into learning taking our perspective on investigating the experience of learning through the experience of the learner. That people differ shows itself here, in that qualitatively different ways of experiencing the tasks were found, qualitatively different outcomes of learning were seen, and these were found to be largely correlated. Thus, we have started to relate empirical evidence indicating that certain approaches to the learning tasks correlate with better results in terms of understanding the object of learning than others do.

### APPROACHES TO LEARNING
### AND CONCEPTIONS OF LEARNING

In Example 2.3 in the previous chapter we described a study in which a broad sample of individuals were asked to read a text about forms of learning (see Fig. 2.6), after which they were interviewed on what the text was about and how they

---

[1]The reader should note that there are different ways of using the terms *what* and *how* of learning, which we clarify in chapter 5.

had gone about the task of reading it (Säljö, 1982). We also illustrated some of the qualitative differences found in the participants' understanding of the text, and we pointed out that these differences were closely related to differences in the partici- pants' ways of approaching the task of learning from the text. Having established that the approach to reading a text and the outcome of the reading are united in the total experience of reading one goes on to ask: "What is it that brings about the different experiences?" If we choose, however, to consider differences in ap- proaches to reading as an explanation for differences in how the text is understood, we could ask instead: "How can we explain the differences in approaches?" If we could answer that question we would have a better idea of the source of better learning, better understanding. How might we go about finding a satisfactory answer to such a question?

We can conjecture that people sitting and reading a text experience the situation through their different biographies. They have all been there before—reading a text with the expectation of being asked about it—and they make one sort of sense or another of the situation. They have different conceptions of what learning is, and because they define this situation as a learning situation, it consequently takes on different meanings for them. In a search for differences in the experience of learning, we could possibly try to trace individual biographies, follow students through many tasks of learning over many years of study, maybe, and try to identify critical aspects of the whole history of their learning. We have not done that. What has been studied by now in different situations and cultures is how students talk about their learning. We have quite simply asked them to tell us about how they see learning, how they go about learning, and what they think it is.

In the study by Säljö (1982) to which we have been referring, prior to reading the text about learning (see Fig. 2.6), those questions were taken up in individual interviews. Some of the participants described how they saw reading as an impo- sition and made sense of the given task accordingly, treating learning as something external to themselves, as a task to perform for later recall. They adopted what we have called a surface approach to the learning task, focusing on the text as such and ending up mainly with the sequential kind of understanding that we have illustrated in the previous chapter. In contrast, others seemed to see reading as a means of finding out about the world around them. They saw texts rather as windows to reality, and they treated the text in the experimental situation accordingly. They adopted what we have called a deep approach to learning and ended up with the hierarchical kind of understanding in which the phenomena the text was supposed to tell them about came to the fore, as we also illustrated in the previous chapter.

Säljö claimed that the relationships between ways of experiencing learning in general (conceptions of learning), ways of experiencing learning through reading the text (approaches to learning), and ways of understanding the specific text hold for the entire group participating in the study, a pattern of relationship that has been corroborated by other researchers (van Rossum & Schenk, 1984). Instead of statistics, Säljö develops six cases that are used to illustrate the differences and the relationships, for which Dave and Suzy were quoted in chapter 2.

The most striking result that comes from these studies is that there are two overriding categories of how students conceptualize learning. On the one hand, there are students who see learning as being intimately related to the actual tasks of learning: They describe learning with a focus on gathering facts and information from a text, and possibly on memorizing them for later use. On the other hand, there are people who see learning as finding meaning through the medium of learning tasks: They see things in a new light; they relate them to their earlier experiences; they relate them to the world they live in; they see learning as changing oneself in some way.

We are first going to relate the results of two such studies into how people conceptualize learning, the results of which have much in common, and, yet again, are strikingly different. The first study is of adult learners at the Open University in England; it followed a number of students through their whole university career, looking at many aspects of their studies and study situations, and always taking up the question of what they understood learning to be. The second study is of school pupils between the ages of 12 and 18 years in Hong Kong; they were asked about what they understood learning to be in the context of the different subjects they met in school. Thereafter, we will return to consider our central question for this chapter: "From where do the different approaches to learning spring?"

## LEARNING AS SEEN BY
## OPEN UNIVERSITY STUDENTS

Of the students who enrolled in the Social Science Foundation Course of the Open University in 1980, 29 were selected for study over a wide range of aspects of their experiences as students (Beaty, 1987; Gibbs, Morgan, & Taylor, 1984; Taylor & Morgan, 1986). They were interviewed at the start and end of their first year of study, and then once in each of the 5 subsequent years until they completed their degree or until they dropped out. In each interview, one topic that was touched on was the students' reflections on their own learning and their progress as learners, and that item from each interview formed the basis for a thorough analysis (Marton, Beaty, & Dall'Alba, 1993) of how these students conceptualized learning at large.

As you know, this was not the first such study. Säljö (1982)had addressed the same question, not only in his six case studies (Säljö, 1982), but also across the whole set of participants in the study (Säljö, 1979). He identified five qualitatively distinct conceptions of learning, and Giorgi, who tackled similar material from the research perspective of phenomenological psychology, verified them (Giorgi, 1986).

Marton et al. (1993) identified six distinct conceptions of learning that fall into the two groups that we have already described in connection with Säljö's (1982) study: One group focuses on learning in the context of tasks of learning (the act and the consequences of the act) whereas the other focuses on the object of learning (finding meaning through the learning tasks). Each group was composed of three distinct conceptions, the first five being isomorphic to those identified by Säljö

(1979) and Giorgi (1986), and the sixth quite new. By conception, here, we mean a qualitatively distinct manner in which the subjects were found to voice the way they thought about learning, whether in respect to themselves, their reflections over their progress, or any other expression. We do not assign a conception to an individual as some sort of mental entity, but see it rather as a telling feature of the whole picture drawn by the group.[2] The most revealing way of introducing the conceptions is through the way they are voiced. (The number following the name of the participant—actually a pseudonym—refers to the interview occasion, 1a and 1b being the first and second first-year interviews, respectively.)

The first group of conceptions are those where focus is on the act of learning itself. For instance,

Accumulation of knowledge (Vincent 1b)

Filling my head with facts (Field 2)

are examples of how students voice the first conception: *learning as increasing one's knowledge* (A). These two quotes point to learning being seen as knowledge in the form of facts and information acquired with consumption as the principal metaphor: filling up, being absorbed, being picked up. Learning is seen in a quantitative light—learners undertake barely specified tasks of learning in order to increase what they know—but otherwise it is seen only as a series of synonyms.

There is a distinct difference in the following quotes:

Learning it up for exams and reproducing it (Field 1a)

Drumming it (text) into the brain and reeling it off (Nelson 1a)

When you have achieved whatever it was learned for, then that's it, it can go away, it's disposable, you can get rid of it (Downs 4)

Rather than focusing only on acquiring knowledge, these students focus equally on what is to be done with it, again purely in a study context. They see *learning as memorizing and reproducing* (B). The consumption metaphor is extended to include the way in which it is consumed: drumming it in, learning by rote, cramming and its eventual use—repeating it, reproduction in exams, and disposal when used.

The next pair of quotes show yet another difference:

Take in information, see how it can be used. (Childs 2)

Turn it around and make use of it in other ways. (Parker 1b)

*Learning as applying* (C), which these two quotes exemplify, has application in focus in addition to getting the knowledge and storing it. In this view, the constraint that learning is confined to study situations has weakened, as the learner becomes prepared to consider the new acquisitions in other, as yet unspecified, contexts. That

---

[2]The notions of conception and experience will be thoroughly treated in chapters 5 and 6.

completes the first group of conceptions of learning, in which the learners thematize the task of learning per se.

Contrast them with the next group of quotes, of which Marton et al. (1993) that wrote "the watershed is meaning":

> Finding out lots of ways of thinking about things, and what view you have yourself (Charles 1a)

> Looking again at things that you know about but with a slightly different perspective—or seeing other people's views on things (Parker 1b)

> To have a process of thought that sort of "sets in motion" when you look at something...tackle looking at something in a far more logical way (Field 2)

These three students are talking about having a view or taking a perspective or looking in a particular way at the things they are learning. Their horizons have broadened with respect to learning; they stand away from the knowledge they are acquiring, or memorizing, or applying and reflect over it. They view *learning as understanding* (D). This involves putting their newly gained knowledge not only into a context of the demands being made by the educational system of which they are part, but also integrating it into their own worlds through comparing and contrasting. The consumption metaphor so dominant in the first two conceptions is replaced by more of a visualization metaphor in which learning has the character of looking at things, seeing things in a new light, taking a view, having insight. Learning is now centred on the learner; it goes from the learner, who examines things critically or considers arguments, into the stuff to be learned, which is tossed around or viewed from different angles.

In the fifth conception, exemplified by the following quotes, understanding is taken a stage further in that not only does the new knowledge act as a catalyst for taking a perspective or view, but it actually makes the world appear in a different way:

> All the time it [what was learnt] keeps cropping up you might just have seen it [what happens around you] in one way before, you sort of see it in different ways. (South 1b)

> Opening your mind a little bit more so you see things [in the world] in different ways (Field 2)

> Being able to look at things, from all sides, and see that what is right for one person is not right for another person (South 2)

These students are voicing *learning as seeing something in a different way* (E). For them learning is not only taking a perspective or view on things, but taking a wider perspective or multifaceted view, thereby bringing about a more fluid or dynamic perspective on the world. Compared with the previous conception, "learning as understanding," the context of learning has expanded, away from the area immediately demanded by the subject of study and toward the world as a whole.[3]

---

[3]Note that an individual is not necessarily restricted to one conception at a time; in this study, Field is categorized as having voiced two distinctly different conceptions of learning in the second interview.

The five conceptions described so far are virtually the same as those identified by Säljö and by Giorgi. Here, however, a sixth was also found:

> I suppose it's what lights you.... It's something personal and it's something that's continuous. Once it starts it carries on and it might lead to other things. It might be like a root that has other branches coming off it.... You should be doing it [that is, learning] not for the exam but for the person before and for the person afterwards .... (Downs 4)

> Expanding yourself ... you tend to think that life just took hold of you and did what it wanted with you.... You should take hold of life and make it go your way. (Field 6)

This is *learning as changing as a person* (F), the most extensive way of understanding learning in that it embraces the learner, not only as the agent of knowledge acquisition, retention and application, and not merely as the beneficiary of learning, but also as the ultimate recipient of the effects of learning.

In these six conceptions of learning, summarized in Fig. 3.1, and more particularly in the two sets of three conceptions, we see the same answer to the question we asked earlier, "From where do different approaches to the tasks of learning spring?" as the one at which Säljö arrived at. The answer lies in the insight that people who embark on learning activities have different ways of thinking about, of understanding, what it is they are doing. Some conceptualize learning as acquiring knowledge, as memorizing for later reproduction, as being able to use what one knows. Others view learning as coming to an understanding of things, taking perspectives, getting a new way of viewing the world, and as ultimately changing as a person. The former think about learning as if it were limited totally to the tasks of learning imposed by a study situation, whereas the latter look beyond the tasks in themselves to the world that the tasks open for them. This is directly analogous to the difference between surface and deep *approaches* to learning: the former focusing on the tasks themselves and the latter going beyond the tasks to what the tasks signify.

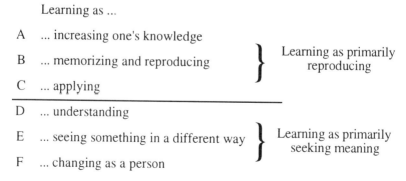

FIG. 3.1. Summary of six conceptions of learning (Marton, Beaty, & Dall'Alba, 1993).

# THE APPARENT PARADOX
# OF THE CHINESE LEARNER

In another part of the world, another question began to arise. If memorization as a form of learning is so closely associated with surface approaches to learning and if surface approaches lead to poorer learning, why do Chinese students, who spend a good deal of time in activities that appear to be aimed at pure memorization, do so well in competition with their Western contemporaries?

There are two stereotypes of the Asian learner or, more particularly, the Chinese learner. The first stereotype, the "brainy Asian," has its source principally in the success of the ethnic Chinese students within higher education in Australia and the United States. This success is evident in comparisons of achievement in mathematics and natural sciences in which students from Hong Kong (and also from Japan) performed particularly well (Torney-Purta, 1990). The second stereotype, the "Asian learner-as-a-rote-learner" (Biggs, 1990; Kember & Gow, 1991), is primarily related to Chinese students, but is also related to Asian students in general.

These stereotypes of the brainy Asian and the Asian learner-as-rote-learner are apparently incompatible; an orientation to rote learning is negatively correlated with achievement, exception for the reproduction of trivial details (Biggs, 1979). Thus, in an attempt to elucidate the matter, studies were made to identify how Chinese students conceptualize learning and go about the tasks of learning. One such study has shown that for the Chinese learner a distinction has to be made between two qualitatively different ways of seeing memorization: on the one hand, memorization with intention to understand and on the other, mechanical memorization (Marton, Dall'Alba, & Tse, 1992). Thus the source of the paradox is revealed: The Chinese learner who is taking a deep approach to learning *is* indeed making an effort to memorize, and is *at the same time* intending to gain understanding.

The results of the study by Marton et al. (1992) shed light on the relationship between memorization and understanding for the Chinese learner. In the process of memorizing, the text being memorized is repeated several times, which may be outwardly suggestive of rote learning. However, a number of subjects in the study, all teacher educators, explained that when a text is being memorized, it can be repeated in a way that deepens understanding. For them, the process of repetition contributes to understanding because different aspects of the text are in focus with each repetition, which is different from the mechanical memorization which characterizes rote learning.

# LEARNING AMONG SCHOOL PUPILS
# IN HONG KONG

A much more detailed analysis of learning among Chinese school children, between 12 and 18 years of age (Marton, Watkins, & Tang, in press) also serves to cast light on and deepen our understanding of the conceptions of learning that we have already presented—those of Open University students in the social sciences.

| learning as committing to memory | (words) |
|---|---|
| learning as committing to memory | (meaning) |
| learning as understanding | (meaning) |
| learning as understanding | (phenomenon) |

FIG. 3.2. Four distinct ways of experiencing learning (Marton, Watkins, & Tang, in press).

Let us first look at the four distinct ways of experiencing learning that were identified in the study, which have a somewhat different disposition from those described earlier. They are given in Fig. 3.2, which shows a distinction between committing to memory and understanding which is akin to the distinction drawn in the earlier study between learning as reproducing and learning as seeking meaning (see Fig. 3.1). A further distinction is seen with respect to the object of learning: In the first of them it is mere words that are to be memorized: in the second and third, meaning itself is the object of learning, whether to be memorized or to be understood; and in the fourth the object lies beyond the words or their meaning and stretches to the phenomenon that the words relate to and the meaning concerns.

Before proceeding with the analysis of these ways of experiencing learning, let us try to catch more of the sense of these categories with the help of typifying extracts from interviews. Contrast this pair of interview extracts (all extracts taken from Marton et al., in press):

I   When will you consider that you have really learned?
S1  I really pay attention when listening in class. The teacher will repeat again and again some important words, then you will absorb them, and you will be able to use those words later, you won't forget.
I   Will different assessment forms affect your study approach?
S2  If the test is not long questions, I will just learn by heart. If I know that the test consists of long questions, then I will madly learn by heart.
I   What do you mean by "madly" learn by heart?
S2  Meaning that I will learn it well by heart at home, and when I get to school in the morning, I will try to learn it by heart and recite it over again.

with this pair:

I   What do you mean by understanding?
S3  To know the meaning, to memorize
S4  I do not like rote learning. I would rather read the things a few more times and try to remember. I do not rote learn because if I do that and get stuck in the middle, then I will not be able to write out the rest of the things. So I would rather think and try to remember it.

All four extracts imply that learning is experienced as reproducing a given content, the difference being that the first pair focuses on absorbing and reciting the very words of the content, whereas the second pair involves memorizing that which has been reached through thinking about and finding meaning in the content. This is the essential difference between the first two ways of experiencing learning.

Now consider the following extracts:

S5   After understanding certain things, to be able to apply them, the knowledge, in answering questions and in other situations, not just in situation A where I learned it, but also apply in situations B and C

S6   You will have to understand very clearly the meaning of the whole passage, and then answer in your own words. If you just copy, you will not be able to get good results.

S7   If you are taught that two plus four equals six and if people then ask you what is four plus two and you do not know the answer, that means that you have not understood. You only know two plus four but not four plus two.

Very clearly, none of these extracts refers to learning in the sense of reproducing, which was the prime characteristic of the previous two pairs. They all mention understanding and talk about learning in terms of abstracting the content to be learned and making it the learner's own in some way. The first speaks of applying that which has been learned in similar but new situations. The second refers to expressing what you have learned in your own words, and the third speaks of taking what you know and knowing it in a different way. In fact, they illustrate three different ways of experiencing how you can make use of your understanding of meaning: being able to do something in different circumstances, being able to do something differently, and being able to do something different.

The fourth way of experiencing learning in Fig. 3.2 is different from this, because now the process of abstraction goes beyond the content to be learned—whether from texts or the teacher's lesson or experiments in the lab—to the phenomenon that the content deals with. Two extracts from the interviews point quite clearly to this experience of learning, even in a school context:

S8   If you look at the sky and wonder how high it is, how the clouds formed and the different types of cloud, you will not be able to understand all this with your present thinking processes. But through learning and explanation from your teachers you will be able to understand all these very clearly.

S9   If you see something in the street and are able to relate back to the example that was given in class, then you have understood that example.

Now learning leaves the schoolroom and finds its application in the world at large. Learning is now characterized as learning about and understanding phenomena as opposed to content.

Let us now turn to the analytical framework that was developed in connection with this study. There are two dimensions: a temporal dimension and a dimension of depth. The temporal dimension was identified in the earlier study (Marton et al., 1993) in connection with the conceptions of learning there described, and has been elaborated in the study of Chinese learners in a more general way. Learning can be experienced as having three distinct temporal facets, which may or may not appear in any one way of experiencing learning. These are the *acquisition* phase in which knowledge is acquired or absorbed; the phase of *knowing* in which the learner possesses or stores up knowledge; and the phase of *making use of,* applying, or exploiting the knowledge.

The depth dimension is more of an intertwining of three distinct aspects of learning: the *agent* of learning, the *act* of learning and the *object of learning.* The two dimensions thus represent two kinds of variation: The temporal facets point to different phases of the overall experience of learning, whereas the depth dimension points to a variation in the temporal experience, and we now elaborate on them in turn.

The temporal facets of learning are apparent to inspection in the interview extracts already quoted. Look, for instance, at the first:

> S1   I really pay attention when listening in class. The teacher will repeat again and again some important words, then you will absorb them, and you will be able to use those words later, you won't forget.

The acquisition phase is explicitly mentioned, "really pay attention when listening in class," and "then you will absorb them." The phase of exploiting the knowledge thus absorbed is also seen in the statement, "be able to use those words later," whereas the phase of knowing as holding it in memory is implied by "you will absorb them" and "you won't forget." Look again at S4:

> S4   I do not like rote learning. I would rather read the things a few more times and try to remember. I do not rote learn because if I do that and get stuck in the middle, then I will not be able to write out the rest of the things. So I would rather think and try to remember it.

This student is not intent on reproducing merely the words of the text but rather the meaning that she has found there. In saying that she likes to "read the thing a few more times" and that "I would rather think and try to remember" she is explicitly stating that this is her preferred mode of acquisition, rather than "rote learning"; the phase of making use of the stuff she has learned is described as "able to write out the rest of the things." Again, the possession of knowledge is implicitly referred to, this time in terms of remembering.

If we focus on the temporal dimension, we obtain a two-dimensional outcome space: By this we mean the 3 x 4 matrix obtained when we analyze the four ways of experiencing learning according to their three temporal phases depicted in Fig. 3.3. Each cell in the space has been filled in according to the characteristics of the depth dimension as we describe in due course. We can see that the three temporal facets occur in the four different ways of experiencing learning in reply to three questions: "How do you acquire that which you learn?" "In what form does it persist?" and "How do you make use of it?" The third way of experiencing learning—as understanding (meaning)—has three differentiated ways of experiencing it in relation to the third temporal facet—making use of that which is learned.

| Ways of experiencing learning | Temporal facet | | |
|---|---|---|---|
| | **acquiring** | **knowing** | **making use of** |
| **committing to memory (words)** | memorizing (words) | remembering (words) | reproducing (words) |
| **committing to memory (meaning)** | memorizing (meaning) | remembering (meaning) | reproducing (meaning) |
| **understanding (meaning)** | gaining understanding (meaning) | having understanding (meaning) | being able to do something<br>being able to do something differently<br>being able to do something different |
| **understanding (phenomenon)** | gaining understanding (phenomenon) | having understanding (phenomenon) | relating |

FIG. 3.3. The outcome space of learning (Marton, Watkins, & Tang, in press).

The temporal facets of the experience of learning focus on the phases of learning, whereas the dimension of depth focuses rather on what it takes to learn. The first of the three intertwined aspects of the depth dimension, agency, refers to what it is that initiates learning, the teacher's teaching or the learner herself; learning is experienced either as being taught or as something one does oneself. In the extracts just presented, S2 talks wholly in terms of an active experience of learning, involving as it does repeating and reciting madly until it is time for the test. S1, in contrast, who also focuses on being able to repeat the words, experiences learning as coming from the teacher's constant repetition of them. The two ways of experiencing the agency of learning are not mutually exclusive and can be expressed in the same breath, as the following extract indicates:

S10   We have to know the things that they (the teachers) teach, have to digest. They impart the knowledge to us so that we learn and are able to use the knowledge later.

Furthermore, there is no distinction in agency when it comes to the different ways of experiencing learning. Teachers teaching and imparting knowledge are part of this experience equally with the student digesting and learning to be able to use the knowledge later. The distinction in terms of agency applies only to acquiring. The teacher may impart the knowledge, but only the learner can maintain it and make use of it. Thus, whatever sort of experience is expressed, it can be initiated or directed by teachers or by learners, but the process of acquisition, retaining and making use of learning is in the hands of the learner alone.

The act of learning is the second aspect in the dimension of depth and can be characterized as having to do with the intentions of the experience of learning, either to memorize or to understand, and this is indicated in each cell of the outcome space in Fig. 3.3. Clearly, all kinds of experience classified in the first two categories, *learning as committing to memory* (*words*) and *learning as committing to memory* (*meaning*), illustrate the memorizing act aspect, while the third and fourth categories, *learning as understanding* (*meaning*) and *learning as understanding* (*phenomenon*), illustrate the understanding act aspect. Again, a single student can report experiencing learning in both ways, differentiating according to context or demand, as, for example, S13 does later. The distinction between the two acts, committing to memory and understanding, does not apply to the third temporal phase, in which new distinctions have to be made in relation to the act aspect, including reproducing, doing, and relating. The act aspect as such is not usefully applicable to the second temporal facet, "knowing," which designates more a state one is in than something one does.

The third aspect of the dimension of depth refers to the object of learning, which in this particular study proves to have one of three foci: the atoms of the content of learning (whether spoken or written words or details), the meaning of the content of learning, or the phenomena to which the content points. The category of experience called *learning as committing to memory* (*words*) clearly relates to the first of the three kinds of object of learning; the second and third categories, *learning as committing to memory* (*meaning*) and *learning as understanding* (*meaning*) relate to the second, meaning, whereas the fourth category, *learning as understanding* (*phenomenon*) relates to the third, phenomena. The object of learning is indicated in brackets in each cell of the outcome space, in Fig. 3.3. We may also point out that the object aspect of the depth dimension runs through, or is applicable to, all three temporal facets. In a way it is what links them together.

The dimensions of temporality and depth are in a sense discontinuities in the experience of learning: they point to distinct differences in the variation shown between individuals. Marton et al. have also drawn from the material a sense of continuity, which leads us to return to the original motivation for the study. The study of Open University students and other similar studies had pointed to memorization for later recall as an essentially surface approach to learning that was known generally to be linked with inferior outcomes of learning (a lesser grasp of the meaning of the content, poorer structure of the message as a whole and poorer recall), whereas observations of Asian learners seemed to indicate that memorization was associated with very successful learning. Studies of Asian learners, however, showed the dangers of generalizing such results without regard to culture, because Asian learners, it was found, treated memorization as a step toward understanding, in that each repetition of a text or lesson gave a new perspective on the content, and so an understanding was built up stage by stage. The parallel was drawn with Western actors learning their parts in a new play: Although rote memorization plays a large part in preparation, each repetition, recall, and rehearsal of the lines reveals a new layer of meaning in the part. An amateur actor who merely learns the lines of the part, maybe by mnemonic tricks, gives only a wooden representation of the character, whereas the professional who has made the lines his own by successive repetition and review has thereby extracted the necessary meaning from the lines and can bring the part to life.

It was with this issue as the point of departure that the study set out to investigate the relationship between memorization and understanding in these Chinese students. They were specifically asked about these two sides of learning, and the relationship was taken up from three different perspectives: in terms of function, in terms of structure, and in terms of the mechanism that might bring one or the other of them about. The functional perspective refers to memorization and understanding being in parallel, understanding stemming from memorization, and understanding replacing memorization. The structural perspective is seen in the categories in which there are levels leading from the former to the latter, from reproducing words all the way to seeing something differently. Continuity in this sense is most obvious in relation to the third temporal aspect: "making use of." The different categories can be seen as forming a logical continuum that ranges from making use in a very narrow sense, exact recall of words or details memorized, to making use in more and more widely varying situations to the case in which the point of centering, the learner's focus, is no longer that which is learned, but the new situations that are seen through, or in terms of, what has been learned. This is what is referred to as "relating" in the final cell of the outcome space in Fig. 3.3.

What is possibly of greatest interest is the mechanism by means of which a transformation between one way of experiencing (and carrying out) learning and another takes place. There is evidence in the data that the student's experience of learning changes with changing demands of school, and in particular the amount of stuff that has to be learned. While the amount is quite small, it can be coped with through rote memorization, but that fails when the amount gets larger. Then one is forced to make a selection, picking on the more important parts to memorize and leaving other things out. Unless specific instructions are given on what to leave out (or hints to the same effect are detected), this necessarily involves reviewing the whole stuff and making judgments on the relationships between parts and their relative importance. Many extracts in the interviews point to just this:

S12 I find that I could not memorize by heart like I did for School Certificate. There are too many things to memorize.

  I Has your study approach changed since Form 1?

S13 Yes ... Many of the subjects in the lower forms require rote learning in answering the tests, the questions can be exactly the same as those in the exercise or workbooks. This encourages and forces you to memorize the information in the books.

  I What about in the higher forms now?

S13 There is so much to learn, you cannot learn by heart, you must rely on understanding, on your teachers' explanation in order to learn. This is the reason for my change in study approach.

## ON THE RELATIONSHIP BETWEEN THE TWO STUDIES

As we mentioned earlier, the outcome of the investigation carried out with Open University (OU) students very closely resembled the results obtained by Säljö (1979) and Giorgi (1986). The secondary school students in Hong Kong were not only much younger than the OU students and culturally different, but they were a more heterogeneous group as well. They varied in age between 12 and 18 years, and they discussed learning in relation to a number of different subjects and individually specific assignments.

As seen in Fig. 3.3, and as should be obvious from our account as a whole, the variation found was considerable. Although it was apparently another kind of variation than the one found among OU students, the two are by no means irreconcilable. As pointed out earlier in connection with the OU study, Marton et al. (1993) remarked that the six different ways of experiencing learning reflected variation in two different dimensions. As a matter of fact, the six different ways of experiencing learning can readily be projected into the two-dimensional outcome space obtained in the Hong Kong study with respect to the temporal facet, inasmuch as all but one of the OU categories brings one of the temporal facets into focus. The exception is conception B, which refers to both memorizing and reproducing, and can thus be seen as being composed of two subconceptions, $B_1$, memorizing, and $B_2$, reproducing.

Neither the variation in depth within the first and second groups of three conceptions, nor possible correspondences between the two studies on the level of categories have been made explicit. Other studies have replicated the findings with educationally and culturally different groups and are beginning to throw light on certain aspects of learning of more general interest as well as raise new questions. For example, in a study of ways of experiencing learning, under-standing, and memorization carried out in Uruguay, by Nagle and Marton (1993) and Marton, Wen, and Nagle (in press) have found that the experience of the acquisition phase of learning breaks down into the experience of three consecutive steps. First is, understanding that which one is supposed to learn, act of understanding that is light, instantaneous, and effortless, for which synonyms such as "you accept it" and "you take it in" are used. The next step is working on that which you have grasped somehow: You process it, absorb it, and you make it really yours. Then in the third step: you *really* understand it—now you have appropriated it. The sequence is thus:

understanding(1)     learning     understanding (2).

Interestingly enough, Mugler and Landbeck (1994) report finding the same pattern among students of the University of the South Pacific in Suva, Fiji, in which the structure of the three steps is the same as above, but the concepts have shifted positions:

learning (1)     understanding     learning (2).

These studies are serving to develop our understanding of the fundamental dimensions of the experience of learning. A picture is emerging of learning being experienced in ways that indicate overlap and complementarity between different groups of learners, potentially within a common framework. This is expounded on further in chapter 6.

## THE ORIGIN OF THE IDEA OF LEARNING

The studies and results described so far begin to give a pretty clear answer to our question: "From where do the different approaches to learning spring?" In general terms, we can say that people at large have distinctly different ways of under-standing (conceptualizing or experiencing) what learning is, and that they act in accordance with these when faced with a task of learning. Now, in more specific terms, we can add that an individual may actually express a variation across these distinct ways of experiencing (understanding or conceptualizing) learning, and these ways of experiencing learning are closely related to the actual tasks to which they are being exposed. We are therefore able to state that the approach to learning adopted by an individual, whether a school or university student, in a particular situation is a combination of the way in which that person experiences learning and the way that he or she experiences the situation. This is where the approach to learning springs from on a task to task basis. But it begs the more fundamental and more tantalizing issue of where the understandings of learning have their origin, what can explain the differences, how far back we have to go to begin to trace the history of the experience of learning. First, we have to ask, "how far back are we able to go, limited as we are by our intention to ask people what they think of learning?" After all, it takes an awareness of what learning is, an awareness of awareness, to be able to discuss it with an interviewer.

Pramling (1983, 1986) carried out an interview study into the ideas of learning held by children between 3 and 8 years old. But even here, because an awareness of awareness is needed, only the oldest children could discuss what learning is in general. The others discussed examples and answered specific questions. The most common examples the children gave when they were asked, "Can you tell about something you have learned?" was learning to ride a bike and learning to swim. In general, the formulations of the nature of learning that the 8-year-olds came up with were something like "if first you are not able to X, and then you are able to X, then you have learned X," where "to X" is mostly "to do something," but possibly "to know something," or infrequently "to understand something." X is about what learning yields. The "some-thing" can be thought of as the direct object of learning. If we were to parse the sentence, "something" would be in the accusative, the remainder of X, the doing, knowing, or understanding that is in sight is the indirect object of learning, which Pramling calls the "what" aspect of learning.[4] We can see how frequently the different age groups gave each of the three kinds of answer in Table 3.1.

---

[4]Pramling's use of the "what" of learning is different from that introduced at the start of the chapter, where it refers to the content of learning, the actual "something."

**TABLE 3.1**
Children's Conceptions of the "What" Aspect of Learning (%)

| Learning | Age | | | | | |
|---|---|---|---|---|---|---|
| | 3 | 4 | 5 | 6 | 7 | 8 |
| To do | 31 | 92 | 100 | 100 | 100 | 100 |
| To know | — | 4 | 11 | 15 | 11 | 28 |
| To understand | — | — | — | — | — | 8 |

*Note.* Each subject may give from one to three responses.
*Source.* Pramling (1986, p. 37)

**TABLE 3.2**
Children's Conceptions of the "How" Aspect of Learning (%)

| Learning | Age | | | | | |
|---|---|---|---|---|---|---|
| | 3 | 4 | 5 | 6 | 7 | 8 |
| As doing | 46 | 50 | 11 | 4 | — | — |
| By getting older | 23 | 32 | 30 | 11 | 4 | 4 |
| By experience | 15 | 64 | 100 | 100 | 100 | 100 |

*Note.* Each subject may give from one to three responses.
*Source.* Pramling (1986, p. 38)

Now if we ask how the children conceive of *how* one learns *to do* something (which can be seen to be by far the most frequent way of understanding the "what" of learning in the sense used here), we find that to begin with, "learning to do" is not differentiated from "doing." Another way of answering the question *how* one becomes able to do something is that you get older and then you can do it. And then among the older children the most frequent answer to the question of how you learn is that, as adults take for granted, you learn by doing it for yourself, or seeing it done—you learn through experience. These results are shown in Table 3.2.

When children realize that they learn either by doing it for themselves or by seeing it done, there is still a distinct difference in how they experience and account for the fact that they learn. In one case they simply point to being involved in something: You learn because you participate in something, as shown in the following example from Pramling (1986, p. 38):

Victoria (7 years 1 month)

V   At the start I had a very small bike with a support wheel and then I got a new one like I have now ... at the start I had to have a helmet on in case I fell and hit my head and daddy was with me and helped me.

I  How did you know you could do it?

V  I could … just suddenly.

From the idea that you learn because *you do* it the idea that you learn because you do it *several times* seems to emerge (Pramling, 1986, p. 39):

Robert (6 years 6 months)

I  If you get a new friend today and want to learn his phone number, what would you do?

R  Then I'd ask him and maybe he'd write it down on a piece of paper and then I'd read it a lot of times when I call him, and then I'd know it finally.

I  Would you be able to call him to-night if I wrote it down?

R  No, it takes weeks, I have to call many times.

Here the idea of practice might appear to be present, but we argue that such is not the case. What Robert says certainly reflects a view of learning that is a precursor to the idea of learning through practice, but is certainly not identical with it. In what he says, learning is a by-product of doing something, but what is done is not done in order to learn. Practice, in contrast, is exactly that: to keep on doing something in order to learn. One could argue that it is exactly there, in practice, that the idea of learning in its most fundamental sense is born, in carrying out acts with the sole purpose of becoming able to do, or to know, or to understand something that was not previously the case. Consider this example from Pramling (1986, p. 39):

Linda (7 years 5 months)

I  If you want to learn something you don't know, what do you do?

L  You practise.

I  How do you go about practising?

L  Well, first, if you want to, for example, learn to walk on a tight-rope, you maybe have it very low and then higher and higher each day in … and then finally you can do it.

As we see in Table 3.3, there is a very clear break in age when the idea of learning as a function of practice is expressed.

In the studies described earlier in this chapter it was adults or teenagers who were interviewed about their views, ideas, conceptions of learning and about their differing ways of experiencing it. Pramling's studies rested on interviews with preschool

**TABLE 3.3**
Children's Conceptions of the "Learning by Experience" (%)

| | Age | | | | |
| Learning | 4 | 5 | 6 | 7 | 8 |
|---|---|---|---|---|---|
| Through incidental activity | 29 | 43 | 19 | 7 | 2 |
| Through practice | 1 | 12 | 23 | 32 | 32 |

*Source.* Pramling (1986, p. 41)

children, but if we are interested in how the idea, the experience of learning evolves, we need to look at even younger children, and we become unable to restrict ourselves to *asking* them about learning. In particular, we should be looking at children who are engaged in learning long before they can talk about learning.

Of course, one can learn something without experiencing it as learning in any reasonable sense of the word, but Lindahl has shown that children as young as 1 year may have an explicitly observable awareness of their own learning (Lindahl, 1996). In an extensive study of how toddlers experience their first months in nursery care, she recorded the first 3 months that 10 children between 13 and 20 months old, spent at a day care center. She was able to identify a great number of episodes in which they engaged in acts that had the sole purpose of learning to do something or finding out what something is like. Each child was followed from her first day at the center and filmed five times a week during the first month, three to four times a week during the second month, and one to two times a week during the third month. By analyzing episodes from these films she concluded that such young children engage in practice in order to become able to do something they want to do, such as ride a three-wheeled bike or slide on their front. They were seen to maintain concentration on certain objects or problems and to keep it there over impressively long periods of time, in spite of strong distractions from peers and adults.

One such episode, for example, involved a little boy not more than 1 year old who wanted to use a swing that two other children were already using. Waiting for it to become free the little boy walked into an adjoining room. A teacher and other children who were seated around a table playing wanted him to join them, but he just stood in the doorway, watching them. From time to time he looked back, checking the swing, until at last it was free; at that his face light up and he ran over to the swing. A full 3 min. and 30 sec. had elapsed. The infants engaged in reflection on features of the world (such as the correspondence between their right hand and a right shoe and their left hand and a left shoe), in solving problems (such as how to reach something that is on a shelf too high up), and in observing other children's acts, such as dressing a doll intensely for extended periods, thereby become able to do the same thing.

To give a flavor of the episodes that make up the units of analysis let us look at 19-month-old Mia, who is trying to master the art of using the slide.

Mia has bit by bit learned to slide sitting up. One day at the nursery another little girl slides down on her front. Mia sees this and says, "Tummy ... Mia tummy a'well." She points to her stomach and repeats: "Tummy, wanna go tummy." Mia climbs to the top of the steps, but sits down and slides down in her usual way. The other little girl carries on sliding on her front. Mia climbs up again, kneels down, and says: "Tummy, tummy a'well," She gets up and waves her hands around in agitation, but eventually sits again and slides down sitting up. This carries on for a while, Mia sliding down the slide several times sitting up. Leaving the slide, she bends over and tries on one of the adults' shoes that is lying on the floor. Then she gets up, goes over to the slide and holds on to it from the front. Straight afterwards she goes into a little closet and draws a curtain over the entrance. She peeps out, but draws the curtain again.

When another child goes into the closet, she leaves it, goes up close to the slide to watch a little boy sliding down. Then she goes straight round to the steps, climbs them, lies on her front and slides down, though a bit awkwardly and with great care. (Lindahl, 1996, pp. 98–99)

This episode involves, according to Lindahl's interpretation, an extensive continuity of intention, repeated and slightly varied attempts, withdrawal, reflection, observation, and sudden insight. Lindahl claimed that such a sudden insight is always preceded by a brief period of withdrawal.

Compared with Pramling's results, Lindahl's study shows convincingly that children's awareness of learning (as a function of practice, observation, reflection) as expressed through acts, predates their awareness as expressed in words by 5 years or more. This difference has to do with the difference between two levels of awareness, which we will deal with later.

Judging from observations such as Lindahl's, we have to conclude that children are indeed aware of learning, in the sense of being aware of not being able to do something, trying to become able to do it, and being satisfied when this is achieved. Looking at this study moves us to reflect on the way the question "*Why* do people learn?" should be addressed. From an experiential perspective, the answer is of a teleological nature: we explain learning in terms of what the learner is trying to achieve. The explanation is an aim, and points to the future, in distinct contrast with causal explanations that point to events in the past; we are saying "people learn in order to ..." rather than "people learn because they have...." Children demonstrate this, but they do not say so. Quite clearly, if they cannot talk (as the infants they are), then they can hardly talk about learning.

But that might well not be the only reason, as we see later. Even when children grow older and more verbal, there are still constraints on what they can say about learning. To be able to describe something we have to be aware of it. Earlier we argued that this is exactly what Lindahl's infants are, aware of their own learning, but to talk about it, to describe it, takes another kind of awareness. We can call it conscious awareness, our awareness of being aware. The difference between the two kinds of awareness is succinctly illustrated by Helen Keller's autobiographical account of the languageless world of the deaf and blind child; although she was aware of the world, in the sense of being affected by it, feeling it, experiencing the presence of things, she was not aware of her own awareness. Hence she was "locked into" every specific situation:

Before my teacher came to me, I did not know that I am. I lived in a world that was a no-world. I cannot hope to describe adequately that unconscious time of nothingness. I did not know that I know aught, or that I lived or acted or desired. I had neither will nor intellect. I was carried along to objects and acts by a certain blind natural impetus. I had a mind which caused me to feel anger, satisfaction, desire. These two facts led those about me to suppose that I willed and thought. I can remember all this, not because I knew that I was so, but because I have tactual memory.... My inner life, then, was blank, without past, present, or future, without hope or anticipation, without wonder or joy or faith. (Keller, 1908, p. 113)

The ascent of the awareness of being aware seems to be linked with the development of language, which is presumably why we remember so little from our early lives before we could talk and understand spoken language.

The kind of learning that was in focus in the investigations carried out both at the OU in Britain and in secondary schools in Hong Kong was learning about the world through symbolic representation, whether written or spoken. It is by far the most common form of learning in educational institutions, and it is this kind of learning about which our entire book is concerned. Quite obviously, it is not the kind of learning dealt with by the children interviewed in Pramling's study, and even less in Lindahl's preschool study, so it might be said that in going so far back in the history of our learners we have passed the point that is of interest: where infants first become pupils and start to cope with the expectations and rigors of mediated learning. Nevertheless, these investigations of very young children's differing ways of experiencing learning throw light on our question: "From where do approaches to learning spring?" by highlighting aspects of learning that are hidden or taken for granted by older learners.

First of all the very idea of learning appears in a pretty straightforward form among 8-year-olds: Learning is a change from not being able to do something to becoming able to do so, due to experience. This is a general aspect of all the different ways of experiencing learning which are confined to the socially shared meaning. For example, "learning to do" is differentiated from "doing," and learning is not seen merely as a function of getting older, but as a result of having some experiences. Another point made clear is that acts of learning, actually what we refer to as learning in the narrowest sense, are acts with the main, even the sole, purpose of bringing such a change about, and that they belong to what we have called the first temporal facet of learning, "acquiring." Differences in this respect are differences in the "how" aspect of learning. The kind of ability or capability that learning yields, whether a capability to do, to know or to understand a certain thing, is one "what" aspect of learning which belongs to the second temporal facet, "knowing." We say *one* "what" aspect because there is another "what" aspect, the specific *content* of learning (e.g., learning to ride a bike, that Bangkok is the capital of Thailand, or that it snows in winter and rains in summer).

## DIFFERENT WAYS OF EXPERIENCING
## THE LEARNING OF MATH

Investigations have been undertaken into this second "what" of learning (the direct object) that actually cast light onto the "how" and the first "what" aspect (the indirect object) as well, one being a study of the experience of what it takes to learn math among three classes of 7-year-old school beginners (Ekeblad, 1995). It differs from other studies in this chapter as far as the content is concerned, aiming at children learning math based on a view of arithmetic skills very close to one we elaborate on in the next chapter (Neuman, 1987), according to which a sensuous experience of numbers counts more than counting, although that is also a necessary prerequisite. But it also differs in the medium of learning, in that Ekeblad had developed several computer games based on that view (Ekeblad & Lindström, 1995), and the children spent their first year in a classroom where there was a computer by which the games were implemented. All the children involved in the study were interviewed at the beginning and end of the year, as well as during the year in conjunction with sessions of computer games. The focus of the study was the nature and development of the experience of number during the first year in school, partly in relation to the children's ways of interacting with the computer games, against the background of their total experience of math during the period.

In describing some distinctly different ways in which children experience their learning of math, Ekeblad focuses very much on the how aspect of learning, the main focus of this chapter, and finds a distinction with respect to agency: In some cases the children see themselves as the agents of learning—"learning is something *I* do"; in other cases the teacher is seen as the agent of learning—learning is brought about by others. There is another distinction, however, which according to Ekeblad's line of reasoning is superordinate to that: In some cases the children seem to see *math learning as a gift,* something that just happens, a sudden revelation, as illustrated by the following interview with Drew:

I   And you don't know why *you* had learned so much either?
D   No. I didn't *learn.*
I   You didn't learn … You just knew without learning?
D   No, but I never knew how it had just *got* there.
I   No.… No no, as a matter of fact I can understand that …
D   … But *I* didn't go around *practising* like that.
(Ekeblad, 1995, p. 10, our italics in Drew for emphasis)

As you can see, there is not much experience of learning for Drew, whose experience is more one of having learned, or having become able (from which one must infer that one has learned). As Ekeblad put it: "So, as you are now able, you must have learned, and the aspects of your experience that might indicate *learning* must be that slight surprise, the excitement, or joy, that feeling of lightness that constitutes an aspect of your first successful performance," in line with the findings on the very first step of the Uruguayan students' experience of the acquisition stage of learning referred to earlier (Marton, Wen, & Nagle, in press).

The alternative to this is the experience of "math learning as work." The importance of repetition or practice may be emphasized as in this case:

I   How did you learn that seven plus three make ten, then?
A   … I … think … that … I … did it so many times in my exercise book.

In other cases, which also reflect the way of experiencing "math learning as work," learning is identified with the actual acts carried out:

I   Do you feel that you've learned something in math that you didn't know when you started?

P  Uhh ... With the hot dogs
I  Hot dogs?
P  Yes, there were hot dogs, you had to shop.
I  What did you learn with them?
P  Uh, that I got to ... uhh—I got to draw, like, rolls and burgers and ... write it, how
   much it cost.
(Ekeblad, 1995, p. 15, Paul)

Inherent in this second way of experiencing learning math, which is in line with
the second step of acquisition as found in the Uruguayan study, is the idea of practice
that is fundamental to our understanding of the phenomenon of learning, as
indicated in our account of Lindahl's toddlers and Pramling's preschool children,
an understanding closely correlated with age. But Ekeblad's interpretation differs
from Pramling's in that she points to the learner's focus in the experience of "math
learning as a gift" being on the object of learning, whereas in the experience of
"math learning as work" the focus is on the act of learning. As Drew did, several
children express a preference for the former while being well aware of the latter.
School certainly cultivates a focus on the act of learning, so it is not surprising that
its frequency increases with life as a pupil. But we have to ask, "Is a focus on the
act of learning necessarily better than a focus on the object of learning?" It is
reasonable to think of it as an advantage if learners can focus on either the object
or the act of learning, but we argue in chapters 7 and 8 that the learner being one
with the *object* of learning is a critical feature of genuine learning.

## WHAT DO WE KNOW ABOUT THE EXPERIENCE
## OF LEARNING?

The reader may find that it has been somewhat bewildering, our bringing together
findings on qualitative differences in the way in which learning is experienced that
originate from studies of learning in widely differing educational contexts, that if
infants, preschool children, secondary school pupils, and university students, and
moreover from such widely differing cultural contexts as Britain, Sweden, China,
Uruguay. Our assumption is that a phenomenon, such as learning as experienced,
can be characterized in terms of the complex of differing dimensions of variation
identified.

The picture that we offer of this complex is incomplete and not particularly well
integrated; most of the studies are very recent, and others are still in progress. If we
return to the question for this chapter, "From where do the different approaches to
learning spring?" it is seen that we have gone far beyond what is needed for a
reasonable answer to be attempted. The different approaches spring from the
different experiences of learning one has and has had, there being variation with
respect to depth (i.e., What agent is held responsible? What acts are considered
reasonable? What is the object of learning felt to be) and time (i.e., where learning
is located in one's temporal sense) and above all what one conceptualizes the
intertwined complex we call "learning" to be directed toward. If we return to our

overriding question, "How do we gain knowledge about the world?" the details of the variation we have identified start to take on a new significance. The agents of learning, the acts and objects of learning are more or less well situated in our world, the world about which we wish to gain knowledge.

The general impression from the results brought together in this chapter is, as we see it, that the ways in which learning is experienced differ in richness (different aspects of learning are discerned and held in focus simultaneously) and situational appropriateness (which particular aspect is held in focus under the prevailing conditions). In this chapter we did not attempt to spell out systematically what aspects of learning may be present simultaneously in the learner's awareness, or how the experience of learning might be structured in awareness, as we did attempt to do in some examples in the previous chapter. That topic is dealt with explicitly in chapter 5.

# 4

## Revealing Educationally Critical Differences in Our Understanding of the World Around Us

In the first three chapters of this book we have surely convinced the reader that learning—gaining knowledge about the world—and the learner's experience of learning are very complex phenomena. According to some lines of thought, the sheer feasibility of learning is logically questionable, but, paradoxically, learning certainly does occur in many forms and in many settings all around us and throughout our lives. We have seen that there is a variation in the approaches learners adopt to their tasks of learning, and that the approaches are profoundly intertwined with the learning outcome. This variation we have related to the ways in which learners conceptualize learning in the actual setting in which learning is taking place, and in chapter 3 we elaborated that notion to analyze the experience of learning in terms of time and depth, and looked at aspects of the development of the experience of learning.

There we pointed out that the way in which learners experience a particular situation, such as reading a given text or solving a particular problem, reflects the ways in which they experience the phenomena that enable them to make sense of the situation. The experience of the learning situation was described as having two intertwined aspects: the "how" and "what" aspects, where "how" refers to the experience of the act of reading, or of trying to solve a problem, whereas "what" refers to the experience of the actual text read, or the actual problem addressed, what we have referred to as the content or direct object of learning. The "how" aspect is then related to one's overall understanding of learning, reading or problem solving, and the "what" aspect is made sense of in terms of one's understanding of the topic dealt with in the text or the phenomena involved in the problem. In the best case, the experience of undertaking such a task as reading or problem solving brings about some change in one's understanding of the phenomena involved therein.

Such a change is more likely, or more visible when texts are read, in that they generally present a line of argument that their readers find more or less novel. The examples of chapter 2 illustrate this, in that novel ways of seeing university reform (selective measures) or how nations benefit from education (the output of the educational system) were being expounded in texts that were chosen to be within the reach of all the participants so that preconceived understandings were not expected to make much of a difference in how they experienced or understood them. The differences in understanding that were found seemed to reflect, as we pointed out before, differences in the participants' approaches to the tasks, and the differences in approaches to learning tasks have been found to reflect differences in the meaning that learning has for the learner. Qualitative differences in how people understand texts that they read in situations considered to be "learning situations" thus also reflect differences in the meaning that learning has for them.

When it comes to problem solving the situation is somewhat different. In problem solving it is often less obvious what changes come about in the problem solver's understanding of the phenomena involved in her isolated experience of a specific problem. On the other hand, it seems more obvious that the problem solver's experience of the specific problem (and her way of going about solving it) reflects, in addition to her preconceived ideas of what it takes to solve a problem—their understanding of the phenomena in terms of which she makes sense of the problem.

In this chapter we once again start from our central question, "How do we gain knowledge about the world?" and consider it in the light of studies into what people in educational settings learn about aspects of and phenomena in the world. In a search for what is educationally critical in the different ways the world around us can be experienced, we will deal with qualitative differences in the learners' understanding of content or phenomena related to the "what" aspect of learning. We present four examples of what we have in mind when we talk about this kind of difference, examples to which we return in subsequent chapters to consider other aspects of them and their implications.

## EXAMPLE 4.1:  ON THE ORIGIN
## OF ARITHMETIC SKILLS

Learning simple arithmetic is one of the most commonly researched fields in education. Moreover, it is one of the few fields in which a large number of researchers have reached a consensus as far as a general outline of a developmental path is concerned. According to this consensus view, arithmetic skills are acquired in three steps, which can be outlined as follows:

1. *Modeling*: Children are using objects or their fingers to model problems. For instance, in order to solve the word problem "2+7= _ " they count up two objects,

then seven objects, and they arrive at the answer 9 by counting all the objects together.

2. *Counting strategies*: Children may count silently or aloud, without using any objects: "1, 2 ... 3-1, 4-2, ... 9-7." They have to keep track of the number of units in the second addend, or otherwise they would not know when to stop. An easier approach leads to them say: "7 ... 8, 9 ... it's nine," having switched the two addends, 2 and 7, to start with the larger. When they count on from the larger addend and utter "8, 9" for the smaller, they can hear its "twoness," and they realize that it is time to stop counting because 9 is the last unit, and hence 9 is the answer.

3. *Number facts*: The children simply know the addition and subtraction tables. By retrieving the relevant combinations of numbers they can solve the various problems they meet.

The characteristics of the different counting strategies—mostly hidden from observation—are not part of the layman's understanding, but they have been revealed by researchers, and their findings have been disseminated to teachers and student teachers. Most adults, however, would probably agree with the following briefer but structurally identical description of how children acquire arithmetic skills: First they count things, then they keep practicing arithmetic tasks with symbols, and eventually they come to know the number facts by heart.

Now, general agreement does not in itself imply correctness, and we want to question the very basis for this agreement. To begin with there is a somewhat surprising finding from Russell and Ginsburg (1984) from a study aimed at comparing the mathematical ability of children with and without mathematical difficulties. They found that the only significant and dramatic difference was that the former (with difficulties) did not have a mastery of the simplest number facts whereas the latter (without difficulties) did. These children have all gone through phases of modeling with concrete objects and practicing counting strategies, but some of them have failed to develop mastery of the simplest number facts. How can this be? These somewhat curious results were in good agreement with earlier work that Eriksson and Neuman had carried out with the same aim (Eriksson & Neuman, 1981). They found that children, in this case 7- to 13-year-olds with difficulties in mathematics, managed to solve only 28% of a set of simple arithmetic problems involving numbers in the range of 1–10 without using strategies for "keeping track" (i.e., counting and at the same time counting the counting words, as we will elaborate on later), compared with 87% success for children in a comparison group.

This research points to the fact that even older children with difficulties in mathematics use strategies for counting and keeping track, rather than number facts, when they deal with very simple arithmetic problems. That means that as much as 6 years of practicing strategies for counting do not necessarily yield a capability for using number facts. The received developmental wisdom, that by using counting strategies you end up with number facts, obviously does not hold water, at least for a fairly large group of children.

It was against the background of these results indicating the importance of mastery of number facts in the range of 1–10 that Neuman set out to investigate the question, "What does it take to master the simplest number facts, those in the range of 1–10?" (Neuman, 1987).

## The Experience of Numbers

Although counting may be both instrumental and necessary in developing the mastery of number facts, the critical issue is not counting as such. Neuman (1989) claimed unequivocally that the critical feature of a child (or adult, for that matter) acquiring simple arithmetic skills is the possession of the capability of experiencing the numerosity of numbers larger than 3 or 4. The numerosity of 3 or 4 objects is something that we can all experience. We *see* that three objects are exactly three, or that four object are exactly four. We can even *hear* the threeness or fourness of three or four words, sounds, or whatever units. Try it! Even very young children can do this; they have the capability of subitizing (instantaneously perceiving) small numerosities. But when the number of the objects (or sounds) is larger, we lose this immediate sense of numerosity—we need to count.

When we experience something, we usually experience it as a whole that is present to us in its entirety. That is the way we experience chairs, dogs, sunrises, gearboxes, or whatever. Even with a book, when we have read it, we (usually) have a sense or grasp of the whole thing, and the same with a painting or piece of music. But what about "seven"? How can we experience the sevenness of seven? Or as Neuman asks: "How can we be sure that seven really is seven?" She believes that this is where the secret of arithmetic skills lies. Unless the child can experience each one of the numbers from 1 to 10 as wholes, no genuine arithmetic skills can develop. The child has to learn to know the numbers, and to know is to be able to experience.

Now, if we assume that Neuman is right, then the child has to be able to experience sets of "things" simultaneously (e.g., see 7 magpies or hear 5 shouts) in order to develop genuine arithmetic skills. Earlier we stated that neither children nor adults can experience more than 3 or 4 objects simultaneously, and yet, quite a few of us do develop genuine arithmetic skills. Are we tripping over paradoxes again? Is Neuman wrong? Well, not necessarily, but it is a dilemma for the moment.

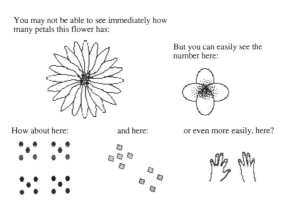

You may not be able to see immediately how many petals this flower has:

But you can easily see the number here:

How about here:          and here:          or even more easily, here?

The petals in the flower of the first drawing need to be counted; those of the second can be subitized. We can perceive numerosity of sets larger than 3 or 4 as long as the units form a pattern as is the case of the two dot patterns and the finger pattern. In fact, a sound pattern works just as well. Think of a radio call signal, such as beep, beep, beep … beep, beep, beep … beep. We can hear the threeness of three beeps, the twoness of the two groups of three beeps, and the oneness of the singular beep. Moreover we might, but not necessarily, be able to experience the whole pattern simultaneously. Radio operators who use Morse code certainly can.

But a pattern thus experienced, visually or aurally, is not necessarily a number. It might be experienced just as a pattern. No, to have a *numerical* experience we must experience the units as such at the same time as we experience them together as the whole, and this offers a solution to the potential dilemma posed by Neuman's claim. Moreover, the pattern represents a number to the extent that the single units form an ordered set. In seven there is a first unit, a second, a third, and so on. This has to do with the dual sense of number. If we enumerate a boat's crew: 1, 2, 3 …, then the number 7 has the meaning "the seventh crew member." If we are counting to find out how large the crew is, and the seventh crew member is the last to be enumerated, then 7 has the meaning: "there are 7 crew members altogether." These two senses of numbers—their ordinal and cardinal aspects: the seven*th*ness of seven and the *sevenness* of seven—are both essential aspects of the experience of number, and we can conclude that we have to experience them simultaneously to grasp fully the structure and meaning of numbers.[1] *This* is what is necessary, we believe, in order to develop arithmetic skills.

**Number Facts.**     But not only that. Neuman claims that the fundamental building blocks of the skills of arithmetic in a denary system are the different combinations of numbers between 1 and 10. In addition to being able to experience a number as a whole *and* as an ordered set, the child has to develop a capability of experiencing each number both as a sum of smaller numbers and as a part of larger numbers. To take 4 as an example, 4 is the sum of 1 and 3 as well as of 2 and 2. At the same time it is a part of all the numbers larger than 4: 5, 6, 7 and so on. In the same way, 7 can be seen as the sum of 1 and 6, 2 and 5, and of 3 and 4, while being at the same time a part of 8, 9, and 10. These are what we will call the part–whole relationships of 4 and 7, respectively.

Now being able to experience numbers in terms of their part–whole relationships is different from remembering number facts. If a child understands 9 as encompassing all the different combinations of its constituent parts then it follows, "If I don't remember how much I borrowed from you yesterday when I didn't have a single

---

[1]We are using the terms *cardinal* and *ordinal* in the sense defined in the article on Set Theory in the *New Encyclopedia Britannica*: "A number used to designate the size of a set (i.e., to answer the question "How many?") is used cardinally. Any use that depends on the position of the number in the prescribed sequence is the ordinal use of the number. The number at the top or bottom of the page is an example of the ordinal use of number" (Hashisaki, 1985). This definition is derived from, and is compatible with more fundamental definitions grounded in the theory of classes.

öre, but the only money I spent was 7 kronor for an ice cream and I have 2 kronor in my purse, then I might well have borrowed 9 kronor from you." Furthermore, all of the following are related perceptions:

"If I am 9 now I must have been 6 years old 3 years ago."

"If I am 4 years old, then my brother who is 9 is 5 years older then I am."

"If it is 7 o'clock and I have to go to bed at 9, then I have 2 hours left to read my book."

"If we have been in the air for only one hour and it takes 9 hours to fly to New York, then there must be 8 more hours to go."

Sheer recall of the number facts involving 9 does not enable such problems to be tackled unless stated in some recognizable way.

The capability of experiencing a number between 1 and 10 as all possible combinations of two parts enables one to handle an unlimited number of situations in which either one of the two parts or the whole is unknown—subtraction and missing addend in the former case and addition in the latter. What is more, larger numbers can now be experienced as combinations of their parts. The numbers between 11 and 20, in the first place, can now be experienced as combinations of numbers between 1 and 20, in particular as combinations of 10 and another number in the range.

The point we are trying to make, if rather lengthily, is that numbers are not only things used for counting or things for which you need to remember facts by heart, but things you *experience* through your senses. In fact, this is the essential difference between our arguments and those used by the researchers who have reached the consensus described at the start of this section: We prioritize the nature and structure of the child's very experience of number over the memorization or practice of number skills. Numbers do not have to be experienced through any particular sense, but what is vital is the simultaneous experience of the different aspects of numbers: cardinality or numerosity, ordinality or ordered units, and constitution or part–whole relationships.

Two questions now demand consideration. First, what makes us so sure that this is a reasonable way of describing critical features of arithmetic skills? Second, if these are indeed critical features, how do they develop?

***Counted Numbers Versus Finger Numbers.*** We consider the first question first. Most school children and adults handle simple arithmetic problems such as the previous examples automatically; they "just know it," a response that does little to reveal how they experience the numbers involved. But there are cases in which we are able to observe ways of experiencing numbers, because they are reflected in the ways the numbers are dealt with when a child, especially a child who has not yet been taught any arithmetic, has to do something in order to solve a problem. Neuman offers some examples including the following, a problem she used in her original investigation in 1987:

If you have only 2 kronor and you want to buy a comic that costs 9 kronor, how many more kronor do you need?

This is known as a missing addend problem: You know that 2 and "something" have to add up to 9. If you do not know the "something" at once, you can count, saying "1, 2" (for the 2 kronor you've got) and then "3, 4, 5, 6, 7, 8, 9" (one numeral for each of the kronor you need). Having said "3, 4, 5 … 9," you need to know how many numerals you have uttered. But you don't! You can't! We have gone to lengths to point out that you cannot hear the sevenness of seven just straight off. Therefore, you have to keep track of the numerals. One way might be to keep track by counting numbers, setting an index for every numeral uttered, saying "1, 2 … 3-*1*, 4-*2* … 9-*7*." You stop at 9, referring to the ninth krona, and you can read off the index, 7, which gives you the number of kronor that you still need to buy the comic. This is an example of so-called double counting, in which the two aspects of number, the ordinal, which refers to which krona you are mentioning, and the cardinal, which refers to how many kronor you have mentioned, are kept separate. You arrive at an answer, but you do not experience the two aspects simultaneously—quite the contrary.

Another form of keeping track and counting numbers is by using fingers to keep count of the numbers as they are uttered. The task would then be solved by saying "1, 2" and then continuing "3, 4, … 9" (raising one finger at a time until 9 is uttered). By now all the fingers on one hand and two on the other have probably been raised, forming a pattern that can be recognized as 7. This is another procedure for keeping track in double counting, and again, the two aspects of numbers—ordinality and cardinality—are kept apart. The ordinal aspect lies in the numerals uttered—3 (= the third), 4 (= the fourth) … 9 (= the ninth)—and the cardinal aspect lies in the fingers raised for later counting. Thus once again, the aspects are not being experienced simultaneously, and neither of these methods of keeping track by counting numbers amounts to the way of experiencing numbers that we believe to be necessary for the development of arithmetic skills.

There is another, quite different way of using fingers, representing another way of experiencing numbers, which can be illustrated using just the same problem, 2+_=9. In this case the child *starts* by raising 9 fingers palm up, opening both hands and folding in her thumb. She looks at her fingers and folds in two more, the two next to her thumb. Still looking at her fingers she usually *sees* that there are now 7 fingers raised, and says: "You need 7 more kronor." In this case, 2 kronor are being taken away instead of 7 being added. The child is experiencing the whole 9 and two parts within it, one of which is known to be 2 and the other of which is unknown but can be found.

With this way of using fingers comes a great discovery: You can switch the parts in a number around; you can put them in whichever order you want; you can add or take away according to need; and you can deal quite simply with the smaller part. Therefore, if you get the problem "You had 9 kronor and lost 7, how many kronor do you have left?" (9-7=_) you can avoid dealing with the larger number 7 and deal with the smaller part instead: You simply add on "7 … 8, 9" and hear or see the twoness of 8 and 9 together. Work through the related problem: "You have 2 kronor and you find 7 more. How many do you have altogether?" Again, you start with the larger number 7 and find yourself seeing or hearing the twoness of 8 and 9 so that you know you have added 2 to 7. If the child uses her fingers, she will almost certainly represent the larger number by a whole hand (the undivided 5) together with one or more fingers of the other hand. Now the finger patterns unify the ordinal aspect (the experience of ordered fingers) and the cardinal aspect (the numerosity of the fingers taken together). Moreover, the hands impart a strong sense of the parts within the whole, which enables the child to cope with any problem when two of three numbers between one and ten are given and the third is to be found.

This comparison between keeping track by counting numbers (whether on the fingers or in some other way) and what we can call "finger numbers"[2] to represent wholes and parts within wholes constitutes our argument in answer to the first question. Extensive use of procedures for keeping track are closely related to math difficulties, whereas an experience of the parts that constitute whole numbers between 1 and 10 leads to knowing number facts. Procedures for keeping track deliberately and inevitably separate the ordinal and the cardinal aspects of numbers, whereas finger numbers as we have described them bring them together in a simultaneous experience of numbers.

**Numbers as Extents and Numbers as Names.**    The three different ways of experiencing the numbers 1–10 that we have described so far—number facts, finger numbers, and counted numbers—all enable children to solve simple arithmetic problems, but there are other ways of experiencing numbers that do not. The most frequent of these among young children is characterized by its focus only on the *cardinal* aspect of number. In such cases, children experience wholes and parts as vague approximate numerosities without experiencing the units that constitute the parts. Imagine a child who is shown 9 marbles and is asked to count them, and who then witnesses them being put into two boxes. She does not see how many are put into each box, but is asked to guess how many are in each of them. Given five guesses, she may say something like "4 in one and 6 in the other" as her first guess and "3 in one and 5 in the other" as her second guess. She has an experience of the relationships between the parts and the whole, but, failing to discern the single marbles experientially, her answers lack precision. This way of experiencing number is called "numbers as extents."

What sense can we make of another apparently mysterious reply to the same question, a child who replies "2 in one box and 9 in the other" as a first guess, and "7 in one box and 9 in the other" as a second guess? He claims that out of 9 marbles there are some in one box and always 9 in the other. We interpret this as manifesting an experience of number that is the opposite of the previous one in that the child experiences only the *ordinal* aspects of numbers, with the numerosity of the set of

---

[2]This is a term introduced by Neuman, which we are using with a slight relaxation; while we, like she, emphasize that numbers are thus made visible ordinally and cardinally at the same time, Neuman also emphasized the undivided order of the fingers.

items failing to come into focus. In this experience of number, the child envisages the marbles placed in a row, let's suppose from left to right. Somewhere in the row there is a dividing line, and those to its left are in one box whereas those to its right are in the other. Furthermore, the marble to the left of the divide is the last marble in the first box. If the child guesses that there are 4 marbles in the first box, then this particular marble is the fourth one. When he counts objects, the numeral he uses to denote the last object is the numeral used to denote the whole set; in other words, the ordinal aspect of the number puts a name on the size of the set. Therefore, if this is the fourth marble then there are 4 marbles in the first box. So far, so good. But in the same way, the marble at the right of the row is always referred to as "nine," so, applying the rule "the numeral used to denote the last one is the numeral used to denote the whole set," there are always 9 marbles in the second box. Figure 4.1 attempts to illustrate this way of experiencing number: All of the marbles are there in a dimly glimpsed background, but the focus is on the dividing line and the marbles at the end of the two parts it forms: 4 and 9.

Children in this case experience *numbers as names*. They are aware of the part–whole relationships, and they are also aware of the ordered set of units, even if they cannot necessarily discern in the example for instance, 4 and 5 units. But they focus on the last units in each of the two parts.

## Qualitatively Different Ways of Experiencing Numbers

The picture that evolves is that in the complete experience of number all aspects are present simultaneously. In a lesser way of experiencing number, different aspects are present in a parallel fashion, side by side but separate. In even less advanced ways, certain aspects are held in focus in one case and others in another. It seems that we can find ways of experiencing numbers that involve fewer and fewer aspects simultaneously.

In Fig. 4.2 we have summarized the five qualitatively different ways of experiencing numbers that we have discussed in this chapter. These can be seen as forming three levels. Starting from the bottom, in "numbers as names" and "numbers as extents" one or the other of the two main aspects of numbers, the ordinal and the cardinal, is focused on and is present in awareness, and that does not give sufficient grounds for solving arithmetic problems. In "counted numbers" and "finger numbers" both the ordinal and the cardinal aspects are produced while dealing with problems (in the first case separately, in the second case in an integrated manner), and arithmetic problems can be solved. "Number facts" refers to the simultaneous experience of the ordinal and cardinal aspects as well as of part–whole relationships. Note, it is not at all about knowing addition or subtraction tables by heart.

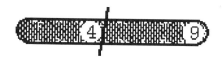

FIG. 4.1. Numbers as names. There is a vague awareness of the members of the set but the focus is on the ordinal aspect of the number.

| number facts | Reflects a complete experience of numbers and their part-whole relationships. A simultaneous experience of cardinal and ordinal aspects is reflected by the way problems are handled, even if there is no conscious awareness of them. |
|---|---|
| finger numbers | Numbers are laid on fingers and made visible. By arranging the largest part first there is usually a pattern of a full hand (the undivided five) plus odd fingers. Numerosity (cardinal aspect) and ordered items (ordinal aspect) can be experienced simultaneously, as well as parts and whole. |
| counted numbers | Ordinal and cardinal aspects of numbers are present in parallel, side by side and separately. Track is kept of numerals that are spoken by counting, either by speaking other numerals or by setting up fingers. |
| numbers as extents | Focus is only on the cardinal aspect of number. Children experience wholes and parts as vague approximate numerosities without experiencing the units within the parts. |
| numbers as names | Focus is on the ordinal aspect of number. Children are aware of the part-whole relationships. They are also aware of the ordered set of units, and they focus on the last units in each of the two parts |

FIG. 4.2.  Five ways of experiencing number.

This characterization of the variation in how numbers are experienced in three levels—of quite a different order from the three levels of the dominant view introduced at the beginning of this section—is partial and oversimplified. It is common for children to alternate between different ways of experiencing number, in the first place within levels, but to some extent between levels as well. Furthermore, there are other ways of experiencing number and there are other aspects of numbers that children become capable of discerning and having simultaneous, focal, awareness of (e.g., singularity of units, units as parts of parts, part–part relations, etc). More detailed accounts of the variation in the experience of number are to be found in other works (Neuman, 1987, 1989), but here we are focusing on educationally critical ways of experiencing number and the development of arithmetic skill.

## The Development of Arithmetic Skills

Neuman suggested finger numbers as the main path toward arithmetic skills, and as we have seen fingers do indeed lend themselves very well to bringing about simultaneous awareness of different aspects of numbers and hence a complete experience of them. She provides a detailed description of how children use their fingers, organizing first the larger number to give a hand or an undivided five, starting with one of the little fingers. Doverborg personal communication also found that children use their fingers quite extensively to make numbers visible, although not always necessarily in this particular way.

The most important argument for the existence of alternative paths to the development of arithmetic skills comes from the study of blind children (Ahlberg & Csocsán, 1994; Csocsán, 1988). Blind children do not seem to use their fingers spontaneously for arithmetic purposes at all. An obvious reason for this is that it is very difficult to sense the numerosity of finger in a tactile way. For example, blind children have difficulty in telling how many of their fingers an experimenter has unfolded from their clenched hands.

Blind children lag about 2 years behind seeing children in the development of arithmetic skills, but they seem to catch up. In a detailed study of blind children between 7 and 8 years of age, Ahlberg and Csocsán (1994) showed that blind children who had developed good arithmetic skills handle and experience arithmetic problems in qualitatively similar, or even identical, ways to seeing children. Furthermore, they try to use structural features of sets when asked to establish their numerosity (they make use of two and three groups of objects which they try to grasp simultaneously as compared to the more frequent double counting of one element at a time).

The different investigations referred to here give support to the thesis that arithmetic skills originate from the sensuous experience of numbers between 1 and 10. Let us briefly reflect on what this means. The dominant understanding of arithmetic skills, in contrast to the proposition we have put forward, is that they originate from counting objects one at a time: The objects themselves are, of course, experienced, and the mathematical aspects such as cardinality and ordinality are abstract, arrived at through the abstracting acts of the mind operating on sensory data. What *we* are saying is that the development of arithmetic skills demands that exactly these apparently abstract aspects can, and in fact must, be experienced sensuously and simultaneously. We need to see, hear, or feel the "sevenness" of seven, for instance, and the "seven*th*ness" of seven. We can then see, hear, or feel that there are seven elements, and we can see, hear, or feel that the seventh element is indeed the seventh element (and is thus preceded by six others). Moreover, we can see, hear, or feel in the seven the one and the six, the two and the five, the three and the four, just as we can see, hear or feel the seven in the eight, the nine and the ten.

Now, we do not know the extent to which such a sensuous and simultaneous experience of the different aspects of number takes place. The point is that it does *not* take place for those who are *classified* as having difficulties with mathematics, and, more important, it does *not* take place for those who *do* have difficulties with mathematics. We also do not know exactly how such development takes place when it does take place. Using fingers to make numbers visible (as opposed to using fingers for counting numerals, double-counting) is probably the most frequent and convenient way. There are also the doubles (two "ones" are two, two "twos" are four, two "fours" are eight and so on), triples (one "three" is three, two "threes" are six, etc.), plus or minus 1 (5 and 3 makes eight because 4 and 4 makes eight), and even double-counting, although it appeared to be a cul-de-sac for the older children in Eriksson and Neuman's 1981 study, might occasionally play some part in development; blind children appear to be experts on verbal double-counting. It may be as Ekeblad (1994) suggested, that the development of a sensuous and simultaneous experience of numbers and their ordinal, cardinal, and part–whole aspects may include keeping track of one numeral at a time, given that children listen to the genuine voices of numbers, by which Ekeblad means not seeing them from one particular point of view only, not dealing with them solely in one way, but trying to capture the richness of the variation in their appearances. Now, if we are right in claiming that a sensuous and simultaneous experience of the different aspects of number is of critical importance for the development of arithmetic skills, we should be able to make use of this insight for developing such skills. We return to this possibility in chapter 8.

## EXAMPLE 4.2: CRITICAL ASPECTS OF UNDERSTANDING RECURSION

For a somewhat different example of an educationally critical aspect of the learner's understanding, we can return once again to the study of students learning to program featured in chapter 2. One notion central to programming in standard Meta-Language (ML), the language these students were studying, and indeed to most modern programming languages, is recursion, and it was also central to one interview a short time after it had been introduced formally to the students.

Whereas the numbers between 1 and 10 need no introduction for the reader, recursion probably does. There are many examples of recursion in everyday life, as well as in mathematics, art, and music, which capture different aspects of the programming concept (Hofstadter, 1979). Take, as a simple example, what happens when you look into a large wall mirror when there is another wall mirror at a slight angle behind you, as most clothes shops cunningly provide. If you look into the mirror straight ahead, you see a reflection of the mirror behind you, and of course you see at least part of your back reflected there. You also see behind you the reflection of the mirror in front, with an image of your face, and so on, ever smaller and, because of the mirror's imperfections, ever less distinctly you see in principle endless copies of your back and of your face. This is in one sense a recursive phenomenon, in that there are large numbers of copies of exactly the same thing, although they are getting smaller and apparently receding in the distance.

The Russian doll is another example, which brings in another aspect of recursion. When you unscrew the top from the bottom of such a doll you find another doll, slightly smaller and painted in a different pattern, nesting inside. Unscrew that and another doll is revealed, and so on, the number of dolls depending on the size of the original. Finally you find nothing but a small polished but plain and solid doll-shape. The set of doll copies has come to an end. This time we have reached a terminating case and there is nothing to do but to set them together again.

A third example comes from the children's book *Cat in the Hat* by Dr. Seuss (1966), in which a cat wearing a hat sets out to help sweep the snow from the pavement. But there is too much for one cat to do, so he lifts off his hat to reveal another slightly smaller cat with a hat, who jumps down and starts to help clear the snow. When it proves too much even for two cats, the second cat lifts his hat and reveals—yet another, even smaller, cat. This procedure continues until enough cats have been called into action to get the snow cleared, upon which, one by one, each leaps back onto the head of the next largest cat, who puts on his hat and repeats the process. Whereas the trick with mirrors and the Russian dolls are both recursive *structures,* in the sense that they involve endless or limited numbers of copies of the same thing nested in one another, the cats perform a recursive *process,* the normal case which is copied being the removal of a hat to reveal a smaller cat nested there, and the terminating case being the ability to clear all the snow. Then there is a return to a normal state by reversing the process.

Recursion is a construct which, as far as it occurs in programmed algorithms, allows the programmer to bring about repetition, in a rather special way compared to the more usual (or, one might say, in other older programming environments) iterative method of looping through instructions until a specified condition is met. For example, a number of cycles has been made, or a required state is reached, or a particular item has been found in the data, or time runs out. To write such a looping algorithm in a program it is necessary to define what should be done each time the cycle is performed and exactly what conditions should call a halt. Recursion, in contrast, is able to bring about repetition through the fundamental property of self-reference: A statement that is to be repeated makes use of itself in a more limited form—thereby getting repeated, until a previously specified terminating case is reached.

The context in which the students in the study met recursion was as a way of writing ML functions that facilitate repetition, brought about by the defined function referring to itself, in an ever diminishing form, until a suitable criterion, or terminating case, is met (Booth, 1992b). As was mentioned in chapter 2, ML is grounded in mathematics, and recursion is directly equivalent to mathematical induction, an approach to proving a mathematical statement by assuming the truth of a similar statement and knowing that one instantiation of the statement is proven true. It should also be said that recursion, like mathematical induction, is a notoriously difficult concept for students to make sense of, and a good deal of research has gone into identifying ways of simplifying it for the learner (Anderson, Pirolli, & Farrell, 1988; Henderson & Romero, 1989). The aim in this study, rather than finding better ways of presenting it, or simplifying it for students, was to reveal how students were actually experiencing it, so that teachers could then exploit that insight.

At some point in the third of a series of interviews, each of 14 students was asked to describe the ideas underlying recursion. From this a discussion ensued in which the interviewer's goal was to probe the student's understanding as far as possible before presenting a simple textbook problem of the kind they had been working on in class. They were asked what the problem meant; then they were asked to try to write a program (a function in ML) to satisfy it. As work progressed the student was asked for clarification of points that were puzzling the interviewer (who was herself quite well acquainted with the field but intent on finding out how the students were thinking), and when they could proceed no further, they were asked to explain what their program, or partial program plus a simple correct program presented by the interviewer, would achieve. (This was part of the material that underpinned the results on approaches to writing programs described in Example 2.5 of chapter 2.)

## Students' Experience of Recursion

As a result of analyzing these interviews three qualitatively distinct ways of experiencing—talking of, working with, thinking about—recursion were identified, reflecting the students' current total experience of recursion. The least developed of the three sees recursion as *a programming construct in ML*. Recursion is seen as a feature of ML that is used for writing programs, with a structure reflected in a small number of standard templates for recursive functions and with gaps that are filled in according to a general case and a terminating case. For example, John says:

> J  I am not going to write any special program, but just write what I normally do. I just write $x::xs$ or something, it's usually *fun* $x::xs$, and then there is usually a variable, say $y$ … We have been doing a lot of different types, but we've done a lot with sets, so I'll write that it's a set $x::xs$ and a number $y$

This focuses on the syntactic meaning of recursion embodied in the syntactic and lexical elements of ML and the standardized format of an ML function.

A second way sees recursion as a *means of bringing about repetition in ML*, as a feature of the language used to repeat a task a number of times. Reference is made to the structure of the list or set of objects to which a recursive function is applied, and as an operation, recursion is seen to work through the list or set element by element. David exemplifies this:

> D  It runs in a loop. If you, sort of … Well, for example, if you have a list, want to do something with every bit of the list, select from it bit by bit, well, sort of like that … Do a mass of functions … then you run in a loop.

This can be thought of rather as a semantic understanding of recursion, focusing as it does on the meaning of what a recursive function can achieve in the context of problems for which models have to be devised.

The third way of understanding recursion is as *self-reference*. It is seen as a feature of ML that brings about repetition of tasks by allowing a function to make use of itself, subject to certain constraints. There is a structure, namely a function referring to (or calling, or being applied to) itself in an ever-diminishing way, together with a nonself-referential terminating case. It is seen to operate by cycling within itself subject to its coming ever closer to the structural constraint of the terminating case and on its stopping when that is met, thus producing (in some possibly unspecified way) a result. Greg voices this third way of experiencing recursion fairly thoroughly:

G   Well, you can say that, that you need a basic assumption, which you might call the
core of it, and then … so you have this core, and then you have another function, and
then you call this function from within the function itself, so it takes it over and over
again until it gets down to the core, well, that's pretty much all I can say.

This third way of understanding recursion is conceptual rather than merely
syntactic or semantic as the previous two were. It relates to the conceptual
framework, the mathematics of programming, and is an abstraction of the iteration
that was the focus of the second way of understanding recursion.

Although the reader might not understand the details of the descriptions, or the
students' quotes, the implications of the quotes are rather plain. The first quote,
from John, although it appears to be a word-by-word commentary on what he is
doing while writing a program, it actually comes from his description of what he
sees as the *ideas underlying* recursion, and indicates that he views recursion as
nothing more than a way of coding a program. The syntactic features that might be
used in any ML program, and a typical example, make up the body of the
description. In the second quote David describes recursion for what it can achieve
in a program, namely repetition, and the sort of structure (i.e., lists) it is most
commonly associated with at this stage. Greg, in the third quote, describes recursion
fairly completely, although in somewhat unconventional terms, in the context of
recursive algorithms, which is the only context so far encountered.

The three ways of understanding recursion become successively more complete,
moving toward the underlying mathematics of programming (induction) through
the functionality (repetition) of the construct, from the least complete notion of the
ML template. Furthermore, they have increasing explanatory power, in that they
enable the student to make sense of recursion in more and more situations, from
writing simple algorithms in ML to solve standard problems to devising programs
in ML that solve problems of a less standard nature to being able to tackle recursion
outside the domain of ML functions. What we are seeing is less and less being taken
for granted, from the taken-for-granted template with its mechanical filling in of
details from simple textbook problems to modeling repetition in problems in terms
of ML functions involving recursion to addressing recursion's fundamental structure and meaning.

## Expert Experience of Recursion

Now, the teacher certainly sees recursion in all the three ways described. It is indeed
a construct in ML. It does indeed bring about repetition, and its fundamental
characteristic is that it is self-referential, subject to constraints. The teacher can
certainly handle it from any of these perspectives, and possibly from others as well.
Indeed, an expert handles recursion in the context of writing a complex program as
being a repetitive construct, and only when a genuinely novel situation is met—a
new programming environment or an otherwise intractable difficulty—is the nature
of recursion addressed (Truvé, personal communication). Referring back to our
description of children's experience of number, we can say that a thorough experi-

ence of recursion amounts to a simultaneous experience of its aspects of programming syntax, looping semantics, self-referential inductive underpinnings, and so on, with different aspects coming into focus in different circumstances.

The first of the three ways of experiencing recursion focuses solely on it as a construct of ML. Any reference to its functionality or conceptual foundation is either missing or fleetingly considered by students who talk about recursion primarily in this way. When it comes to writing a program, they are fixated on mechanically filling in the details of one of a number of templates they have met for writing recursive functions. Now, some researchers into the psychology of programming, and in particular, those with an interest in developing expert systems for inclusion in intelligent tutoring systems (ITS), focus on this way of handling recursion as an ideal (Andersson et al., 1988). Their model for accepting a solution to a recursive problem is that an appropriate template is chosen from a set on offer, and that details are filled in to satisfy the demands of the problem. This is very much in line with the cognitivist view of learning described in chapter 1: training the student to grapple with our sixth paradox of learning, that of recognizing schematic solutions to problems. If a student (or a user in the case of an expert system or ITS) strays outside this ideal behavior, he or she is brought back into line with corrective advice, built around the structure of the template and the repetition that the problem demands, by the conditions for the terminating case being brought to the student's attention, for instance, or by the correction of a syntax error. This reflects the second way of understanding recursion. Referring again to the cognitivist view of learning, the advice can be seen as "piloting" the student toward the schematic ideal. What appears not to be highly prized, or brought to students' attention is the fundamental idea of self-reference, or the mathematical analogy of induction. The goals of such studies are to get students around the conceptual difficulties of recursion (and induction) and get them writing efficient and correct programs just like experts do. After all, teachers are experts, and the expert systems that lie at the heart of intelligent tutor systems are devised according to their habits and priorities.

## Educationally Critical Aspects of Understanding Recursion

For experts, as mentioned earlier, self-reference only needs to come into the picture when and if some unexpected or genuinely new aspect of programming crops up, when the meaning and structure of recursion can no longer be taken for granted. Templates for algorithms become ever more intuitive and adaptable to problems that become increasingly familiar and routine. But what about students? They, in a serious education for potential professionals—potential researchers and teachers among them—are constantly meeting recursion (and induction) in unexpected and genuinely new guises: new languages with unfamiliar implementations, data structures and data types, arguments and proofs. They need to be readily aware of the self-referential nature of recursion. This third way of understanding recursion has greater power for the furtherance of datalogical development, whether for the individual learning student or for the collective field of computer science development and research.

Some of the students, however, had not come beyond the first (the construct) at the time of this interview, when considerably more complex problems were being tackled in class, and moves were being made toward new contexts for recursion. It is suggested that, just in the way that finger numbers might be critical for most children to be able to develop a mathematical understanding that can develop toward general arithmetic skills, it is possibly critical for these students to become capable of experiencing recursion such that its self-referential and induction-like aspects come readily into focus if the students are to develop into reflective computer scientists rather than routine-bound producers of program code.

One instructional shortcoming can be seen in the lack of observability of recursive self-reference. With their wish to focus on the specification of programs rather than on the computer's actual workings, the teachers of this course deliberately avoided discussion of recursion's implementation. It was not a central subject of instruction, nor was it made visible within the computer system. Thus one basic aspect of recursive programs was not available to students' awareness. One student, Neil, expressing something very close to the conceptual understanding of recursion, said:

> N  … In this case, with a function, (you do) a part of the program until you come to the base case, and when you have found that you go up again, the partial things you have done … *I think it's terribly difficult to explain in any sensible way.* Well, you have something and so you do to the base with it, and then when you have come to the base then you go back again and do each item that you should have done … *Nobody has explained in purely technical terms how it works.*

Neil is clearly grappling with a partial understanding of the concept: "It's terribly difficult to explain in any sensible way," maybe precisely because "Nobody has explained in purely technical terms how it works." Thus, the ideas have not been adequately grounded in this student's framework of what it takes to understand a programming concept, not only the abstract but also the technical. He feels unable to discern the technical and mathematical underpinnings that would enable him to keep a check on the functionality he is trying to achieve in the program.

This is an example of the teachers' understanding of the central notion of instruction being at odds with the ways many of the students were understanding it, and of their ways of instructing being inadequately grounded in the students' experience of what it takes to program and to learn to program. What is even more striking in this example of recursion is that students with no more developed understanding than of recursion being some way of writing programs in ML could actually produce correct and functioning programs through recourse to memorized templates, whereas those who were struggling with more advanced ways of understanding were producing seriously flawed programs (Booth, 1992a). Thus, written work such as examination questions and lab exercises were not capable of differentiating between different levels of understanding, and students with undeveloped notions of recursion stood to succeed better in examinations than those who had come a bit further in their understanding without having gone all the way.

Descriptions of the three ways of experiencing recursion identified here em-power the teacher to address inconsistent or apparently nonsensical difficulties students have with recursion. In particular, it offers a framework other than that of the discipline of computer science within which the teacher can consider recursion as an algorithmic construct in ML and identify what aspects of the total under-standing are essential for adequate future development. But most important, it forces the teacher to consider ways of bringing about such a focus in understanding and of testing it.

## EXAMPLE 4.3:  NEWTONIAN MOTION

Mechanics is an aspect of classical physics that has an undisputed part in any physics curriculum at the upper secondary school, as well as in engineering, mathematics, and physics degree courses. A large part of classical physics rests on the work of Newton, published in the three books of his *Principia* in 1686, the culmination of twenty years of work. In the introduction to *Principia*, having defined fundamental quantities of mass, momentum, inertia and force, he goes on to state the laws that these quantities must obey. In a modern commentary on the work, Roche (1988) wrote:

> *The first law*, derived from Galileo, Gassendi and Descartes, declares that *a body will rigidly maintain its state of uniform motion in a straight line, or its state of rest, unless it is acted upon by an impressed force.* Today this law is known as the *law of inertia.* (p. 50)

The introduction goes on to state the second and third laws, which also have their roots in what other natural philosophers had written earlier, Newton's contribution being, as Roche described it, "to express these three laws in an economical and quantitative form, and to gather them together as the foundation of theoretical mechanics" (p. 52). That was only the introduction. The three books went on to introduce Newton's symbolic tools for handling theoretical mechanics: differential calculus,—as well as the overall project of reaching (among other things) a quantitative description of empirically derived laws of motion in the solar system. Prior to Newton's *Principia* there had not been a clear articulation of cause and effect in the realm of motion, nor, more critically perhaps, had there been the conceptual and symbolic tools with which to make such an articulation.

Three hundred years is long enough for the laws of motion to have become taken for granted by physicists, and indeed to have been superseded at the very large and the very small scales. But we expect our students to make the leap that took the genius of Newton, tackling the radical problems presented by a revolution in astronomy, a few weeks of part-time study. They tend to cope admirably well with the calculus, the symbolic and algorithmic side of the topic, but fall down on interpreting and modeling situations that involve motion. There have been a number of studies of how students think about Newton's laws and related topics, and we describe one carried out in Göteborg that will also be referred to in later chapters.

Before going into the details of the study and its results, let us think about a rocket on its way to one of the outer planets, say Saturn. It is launched from earth with some sort of—by terrestrial standards—enormous investment of energy in a multistage launching vessel, and starts off in a partial orbit of the earth. Bit by bit the launching stages are ejected, and with every loss the rocket changes orbit somewhat in carefully calculated steps toward the trajectory needed to escape from the earth's gravitational attraction. Thereafter, it is on a more or less straight path for Saturn. The relative positions of the earth, moon, and rocket will have been predicted and taken into account in planning the trajectory, as will possible close contacts with other planets. But apart from that, after reaching a certain point when the rocket's motors are switched off to retain just fuel enough for forced maneuvres, for example on entering orbit around Saturn, what happens? The rocket simply carries on, moving forward. For how long? Does it slow down and stop at some point? If all the predictions and calculations have been successful, it should slow down on encountering Saturn and then go into a planned orbit. But what would otherwise happen? What if it were to fail and miss Saturn? Everything tells us that it would continue to recede from the earth, even from the solar system, until it encountered something forcing it to change its path, an asteroid maybe, or some other star out in space. We might ask, "What keeps it going?" Its fuel is spent. In the normal course of a journey through space there is no more fuel to be had. It just keeps going, uniformly, neither speeding up nor slowing down, certainly not stopping. Newton might have found such a thought experiment unfathomable, but he would nonetheless have asked a different and more meaningful question, "What *would* make it stop?"

The nature of uniform motion is expressed succinctly in Newton's first law, which can be expressed as Roche quoted (earlier), or more simply, that *a body remains in its state of rest or uniform motion unless a force be applied to change it*. This draws a critical distinction between, on the one hand, rest or uniform motion implying the net absence of force (equilibrium of forces) and, on the other hand, change in uniform motion (acceleration or deceleration) implying the net presence of force (nonequilibrium). In contrast, in common belief, and as attributed to Aristotle, the distinction occurs between rest (implying the absence of a net force) and motion (implying the presence of a net force), an intuitive understanding that proves particularly resistant to change. Right here, we can identify an educationally critical aspect of the content of a course in mechanics: The students should understand the relationship between the state of a body's motion and the net forces acting on it in a way consistent with Newton's conceptualization. This is an insight that has parallels in other fields of knowledge. In the history of the field there are a number of ways in which phenomena have been conceptualized at different epochs, and there is a likelihood that students of the field will tend to those that are more intuitive than the sometimes counterintuitive scientific conceptualizations presented in instruction.

However, the mere knowledge that such a critically important confusion is common does not go far toward devising a remedy. For that we must know more about how students actually experience the relationships between force and motion.

A rigorous study into how university entrants understood such notions of mechanics as Newton's first law of motion confirmed the split between Aristotelian and Newtonian thinking and went some way toward analyzing its roots (Johansson, Marton, & Svensson, 1985; Svensson, 1989). Prior to taking a course in mechanics at the university, 30 students were interviewed and asked to comment on some simple problems as points of departure for a deep analysis of their qualitative understanding of the field. Most of these students (24) were reinterviewed after the course and given similar problems to discuss. To give a taste of the problems, one went thus: "A car is driven at a high constant speed straight forward on a motorway. What forces act on the car?" Another was stated this way: "A ball leaves the hand of its thrower. Describe what happens!" It can immediately be seen that these two problems represent, respectively, cases of uniform motion and of deceleration and acceleration.

Now, Newton's first law can be stated as it was earlier in this section in terms of Newton's predefined quantities, or it can be correctly described in other ways as well, capturing its quality with recourse to properties such as motion, velocity, rest, change of velocity, energy, and force. Students entering university were found to describe the situations presented in the problems in an even greater variety of ways (not necessarily correct) using versions of these properties, including inherent and external forces, motive force, pushing force, and motive equilibrium.

Two qualitatively different ways of understanding uniform motion, as presented in the first of the two problems given above, were found. To quote Johansson et al. (1985):

> A body in this kind of motion was apprehended either as (a) having *constant velocity*, due to the equilibrium of forces, or (b) *moving*, due to a "motive inequilibrium" of forces. (p. 239, italics added)

The significant difference is that the first focuses on equilibrium and steady state in relating constant velocity to a balance of forces; the second focuses on motion, and posits a causal net motive force in all cases other than rest. This is exactly the Newton–Aristotle divide.

Consideration of the case of deceleration and acceleration, as exemplified by the second of the two previous problems, reveals a wider spread of variation among the course entrants. One way of understanding decelerating motion is in agreement with physics: *having a velocity that diminishes* (i.e., decelerating) *due to forces opposite to the direction of motion*. This is in agreement with Newton. Other ways of understanding it refer to such supposed properties as *inherent force* (and in some cases inherent kinetic energy), which diminishes owing to totally greater forces in the direction opposite to that of the motion, impling that in the case of the thrown ball the thrower is seen as transferring a propellant force or kinetic energy to the ball at the instant of throwing. Others see the ball as having an inherent *motive force* acting in the direction of motion (or occasionally as receiving a motive kinetic energy), which diminishes as the forces in the opposite direction oppose it. Yet others imagine an external *pushing force* that diminishes owing to opposing forces.

All of these three categories associate motion with the application of a force, as did Aristotle.

As we pointed out earlier for the three ways of understanding recursion, these different ways of understanding motion vary as to completeness, their degree of explanatory power, and the extent to which they take aspects of the situation for granted.

## EXAMPLE 4.4: THE NATURE OF MATTER

The final example of studies that have sought successfully to reveal educationally critical differences in ways of understanding an aspect of school curriculum is one that set out to chart the ways in which school pupils in the age range 12 to 16 years conceptualized the nature of matter (Renström, 1988; Renström, Andersson, & Marton, 1990). As in the case of the study of motion related earlier, the educationally critical way of experiencing matter was already defined by the school curriculum to be the atomic hypothesis: "that all things are made of atoms, little particles that move around in perpetual motion, attracting each other when they are a little distance apart, but repelling upon being squeezed into one another" (Feynman, Leighton, & Sands, 1963). It was known that students found the notion difficult to grasp, and that the ways in which they reasoned were at odds with the teacher's goals. For example, Andersson and Renström (1979) found in a study of how 13- to 16-year-old pupils reason about change of state, that over half their sample thought "that boiling means that air leaves the water (in the form of bubbles) rather than that water in liquid form turns into water in gaseous form" (Renström, Andersson, & Marton, 1990, p. 555). This study set out to reveal what aspects of an overall understanding of matter supported or hindered pupils' development of the desired understanding.

In the study, 20 students between 13 and 16 years of age were interviewed. The body of the interview required the subjects to talk about 9 different substances (such as salt, water, oil, carbon dioxide), referring to three properties: the structure of the substance; division of the substance into smaller and smaller pieces; and changes due to heating, cooling, or dissolving it. The substances were present for the subjects to handle, and they could draw or write if they wished. For example they were asked to develop their ideas about the nature of salt through crushing it while talking about its smallest parts, and by drawing such small parts.

The analysis of the interviews resulted in six ways of understanding matter, as outlined in Fig. 4.3. (By "substance unit" is meant a unit of the stuff under discussion, e.g., a drop of water or a grain of salt.) The different ways of understanding matter shift successively from (A) a largely undifferentiated idea of matter as homogeneous and continuous, which is unable to explain even the most elementary chemical properties of matter. As notions of atoms and particles enter their vocabulary, the pupils voice understandings of the nature of matter involving first (B) in which substance is in discrete units, sometimes with kernels and always with shells to hold the unit together. This progresses to (C), the idea of units that

| A | Matter as homogeneous substance. | Matter exists and is a continuum. Something typifies a substance and is immutable, otherwise it would not be recognizable. Different phases of a substance are thought to be different substances. Different substances can exist within one another; explanations given in terms of relative proportions of such components. |
|---|---|---|

Examples: Salt consists of substance that is uniform and can be divided (i), and endlessly (ii), given machines to do it. Water (iii) contains impurities and can be divided until there is none left.

| B | Matter as substance units. | Matter exists as small delimited units—drops of water, grains of salt—composed of a border or shell, its contents, and a nucleus, each of which is a form of the substance. Thus the phase notion becomes meaningful. Focus on border, content, or both. |
|---|---|---|

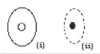

Examples: A grain of salt consists of a nucleus and a shell (i). Oxygen is a kernel with a shell of nothing around it (ii). Iron consists of little bits pressed together (iii).

| C | Matter as substance units with "small atoms." | Matter comprised of substance units, as above, but now studded with small atoms or particles of some sort. Atoms are of the same substance as the surrounding content, but with different properties. Focus on border/nucleus/content of the substance unit and/or the "small atoms." |
|---|---|---|

Examples: Salt consists of salt atoms in dried sea water (i). Wood has nerves with molecules (ii). Oxygen consists of oxygen atoms and protons, in a cloud of oxygen (iii).

| D | Matter as aggregate of particles. | Matter consists of infinitely divisible small particles, which are kept together by the border of the substance unit, and either (a) contain homogeneous substance or (b) have an atomlike character (i.e., not homogeneous). Particles have no attributes, but can still be used to explain phase change and atomic structure, leading to a paradoxical, "atoms contain atoms." Both (a) and (b) can focus on either the substance unit or on the particles themselves. |
|---|---|---|

Examples: When salt dissolves in water salt molecules float in the water (i). Iron comprises iron atoms that are stuck together in iron molecules (ii). When iron is heated some of the atoms drip off (iii).

| E | Matter as particle units. | Matter consists of particles that are not further divisible, and have specific attributes, such as form and structure. Distinction (a/b) as in D above. Within each of these further focal distinction: ($_1$) a single particle, or ($_2$) two or more particles and the relationship between them. Thus four distinct structures: ($a_1$) one substance particle, ($a_2$) several related substance particles, ($b_1$) one atomic particle and ($b_2$) several related atomic particles. Students focus either on the particle itself, without attributes, or on the attributes related to the particle or system of particles. With $b_2$, form and structure of particles and relationships between them can account for macroproperties of substances. |
|---|---|---|

Examples: Water molecules are lots of round things sitting together, connected (i). Air comprises air molecules (ii). When water boils "wet hydrogen will stay in the water and the oxygen will leave" (iii).

| F | Matter as systems of particles. | Matter comprises systems of interrelated particles (or subparticles). Now links can be established between the properties of the substance and the properties of the systems of particles. Closest to the atomic hypothesis, though not found to be complete, in that focus was always on the particles present and never on the space between particles (as would be required to explain the variation in spatial properties). |
|---|---|---|

Examples: Carbon dioxide consists of particles of carbon bonded with oxygen, which itself consists of protons and electrons (i). Iron consists of a nucleus of protons and neutrons with electrons in orbit around it (ii). Ice consists of water molecules with space between them (iii).

FIG. 4.3. The categories of description for pupils' understanding of the nature of matter (based on Renström, 1988).

themselves contain particles or atoms, still held together with a shell around the unit as a whole, and then to (D) that sees matter as aggregates of particles, which is both more complex and more capable of differentiation. Thus some pupils that express a (D) understanding focus on the *unit* that contains the particles, and others on the *particles* contained in the unit. Then (E) and (F) are more closely related to the theoretical picture of matter that is aimed at in instruction, in which the structure of matter becomes more differentiated. The particles referred to as comprising matter take on more attributes, and successively the relationships between particles come into the picture.

In Fig. 4.3 the features of each category of description are summarized, and some replicas of the pupils' accompanying drawings are given to illustrate the sort of things they were saying. The full flavor only comes out of much larger bites of the interviews, and the reader is directed for more detail to the original works (Renström, 1988; Renström et al., 1990). The successive understandings increase in completeness as they move toward a theoretical understanding, as indicated in Fig. 4.4.

With each new way of understanding matter, new properties of matter can be reasoned about. For example, A permits only static matter to enter the argument, whereas with B there is potential for discussing phase properties of matter. C brings atoms into the picture and D other particles, whereas E and F extend these first to greater differentiation between particles and then to relating the particles into systems.

In such reasoning as we have been pointing out, different aspects of a single item of the outcome space can be in focus: One aspect is figural against the background of the other. In item B, for instance, although matter as a whole is experienced as units of substances (drops of water or grains of salt), the content of the unit might be figural against a background of its being delimited in some way, or the actual delimiting boundaries might be figural.

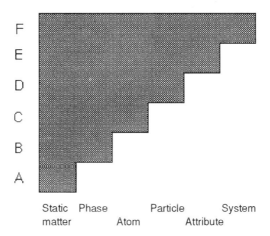

FIG. 4.4. Relationship between ways of experiencing matter and aspects of matter (Renström et al., 1990, p. 566).

In the more advanced understandings, these figure–ground distinctions take on a more significant meaning as they prepare the way for more complete understanding or hinder it. As we indicate in Fig. 4.5, the most advanced notion of matter, F, demands that the relationships between systems of particles or subparticles are considered, and that the particles are seen to have attributes that are different from the substance itself. It is, for instance, realized that sulphur atoms are not yellow, and that water molecules are not wet. This stems from being able to focus on the "small atoms" in a C-like understanding (as opposed to the substance that contains them), shifting to a capability to focus on nonhomogeneous atomlike particles (rather than homogeneous substance particles) that make up the substance in a D-like understanding. Thereafter, in an E-like understanding, a capability to reason in terms of more than one particle and the relationships between them can lead to the F-like, atomic hypothesis way of understanding matter.

It is now seen that at each of the Levels C, D, and E there is a vital distinction in what is held to be figural, if the atomic hypothesis is to be reached. At level C, a student must be able to hold the "small atoms" in focus against a background of the substance in which they are thought to be embedded, in order, at the D level, to see particles as atoms rather than substance particles. At Level D, it is important that it is the particles that are focused on against a background of the substance they constitute, in order to be able to see the particles as being indivisible and as

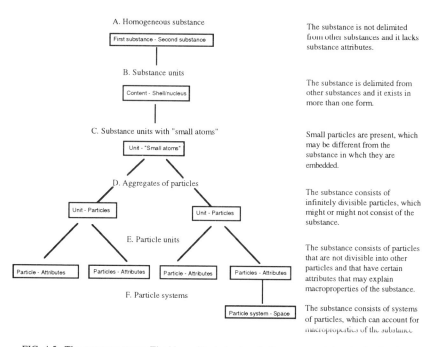

FIG. 4.5. The outcome space. The hierarchical structure indicates potential paths for development and potential obstacles (Renström et al., 1990).

possessing characteristics of form and structure for Level E. Then, at Level E, it is important that students reason about more than one particle at a time, in order to become aware of the relationships between particles that are vital to seeing matter as systems of particles as in Level F. Even at Level F there is a vital distinction that would lead to a way of understanding matter that was not observed in the study, namely that the space between particles has to be figural in reasoning about the spatial relationships between particles, such as rearrangement during chemical reaction or as in crystal structure.

Inspection of textbooks showed woeful lack of support for moving from one way of understanding to another. One central failing is the lack of treatment of matter in terms of models, and a preference for dealing with the "facts." Thus learners are encouraged to look upon what they read or hear as absolute truths, and to view their own development of understanding as confusion. Then, when different sorts of concrete models are presented to describe or illustrate different facets of the whole topic, students fail to make the distinction between model and reality, and are unable to take the different perspectives necessary to further their own understanding.

The notion of a developmental succession between levels of an outcome space, based on the capability of bringing one or another aspect of a level into figural consideration when reasoning about a subject, was the central contribution of this study to the overall project of identifying educationally critical aspects of particular topics. The categories of description had not hitherto been systematically analyzed into figure–ground structures.

## WHICH DIFFERENCES ARE CRITICAL?

The four examples we have related here are four among many, and have been chosen to illustrate four different aspects of the educationally critical differences in which the stuff of learning is understood. The first study, of ways in which children experience numbers between 1 and 10, brings out the potential, and lack of potential, of certain ways for the development of higher order skills, in this case arithmetic. It also illustrates a distinct difference between our views of research into learning and those of the dominant research community.

The second study, of university students' initial understanding of the central notion of recursion, highlights two aspects of our main message, both referring to the observed fact that an educationally critical aspect of recursion is at odds with the taken-for-granted "expert" understanding.

First, the different ways in which students understand recursion focus on its syntactic, its semantic, and its conceptual meanings, and instruction often focuses on the syntactic and semantic at the expense of the conceptual. Indeed, successful programs can be written with the help of syntactically correct templates, a method developed at length by teachers and taken for granted as effective by many psychologists of programming. Here, however, it has been shown to be inadequate for developable learning, learning that can be extended to or built on in new problem areas. The specific aspect that is critical for complete understanding—here seen to be self-reference—should be made figural in instruction, here suggested to be, with reference to students' experience of what it takes to program and to learn to program, making the technical implementation of recursion visible in some way.

Second, traditional examination forms, in which students have to write programs for rather limited problems in more or less well-known situations, do not test conceptual understanding of recursion, in that perfectly acceptable programs can be written with no more than the syntactic template understanding. Thus, what is to our mind the educationally critical way of experiencing recursion is not favored by the teachers in their praxis of instruction and examination.

One thing shown by the third study, on students' experience of Newtonian motion, is that critical differences of understanding found in students have also been the subject of profound shifts in understanding on an historical scale. This is one way in which one might begin to identify such differences. As with the results on recursion, it was also seen that students can succeed in quantitative, algorithm-dependent problems without having a well-developed qualitative understanding, and that the specific notions of equilibrium and change need to be focal in considerations of motion.

The fourth study also shows parallels between how students experience a subject and how it has been understood in different epochs in history. But, more interesting for our purposes, it indicates an analytical path toward a developmental scheme through recourse to the figure–ground analysis of categories of description or ways of understanding the topic in question. Thus, not only are educationally critical differences in understanding revealed, but a notional path of developmental foci for instruction is identified.

# 5

# The Anatomy of Awareness

In the previous chapter we raised the issue that undertaking a specific learning task—reading a text, or solving a problem, or whatever—to some extent *reflects* one's understanding of the phenomena involved, and to some extent *changes* one's understanding of the phenomena involved. It can be said that when an individual encounters a learning task—a text to be studied, a problem to be solved, or whatever—her understanding of the text, or of the problem, or indeed, of the learning situation itself and her understanding of the *phenomena* that are relevant to understanding the text, problem, or situation are somehow related.

We deal with this issue and others in terms of the *nature of awareness*, an explanatory framework that has, in fact, been foreshadowed in the previous chapters. We have referred in passing to features of the learner's awareness: that certain structures of awareness are implied by certain ways of understanding; that the learner is simultaneously aware of certain aspects of a situation or a phenomenon; that her awareness of certain aspects logically imply a tacit awareness of other aspects; that certain aspects become figural, in focus or focal, whereas other aspects recede to ground, and so on. In this chapter we attempt to develop this framework in the context of the studies described so far, in order to progress toward a more illuminated view of learning in the chapters to come.

## PHENOMENA AND SITUATIONS

We have to be clear about one important distinction, that a *situation* is always experienced with a sociospatiotemporal location—a context, a time, and a place—whereas a *phenomenon* is experienced as abstracted from or transcending such anchorage. In the learning situation that prevails, however, the two are inextricably intertwined. That nobody can experience a phenomenon in the absence of a situation is strongly intuitive. That a situation can be experienced only in terms of that which transcends it follows from our ability to make sense of the here and now only through the experiences which precede it: The here and now is experienced in terms which link it with the past and reflect experienced similarities, differences, or both. We refer to the wholeness of what we experience to be simultaneously present as a *situation*, whereas we call entities that transcend the situation, which link it with other situations and lend meaning to it, *phenomena*.

Exactly this idea was expressed by Aron Klug, 1992 Nobel laureate in chemistry, in a discussion broadcast on Swedish television and used as data in the study by Marton, Fensham, and Chaiklin (1994) referred to in Example 7.8 of chapter 7:

> One doesn't see with one's eyes, one sees with the whole fruit of one's previous experience.

We cannot separate our understanding of the *situation* and our understanding of the *phenomena* that lend sense to the situation. Not only is the situation understood in terms of the phenomena involved, but we are aware of the phenomena from the point of view of the particular situation. Furthermore, not only is our experience of the situation molded by the phenomena as we experience them, but our experience of the phenomena is modified, transformed, and developed through the situations we experience them in.

Although situation and phenomena are inextricably intertwined in experience, as researchers we may opt to focus on one or on the other. In the light of this statement, you will see that the three previous chapters actually deal with research into different aspects of the whole learning experience. Chapter 2 describes research that focuses on the learner's experience of learning in specific learning situations, in terms of the *act* of learning and the *content* of learning and the relationship between them. In chapters 3 and 4, respectively, research is described that has focused on these two aspects of the experience of learning alone. In chapter 3, the learners' experience of the *act* of learning is to the fore, as it has accumulated through a history of different learning situations related to different phenomena, whereas in chapter 4, focus has been on learners' understanding of some particular *content* that reflects their cumulative experience of the specific phenomenon across different learning situations. Naturally, the results described in chapters 3 and 4 both have to be seen against a background of the actual research situations that pertained to them.

The researcher may thus opt to focus mainly on ways of experiencing the situation or on ways of experiencing the phenomenon. But the learner, as well, may focus mainly on the situation in which the phenomenon is embedded or on the phenomenon as it is revealed in the situation, as reflected in the different approaches to learning described in chapter 2. Thus we have to realize that the researcher might be primarily interested in exploring the variation in the learners' experience of the situation and discover that some of her learners are largely oriented toward the phenomena that are present there. Yet again, the researcher might be primarily interested in exploring the variation in the learners' experience of a certain phenomenon and find that some of the learners are largely oriented toward the situation in which the phenomenon is embedded.

## INTENTIONALITY

The inextricable relatedness of the two aspects of learning to which we have referred throughout—the *what* and the *how* aspects—is a special case of the notion of intentionality. Franz Brentano, a 19th-century Austrian priest of unusually distinguished features and philosophical turn of mind, pondered over a question that might appear obscure to most people: How can one tell those phenomena that are psychic (or what we would today call psychological) from those that are not? The solution he arrived at can be embodied in the term "intentionality," which, simply put, says all that is "psychic" refers to something that is beyond itself. For example, a thought is psychic, and we cannot imagine a thought without an object to which it refers: A thought of a dog refers to an object, a dog, that is beyond the thought itself. All psychic acts are thus intentional. In Brentano's own words:

> No hearing without something heard, no believing without something believed, no hoping without something hoped, no striving without something striven for, no joy without something we are joyous about, etc. (Spiegelberg, 1982, p. 37)

The research carried out by Marton and Säljö and described in chapter 2 was presented in a paper symposium published by the *British Journal of Educational Psychology*. The preface to the symposium, written by the then editor, Noel Entwistle, was entitled "The Verb to Learn Takes the Accusative" (Entwistle, 1976), thereby indicating an awareness of the idea encapsulated by Brentano's notion of intentionality in spite of the being ignorant then of its formulation, or even of its existence. Both the empirical research of chapter 2 and the philosophical stance of Brentano enables us to picture the basic structure of learning as in Fig. 5.1, in terms of the *how* and the *what* of learning.

Thus, the verb "to learn" has to have an object, but the blunt grammatical statement hides the fact that, as we pointed out earlier, in a sense it actually has two objects! The principal object is the direct object: the content that is being learned. But in addition to that there is a sort of indirect object that refers to the quality of the act of learning, and which, in its simplest form, refers to *what* the act of learning aims at. The examples of chapter 3 nicely illustrate that learning might be aimed at reaching the phenomena the act points to, at understanding that which is being learned, or at committing it to memory. Thus our simple diagram has to be elaborated as in Fig. 5.2. Now the how aspect of learning has its own aspects of how and what, the former referring to the experience of the way in which the act of learning is carried out (we will refer to this now as the act of learning), the latter referring to the type of capabilities the learner is trying to master (which we are calling the indirect object of learning).

FIG. 5.1. Learning can be analyzed as having a how aspect and a what aspect.

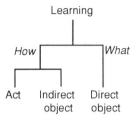

FIG. 5.2. The how aspect of learning can also be analyzed into how and what aspects, the act of learning and the indirect object of learning, respectively.

It is not our intention to try to integrate our earlier characterization of the experience of learning in terms of the two-dimensional outcome space originating from the study of how Hong Kong students experience learning (see Fig. 3.3, and the schematic representation used to depict the experience of learning in Fig. 5.2). We can just mention briefly that "learning" in a narrow sense is restricted to what is referred to as "acquiring." The indirect object of learning is the kind of capability the learner is trying to develop. This is represented in the second and third facets of the temporal dimension of learning (i.e., "knowing" and "making use," in the two-dimensional outcome space in chapter 3. The indirect object of learning, in the sense of acquisition, thus projects itself into the other two temporal phases, toward that which is beyond the actual learning event in the narrow sense, (i.e., the learner's confrontation with something new).

In the Hong Kong study we found a variation in agency. In some instances the teacher and not the learner was seen by the learner as the agent of learning. This is the reason why subject is an aspect of the depth dimension there, and it reminds us of the danger of failing to distinguish between the level of specific empirical studies on the one hand and theoretical and supposedly generalizable concepts on the other. The Hong Kong study is clearly of the former kind, whereas the schematically depicted structure of the experience of learning (see Fig. 5.2) is clearly of the latter. In chapter 3 we tried to move toward an empirical integration of diverse studies of the conceptions and experiences of learning. The time is not yet ripe for a full-blown theoretical integration of them, nor is it likely to be so before this book reaches completion, because there are currently several other relevant studies being carried out in different cultural contexts.

This book is above all a study of learning from the learner's perspective, and in terms of this diagram, chapter 4 has been concerned mainly with qualitative differences from the perspective of the direct object of the verb "to learn," and chapter 3 took mainly the perspective of the indirect object. Chapter 2 was concerned with the how and the what perspectives. We must state again that these distinctions are analytical, they are introduced to distinguish between different research points of view and have no actual existence as separate entities. They are different facets of an undivided whole.

Within this undivided whole of the experience of learning the learner's, as well as the researcher's, focus may be on one or the other of these aspects according to the situation in which she finds herself. When learning, the learner is, or is at least supposed or presumed to be, focusing on the content of learning, the direct object of learning, qualitative differences inthat we described in the previous chapter. If a researcher carries out an interview study, on the other hand, the learner can be brought to reflect on her *way* of learning, and she will then most likely talk about what kinds of outcome she is aiming at, thus the how aspect of learning, specifically the *indirect* object of learning. She will also, to an extent that depends on the researcher's interest, comment on what she does to learn, again the how aspect of learning, now specifically the *act* of learning. The qualitative differences in ways of experiencing learning described in chapter 3 reflect differences in relation to both aspects of the how of learning, more in relation to the indirect object of learning than to the act of learning.

## WHAT DOES IT MEAN TO EXPERIENCE SOMETHING IN A CERTAIN WAY?

Let us briefly remind ourselves of the main question of our book: "How do we gain knowledge about the world?" What we have written so far indicates that the act of gaining knowledge about the world involves qualitative differences across the populations involved in it. When we say "qualitative differences" here, we are implying qualitative differences in the way things are experienced (understood, conceptualized, apprehended, etc.)— as phenomena, situations, or learning itself. The question that now becomes interesting is that of what it means and what it takes to experience something in a particular way, and it is this question that we now address: "What does it take to experience something in a certain way?" First we consider a concrete form before going on to conceptual forms.

We are constantly surrounded by a more or less complex environment. To experience something emanating from that environment is, for the first thing, to discern it from its context. When we look around a room at four walls, floor, ceiling, one door, two windows, a table and chairs, and a book-shelf half-filled with books, we give no pause to what is what, what is one thing and what is another, where a thing starts and where it ends. We know all this because we have grown up in rooms like this. If we had never seen a house and all its furnishings, it might not be so apparent that the table is separate from the floor, and that the books are separate from the shelf, that windows open to let in fresh air.

Studying by reading books, which is one form of learning taken up in this book, has often more in common, however, with walking through the woods at night than with moving around in a familiar and normally furnished room. What does it take to see a motionless deer among the dark trees and bushes of the night woods? To see it at all we have to discern it from the surrounding trees and bushes; we have to see its contours, its outline, the limits that distinguish it from what surrounds it. We have to see, at least partially, where it starts and where it ends. But seeing its contours *as* contours and as the contours of a *deer* implies that we have already *identified* it as a deer standing there, which is exactly where the enigma of what it takes to experience something in some context lies. On the one hand, in order to see something *as something* (the particular configuration in the woods as a deer, in this instance, and not as a truck or a UFO) we have to discern that something from its environment. But on the other hand, in order to discern it from its environment we have to see it as some particular thing, or in other words assign it a meaning. Structure presupposes meaning, and at the same time meaning presupposes structure. The two aspects, meaning and structure, are dialectically intertwined and occur simultaneously when we experience something.

Thus we can state that an experience has a structural aspect and a referential (or meaning) aspect. To elaborate first on what we mean by structural aspect, we need to point out that to experience something in a particular way, not only do we have to discern it from its context, as a deer in the woods, but we also have to discern its parts, the way they relate to each other, and the way they relate to the whole. Therefore, on seeing the deer in the woods, in seeing its contours we also see parts of its body, its head, its antlers, its forequarters, and so on, and their relationships in terms of stance. The structural aspect of a way of experiencing something is thus twofold: discernment of the whole from the context on the one hand and discernment of the parts and their relationships within the whole on the other.[1] Moreover, intimately intertwined with the structural aspect of the experience is the referential aspect, the meaning. In seeing the parts and the whole of the deer and the relationships between them we even see its stance—relaxed and unaware of our presence or alert to some sound unheard by us—and we thus discern further degrees of meaning.

We need more terminology to develop our argument, and we borrow from phenomenology, which provides us with a conceptual framework for many of the distinctions we want to introduce.[2] That which surrounds the phenomenon experienced, including its contours, we call its external horizon. The parts and their relationships, together with the contours of the phenomenon, we call its internal horizon. Thus, the external horizon of coming on the deer in the woods extends from the immediate boundary of the experience—the dark forest against which the deer is discerned—through all other contexts in which related occurrences have been experienced (e.g., walks in the forest, deer in the zoo, nursery tales, reports of hunting incidents, etc.) The internal horizon comprises the deer itself, its parts, its stance, its structural presence.

Now we can characterize the basic unit of a possible science of experience, a way of experiencing something, and illustrate it schematically as in Fig. 5.3.

As our examples in chapters 3 and 4 showed in abundance, phenomena (learning, numbers, recursion, physical laws) can be experienced in different ways, and we are now in a position to characterize this variation with recourse to the basic unit of a way of experiencing something. Let us consider an example to clarify this.

---

[1] This is in line with the way in which Svensson (1984a) characterized the conception.

[2] We may, however, use them somewhat differently, stretching them to meet our own approach.

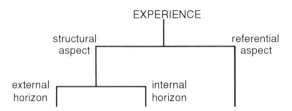

FIG. 5.3. The unit of a science of experience, a way of experiencing something.

## Example 5.1: Experiencing Figures

The "something" of this example is a series of numbers to be found in George Katona's book *Organizing and Memorizing* (Katona, 1940). This is the way it looks:

581215192226

Go ahead and experience it! It seems pretty straightforward, in fact so straightforward that to call what you have a "way of experiencing" might feel rather over the top. Without further reflection, we experience it as just a sequence of 12 numbers:

5 8 1 2 1 5 1 9 2 2 2 6

Each one of them is as important, or unimportant, as all the others. But there *are* other ways of experiencing it. What about this way of experiencing exactly the same series of figures?

5  8  12  15  19  22  26

Now we see a series of numbers where the difference between consecutive terms alternates between 3 and 4. There are now three important numbers: 5, 3 and 4. Given those, we have a rule for constructing or reconstructing the initially featureless series.

Now, what does it take to experience the sequence in that way? Obviously, to see the regularity we have to group the numbers in a particular way: as 5 and 8 and 12 and so on, instead of as 5 and 8 and 1 and 2 and 1 and 5 and so on. But why on earth would we do that? Well, possibly because we have spotted the regularity, so just as with the deer in the woods, finding the meaning (the rule) presupposes finding the structure (the particular way of grouping the numbers); and vice versa, the structure springs from the meaning found.

When we talk about structure in the two distinct ways of experiencing these numbers, the differences in the respective internal horizons are readily visible. What we are discussing is how different parts are discerned (either as one figure at a time or as a progression of 5, 8, 12, 15, …), how they relate to each other (either not at all or through the alternative differences of 3 and 4), and how they make up the whole (either as an arbitrary list of figures or as a number series generated by a rule).

Consider also the external horizon, the other facet of structure, are there any differences in that respect? We stated earlier that the external horizon refers to the way in which the phenomenon we experience in a certain way is discerned from its context, and to be more precise we should add, how it is related to its context as well. The point is that to experience something is not only to pick it out from its context, but also to relate it to its context, and even to other contexts as well at the same time. For instance, when the example of Katona's number sequence has been given in lectures, there are usually some people in the audience who think of IQ tests, the sort for which you have to find the rule that generates a series and predict the next two numbers. Now, merely by relating the number sequence to just such a context you increase the likelihood of finding a regularity, simply because in that context—not now a lecture—you would be looking for one.

As a matter of fact, in Katona's book where this number sequence appears, there is another distinctly different way of experiencing it, namely as:

$$5\ 812\ 151\ 922.26$$

In one of a series of experiments conducted with adult participants in the United States in the late 1930s, the same figures were presented in the same order to one group of experimental subjects, but in the form of a factual statement: "The Federal expenditures last year amounted to $5 812 151 922.26." Seen in *this* context our way of experiencing the number sequence is changed radically, taking on quite a different meaning. The change in the referential aspect of our experience—the national economy of the United States—is intertwined with a change in its structural aspect. Of the external horizon we can say that there is a change of context bringing about a change in the meaning of the number sequence. As far as the internal horizon is concerned, the leftmost figures gain significance, the rightmost lose. What the sequence says is that the federal expenditure during the previous year was nearly $6 billion.[3]

If we return to the deer in the night woods, we now see that to experience it as such we have to discern it from what surrounds it while at the same time relating it (seeing it in relation to, or against the background of) what surrounds it. We cannot experience anything without a context. Once the deer is discerned it is probably not only related to the surrounding trees and undergrowth, but to other contexts as well, such as hunting, maybe to a fear of drunken hunters aiming wildly, or to the context of getting lost in the dark. Now, one might argue that trees and undergrowth comprise a material context, whereas "getting lost in the dark" or "drunken hunters aiming wildly" are abstract contexts in the sense that they exist only in the minds of the experiencers. Here we will lump these apparently different kinds of context together and call them simply "contexts," which is, after all, what they are.

---

[3]See also Svensson (1984b, pp. 59–60) for a similar analysis.

## Example 5.2:  Experiencing Numbers

Let us look at another example of how the structural and the referential aspects of a way of experiencing something are intertwined. This example illustrates a sudden change from one way of experiencing something to another way of experiencing the same thing—akin to what might have happened to you when as you progressed through the three ways of experiencing Katona's numbers. We return to our description of some qualitatively different ways of experiencing numbers, that appeared in the previous chapter.

A 7-year-old boy in Neuman's (1987) study is trying to solve this problem: "If you have 2 kronor and you get another 7, how many kronor do you have altogether?" He says, "1, 2," then pauses briefly to resume, "3, 4, 5, 6, 7," after which he pauses again, a light dawns on his face, and he continues, "8, 9." Then he says, "9, I've got 9!"

What is happening here? The little boy starts by enumerating the two units in the first addend, saying, "1, 2." Then he makes a pause and he starts enumerating the units in the second addend by "counting on" and saying "3, 4, 5, 6, 7." It is highly unlikely that he knows how many units he has enumerated in the second addend by now: "3" was the first unit, "4" was the second and so on, but he can not possibly know that "7" is its fifth unit because he is quite unable to keep count that far. He should stop only when he has counted seven more units, but he cannot possibly know when that happens.[4] But somehow he is aware of his dilemma, and at the instant he utters "7" he has a brilliant insight. The "7" does not have to refer to one of the units in the second addend—God, by now, only knows which one. It can refer to the last unit of the first addend if the two addends (2 and 7) are switched. The "7" he has uttered can instead be the seventh unit in the first addend in the reformulated problem. The little boy has now to add the second addend, 2, so he says "8, 9," thus uttering the first and second units of the new second addend. He can hear the "twoness" of 8 and 9 together, so the problem is thus completed. He has enumerated 9 units—"9, I've got 9!"

Now, what happens at the very instant the little boy says "7" is a restructuring of the field, as illustrated in Fig. 5.4.

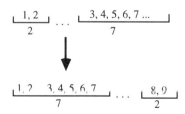

FIG. 5.4.  Restructuring the field of the addition 2+7.

----

[4]We have argued this point more extensively in chapter 4.

In the previous chapter we discussed some of the qualitatively different ways in which children have been found to experience number. In this example we have qualitatively different ways in which a child understands something where the difference is brought about by a manifold change in the child's experience of a problem. At one level, the *meaning* of "7" changes from being a reference to one of the units within the second addend to being a reference to the last unit of the first addend. This change in meaning is intertwined with a change in the *structural* aspect (external horizon) of "7" in the sense that the immediate context of the spoken "7" changes. At a second level, and simultaneously, the whole sequence of numbers changes *meaning* from "2 add on 7" to "7 add on 2," a change in meaning which is intertwined with a change in the *structural* aspect (internal horizon) of the number sequence: The parts and the relations between them are discerned differently in the two cases.

At both levels, the change in the referential aspect (i.e., meaning) of what is experienced is intertwined with a change in the structural aspect, in the first case in the external horizon and in the second in the internal horizon. The complementary facets, the internal horizon in the first case and the external horizon in the second case, remain unchanged, or, at least, we have not observed any changes there.

## Example 5.3: Experiencing Learning

Earlier in this chapter, we characterized the way in which fundamental aspects of *learning,* the how (the indirect object and the act of learning) and the what (direct object), are related to each other, and we have depicted the basic unit of *experience* in terms of referential aspect (meaning) and structural aspect with internal and external horizons. Now we can describe the experience of learning in these terms, as illustrated in Fig. 5.5.

The right-hand branch, the "what" aspect of learning, refers to the way in which the direct object of learning is experienced or understood, and was illustrated through the previous two examples as well as through specific contents of learning

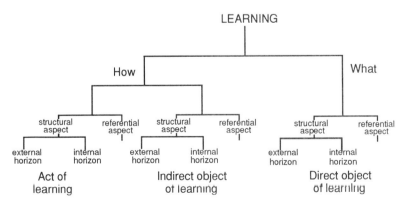

FIG. 5.5. The experience of learning.

in chapter 4. The left-hand side of the figure depicts the experience of the "how" aspect of learning, which was dealt with in chapter 3. Learning yields a capability that can be experienced differently, amounting to a variation in the indirect object of learning, and the learners go about their tasks in diverse ways that constitute the variation in the act of learning.

Referring in particular to the study of how students in Hong Kong experience learning, described in chapter 3, the different ways of experiencing the two aspects of the how of learning, the act and the indirect objects respectively, were described in terms of their referential aspects, such as "committing to memory (meaning)" or "relating." The structural aspects have remained implicit, but as far as "committing to memory (meaning)" is concerned, the internal horizon can be characterized as the distinction being made between the text and its meaning, the latter being figure and the former being ground, whereas the external horizon is in the first place the discernment from and relating to school. To take another example, experiencing learning as "understanding (phenomenon)," for which "relating" describes the temporal facet "making use of," the internal horizon comprises the open class of novel situations to which what one has learned in school is potentially relevant; the temporal facet of "knowing" is characterized as "having understanding (phenomenon)", through which those situations are endowed with meaning that they would not otherwise have. It is thus from the point of view of those situations one encounters that the relatedness of learning to knowledge obtained in school is seen. Both school and the world outside make up the external horizon of this way of experiencing learning.

All the different aspects of the experience of learning illustrated in Fig. 5.5 are present in every experience of learning. But they are surely not always—probably never—present in all *accounts* of the experience of learning. It would be overwhelmingly tedious if every learning experience were described with respect to all its aspects on all occasions. We really don't want to be accused of being tedious, but we do want to indicate that there *are* different aspects of ways of experiencing learning that can be described and commented on.

## ANALYZING EXPERIENCE

If we reconsider some of the examples in the previous chapters we can see how the conceptual apparatus just presented can be used to characterize qualitatively different ways of experiencing particular phenomena.

### Example 5.4: Ways of Experiencing Numbers

In Example 4.1 of chapter 4 we described five different ways of experiencing numbers in the range 1–10 (see Fig. 4.2). For all of them, the external horizon extends from the boundary, the context of the arithmetic problem that the number occurs in, to embrace earlier encounters with similar school problems and encounters with numbers in other contexts such as nursery rhymes and counting games.

The internal horizon comprises the problem and the part–whole structure discerned therein.

If we start with *numbers as names* in Fig. 4.2, we see that this way of experiencing numbers has a part–whole structure, but the sense is somewhat elusive. A number is a name; it is the name that is generally the last to be spoken when a set of objects is counted; it is the name of the set of objects. But that does not prevent parts of the same set of objects from having other names. Thus, when a child is asked how many more kronor she needs to buy a 9-kronor comic, if she already has 2 kronor, she might respond "9 kronor"; obviously, she needs a set of coins of which the last one is called 9. But if, when 9 marbles are placed in two boxes she is asked how many marbles might be in each of them, she might respond "2 in that one and 9 in the other," or "5 in that one and 9 in the other." Now, "9" is still the name of the total set, so clearly there must be 9 marbles in one or the other box; but in the other box there could be 2 or 5, or any other number less than 9. Thus, the 9 can have parts within it, each of them having its own name, so, the structural aspect of this way of experiencing numbers points, on the one hand, to the name of an object, and on the other hand, to what delimits the number in an ordinal sense. The *last item* is thus in focus, and provides the set with its name. The experience lacks cardinality in that there is no sense of numerosity, but it has a weak sense of the ordering of numbers, if only as a succession of names. The referential aspect is simply the number as a name, a name used to refer to that number in many different contexts.

In *number as extents*, the focus is different, in that there is now a weak sense of cardinality. There is a vague numerosity, a sense of relative sizes of numbers that form part–whole relationships in accordance with the demands of a particular arithmetic problem. These are not relationships in a numerical sense, but in the sense that a number is constituted of complementary parts that are separable; in "numbers as names," in contrast, they are not separable but fixed by one another as determined by the list of number names. The referential aspect pertains to the size of the number.

In *counted numbers*, the structural aspect delimits the set of units, which are counted in order to arrive at the numbers demanded of the arithmetic problem in question. The referential aspect is the act of counting that both leads to the required number and lends it meaning.

*Finger number*s have as their essential structural aspect the finger-based "5 + something." The individual fingers are seen as well as the fingers together, forming a pattern, and it is this that lends a number its simultaneous cardinal and ordinal meaning (i.e., its meaning or referential aspect).

In *number facts* units are no longer thematized, but numbers are experienced in terms of all of their part–whole relationships. As with finger numbers, the simultaneous cardinality and ordinality constitute their referential aspect or meaning.

Now we have described five different ways of experiencing number, and we have said that the external horizon extends from the situation of the arithmetic problem through similar problems and other, unspecified, encounters with numbers. Let us look at another way of experiencing number in which we can be more specific. There are children who, when asked how many marbles there might be in each of the two boxes, might point and reply, "2 in that one and 2 in that one" or "5 in that one and 5 in that one" or "9 in that one and 9 in that one." This is a way of experiencing number that has been called "fair shares" (Neuman, 1987). In such a case, we believe that the external horizon embraces the set of situations that all children have been part of (sharing), and the most primitive form of sharing is sharing equally between two recipients. Thus the meaning of the arithmetic problem extends beyond the problem itself to dealing cards or sharing sweets.

### Example 5.5: Ways of Experiencing Recursion

Let us now analyze ways of experiencing recursion in a similar manner, following our description of the ways in which students of computer science and computer engineering were found to experience it during their initial studies in programming (see Example 4.2). Note that "structure" as used earlier refers to the structure of recursion or recursive functions, whereas here "structure" refers to an aspect of the ways in which recursion as a phenomenon is experienced. The names given to the categories of ways of experiencing recursion all refer in fact to their referential aspects.

In experiencing recursion as a *construct,* the meaning of recursion (its referential aspect) is that it is something that exists to be used in the programming environment in question, which has recently entered the repertoire of ML constructs that can be used, and which has a particular syntactic form. In experiencing recursion as *repetition* recursion means, in addition, that one now has the ability to bring about some repetitive process over a list of natural numbers or equivalent data structure with which one is able to model the repetition indicated by some aspect of a problem. In the experience of recursion as *self-reference* its meaning extends to the self-referential abstraction of iteration, possibly mathematical induction and the resulting capability to prove the correctness of programs.

The structural aspects of the ways of experiencing recursion have to do with how recursion and its component parts are delimited from and related to the rest of programming and mathematics (external horizon) and with the way its parts are related to each other (internal horizon). In experiencing recursion as a *construct,* it is the set of typical forms of templates that is the boundary of the external horizon (the existence of templates and their particular formats are what differentiate recursion from the rest of programming in ML) and the syntactic and lexical details of ML functions (the function definition and ways of expressing lists, and so on) form the internal horizon of recursion.

In experiencing recursion as the means of bringing about *repetition,* it is the semantics of the template, the recursive case and terminating case, that form the boundary of the external horizon, extending to the notion of repetition in other contexts (i.e., in problems and in other programming environments). It is the ML expressions for the individual recursive case and the base case as demanded by a particular situation that form the internal horizon.

The experience of recursion as *self-reference* also has the semantics of the template as its external horizon, but now with the essential abstraction of self-reference, the way in which the recursive case will lead to the constraint of the terminating case, the mathematical correctness of the program, as well as the repetition that is facilitated. The internal horizon, again as in the experience as repetition, has the recursive case and the terminating case as internal horizon, but in addition sees the relationship between them in terms of a whole recursive functional expression.

## Example 5.6: Ways of Experiencing Newtonian Mechanics

In chapter 4 we also looked at different ways in which university students experienced the sort of motion that we usually refer to as Newtonian motion or motion governed by Newton's first law: A body remains in its state of rest or uniform motion unless a force be applied to change it. We considered students' experience in the light of two problems they were asked to discuss: "A car is driven at a high constant speed straightforward on a motorway. What forces act on the car?" and "A ball leaves the hand of its thrower. Describe what happens." The significant aspect of Newton's law, as far as students' experience is concerned, is that rest and uniform motion are the simpler, taken-for-granted states of motion in which forces are in equilibrium, whereas change in uniform motion (acceleration or deceleration) is more complex and needs to be explained in terms of net force.

Experiencing this sort of motion in what amounts to an Aristotelian way is most significantly different from the Newtonian way in terms of its external horizon. Students who describe the car as having a motive force propelling it forward or the ball as having an inherent kinetic energy are seeing the problem within the world that they inhabit where, for example, friction and gravity are taken for granted, a world in which bodily force is needed to move something. It is this world that is the external horizon of such a way of experiencing motion. Those students who describe the car as being in a state of equilibrium, a Newtonian description, see the problem within a scientific world, a world in which certain abstractions have to be considered. In this world the everyday, taken-for-granted forces due to friction and gravity have to be accounted for and seen in the equilibrium—or lack of it—that prevails.

The internal horizon of the structural aspect refers to the set of physical concepts associated with the problems in question—forms of motion, including rest, velocity and acceleration; states of equilibrium and nonequilibrium; forces including gravity, friction, and resistance—all of which can be discerned in the stated problems. Distinct for the Aristotelian way of experiencing motion is the relationship perceived between rest and equilibrium of forces, and between motion and nonequilibrium, which is expressed through the introduction of some sort of motive force. The Newtonian experience, in contrast, relates the concepts in such a way that rest and uniform motion are associated with equilibrium, and the presence of force is associated with change of uniform motion (acceleration or deceleration).

In each case, the referential aspect consists of the configurations of forces, velocities, and accelerations associated with the problem, and the equations that express relationships between them, but with a motive force accounting for motion (i.e., nonrest) in the Aristotelian case and with an equilibrium of forces at rest or in uniform motion in the Newtonian case.

### Example 5.7: Ways of Experiencing Matter

Returning to the last example we gave in chapter 4, ways of experiencing matter, it is obvious that the external horizon limited to the immediate experience is no more than the experimental situation, in which the pupil considers certain substances and their forms, discussing them with the researcher. The external horizon of the experience in a more complete sense, however, embraces the pupil's overall history of dealing with matter in all its forms. This is different for the six ways of experiencing matter that were identified, and at the two extremes can be described as (A) a totally taken-for-granted uniformity of kinds and forms of matter, which are distinguished only by appearance and other perceptible attributes, and (F) an analytical, scientific, view of matter, at least when tackled in such a situation as this.

A further analysis of the six categories is given in Table 5.1, in which the column "structural aspect" indicates the alternative foci that were found when students described matter from a variety of different perspectives, with the exception of the least complex way of experiencing matter, A. Students seemed to take one focus or another, hold one aspect of the phenomenon figural while the other remained in the background. One pupil experiencing matter according to C, for example, might have described the various substances and changes in substance in terms of units of the substance, whereas referring to the "small atoms" only in passing, while another might have phrased descriptions in terms of the "small atoms," taking the units of substance for granted. The particularly interesting thing here is that the alternative foci can be seen to lead from one way of experiencing matter to the next: Focus on the "small atoms" in C can lead to seeing matter as units of substance comprised of aggregates of atom-like particles, as in D(b), and there in D(b), focus on the atom-like particles can lead to experiencing matter as being constituted of particles and systems of particles, as in E and F.

### ON AWARENESS

In the previous section we made great efforts to communicate the nature of our basic unit of investigation: a way of experiencing something. But there is something missing. Our descriptions of ways of experiencing are descriptions of an abstraction: The children who experience number in one way or another, for example, do not experience only number but number in some wider context. No, it is impossible to experience anything in total isolation. Our experiences of anything are always embedded in a context.

**TABLE 5.1**

Analysis of Ways of Experiencing Matter

| | Referential aspect ... | Structural aspect | Internal Horizon |
|---|---|---|---|
| Matter comprises ... | | Focus on... | |
| A | ... homogeneous continuum of immutable substances | | Mixtures of substances in varying proportions |
| B | ... delimited units of substances | ... either on the content of the unit or on the border and/or nucleus | Units, their border or shell, their content, and a nucleus |
| C | ... delimited units of substance with "small atoms" being of the same substance but having different properties | ... either on the unit of substance and/or the "small atoms" | Units, their border or shell, their contents, and the "small atoms" |
| D(a) | ... units of substance containing aggregates of infinitely divisible particles of homogeneous substance | ...either on the substance unit or on the substance particles | Units of substance, their borders which keep the particles together and the particles of substance themselves |
| D(b) | ... units of substance containing aggregates of infinitely divisible particles with atom-like nature but no other attributes | ... either on the substance unit or on the atom-like particles | Units of substance, their borders that keep the particles together, and the atom-like particles themselves |
| E(a) | ... particles of substance that are not further divisible and that have attributes of form and structure | ... either on the substance particle(s) or on their attributes | Substance particles and their attributes, either (a₁) singly or (a₂) in groups with relationships between them |
| E(b) | ... atom-like particles that are not further divisible and that have attributes of form and structure | ... either on the atom-like particle(s) or on their attributes | Atom-like particles and their attributes, either (b₁) singly or (b₂) in groups with relations between them |
| F | ... systems of interrelated particles or subparticles with attributes of form and structure | ... either on the system of particles and subparticles, or on the space between them | Particles or subparticles, their attributes, relationships between them, links between microproperties of the system and macroproperties of the matter |

Let us, for the sake of example, envisage a reader of the present text. When reading this very sentence she is aware of the overall topic of the book; she is aware of what kind of book this is a chapter of; and she is aware, at least to some extent, of the gist of the argument. She may have some previous experience of the topic, and to that extent her previous experiences form a background for her present reading. She is aware of why she is reading this chapter and how she feels about it while reading it. She is also aware of who she is, of where she is sitting, what time of year and day it is, and what she is going to do for the rest of the day. She is aware of her own name, of whether or not she is married, if she has any children, if her parents are alive, and much more besides. Although she is aware of innumerable things simultaneously, she is certainly not aware of everything in the same way. Our awareness has a structure to it. At any instant certain things are to the fore—they are figural or thematized—whereas other things have receded to the ground—they are tacit or unthematized. But to stress the dichotomous nature of awareness—figure–ground, thematized–unthematized, explicit–implicit—would be to oversimplify. There are different degrees of how figural, thematized, or explicit things or aspects are in our awareness.

When you, our reader, read this chapter, we hope (very much) that its meaning is at the focus of your awareness, and not the weather or your family troubles. While reading the text, things that are related to its content come to the fore in your awareness, maybe how your own children or your students might experience number or Newtonian motion. Gurwitsch (1964) made a distinction between the object of focal awareness, the *theme*, and those aspects of the experienced world that are related to the object and in which it is embedded, the *thematic field*. As you read this, the text is the theme of your awareness, and issues such as the nature of experience, understanding, phenomenology, and ways of experiencing number belong to the thematic field. The same theme (this text) might, of course, be seen against the background of different thematic fields. For example, if you happen to be engaged in translating this book into German, the thematic field might extend more to your potential audience and related German literature than to the educational research interest that lies behind the book.

Furthermore, there are things that are temporally and spatially coexistent with your reading of the text, such as the room in which you are sitting, your marital worries, the bus you have to catch at 4:30, or maybe the dead-line the publisher has set for your translation, and so on. All that which is coexistent with the theme without being related to it by dint of the content or meaning, Gurwitsch called the *margin*.

The thematic field or fields and the margin belong to the external horizon of the experience. Thematic fields relate to other thematic fields and the margin stretches indefinitely in space and time. In a sense we could say that we are aware of everything all of the time. But we are surely not aware of everything in the same way. Certain things are focused, others less and less. Of most things we are only very, very marginally aware. Then the situation may suddenly change and with it the structure of our awareness. Something else will be come to the fore and other things will surround it closely while yet others will recede into peripheral awareness.

We would like to elaborate somewhat on Gurwitsch's description of human awareness, limiting ourselves to awareness in the context of learning in educational settings. Gurwitsch distinguishes three constituents of awareness: the theme, the thematic field, and the margin. They are related to one another by relevancy both in an instantaneous, snapshot mode and in a fluid, dynamic mode. In other words, at any instant, the current thematic field is constituted of aspects of awareness that are pointed to by relevancy from the current theme, and from instant to instant, one theme replaces another in awareness also according to the relevancy one has for the other. Now, in a snapshot of a learner learning (or reporting on some aspect of the experience of learning) we are able to distinguish, at two extremes, what it is that makes up her theme (of what she is thematically aware and concentrates on) and what is relegated to the margin (what is ignored in this learning effort). The thematic field can be seen as a single structure of relevance surrounding the theme, but for our purposes it can be useful to consider the thematic field in terms of constituent fields related to the theme according to one sort of relevance or another. The sight of a deer in the dark forest points to external horizons (constituent thematic fields) related to anecdotes about hunters or to nursery tales, from which different ways of experiencing the deer are born. In the same way, for the learner, the learning situation points to one or another constituent thematic field that can serve to bring now the constraints of the actual task, now the demands of the educational setting, now the phenomena involved closer to focal awareness. These constituent thematic fields extend into the very life world of the learner, both back into her learning history and forward into the way she proceeds with her learning.

## APPRESENTATION

There is one highly critical aspect of awareness (and we use the term throughout as synonymous with consciousness) that is captured by the phenomenological concept of *appresentation*. When we have a perceptual or sensuous experience of something, which is to say that we see, hear, or smell it, we can talk about the mode in which it presents itself, that is, the way in which it appears to one or more of our senses. But in addition to what is "presented" to us—that which we see, hear, smell—we experience other things as well. If we look at a tabletop from above, for instance, we hardly experience it as a two-dimensional surface floating in the air, in spite of the fact that what we see is, strictly speaking, a two-dimensional surface separated in some mysterious way from the ground. But in looking down on a tabletop we experience the legs that support it as well, because the experience is not of a two-dimensional surface, but of a *table*. Thanks to our previous experiences of tables, and of the particular table we are looking at, we have learned to know tables in general and this particular table as well. We are familiar with them so that when we see a part of a table we are aware of the presence of the table as a whole. In a similar way, in the sound of a tram that has not yet come around the corner the tram itself is presented. In the voice of a loved one, she or he is present, or to use in the phenomenological term, is *appresented*. When we look at a face, we experience a human being, a female or a male body, but even more, a person. That which is not seen, is not even visible, is *appresented*. When we face a house, in particular our own home, we do not experience the facade as merely a facade, but we experience it as a house, while its elements—rooms, doors, floors, a staircase perhaps, are inherent in our experience—are *appresented*.

We wish to apply the concept of appresentation to experiences of abstract entities as well as concrete ones. If we think of the gravitational constant, $g$, for instance, then the highly abstract formulation made by Newton of how bodies affect one another at a distance is appresented, given that we have acquired sufficient education in and experience of classical physics. "Appresentation" refers to the fact that although phenomena are, as a rule, only partially exposed to us, we do not experience the parts as themselves, but we experience the wholes of which the parts are parts. We do not experience silhouettes but phenomena (material or conceptual) in all their complexity of space and time.

## ON AWARENESS, DISCERNMENT, AND SIMULTANEITY

Earlier we claimed that our awareness can be characterized in terms of a generalized figure–ground structure: Certain phenomena or particular aspects of certain phenomena are figural and make up the core of our awareness, whereas other phenomena or other aspects of phenomena are nonfigural and constitute the field surrounding and temporally concomitant with the core. This brings us to another issue closely related to appresentation, which has to do with which phenomenon or aspect of a phenomenon we experience as being figural (i.e., in the fore or thematized, and which phenomenon or aspects we experience in the ground; as nonfigural, unthematized, or tacit). As we keep pointing out, structure and meaning are two dialectically intertwined aspects of a way of experiencing something, whether a situation or a phenomenon. A way of experiencing something can thus be described in terms of the structure or organization of awareness at a particular moment. Similarly, qualitatively *different* ways of experiencing something can be understood in terms of differences in the structure or organization of awareness at a particular moment or moments. Structure, once again, refers to the way in which the whole is discerned, how its parts are discerned and are related to one another and to the whole; it refers to the perspective it is viewed from, what is held in focus and what is not. The whole, the parts, and the relationships between them are discerned in terms of various aspects such as cardinality, ordinality; velocity, frames of reference; systems of particles; topics, subtopics, and so on. Such aspects represent dimensions of explicit or implicit variation in awareness. If we notice *a* change in a particular aspect of a phenomenon (e.g., the level of water in the bath rises as we step into it) then the variation is explicit. If we notice that something *is the case* (e.g., there are 7 marbles hidden in one box), the variation is implicit; there is an implication that there could have been 6 or 8 or some other number of marbles, but we do not focus on it. The dimensions are discerned in relation to the thematic field against the background of which the phenomenon, and the situation in which it is embedded, is seen. The aspects discerned thus derive from and point to the external horizon of the phenomenon in the sense of the thematic fields.

The aspects of the phenomenon and the relationships between them that are discerned and simultaneously present in the individual's focal awareness define the individual's way of experiencing the phenomenon. Being focally aware of the weight of a body immersed in some fluid as compared to its weight when not immersed, of the fact that a certain volume of the fluid is displaced by the act of immersion, of the weight of the fluid displaced—all at the same time—amounts to what it takes to discover, or to understand, Archimedes' principle. The key feature of the structural aspect of a way of experiencing something (and thereby also of the referential aspect with which the structural aspect is intertwined) is the set of different aspects of the phenomenon as experienced that are simultaneously present in focal awareness.[5]

If we reflect on the nature of reality, we readily see that it is fundamentally inexhaustible. There is no way of arriving at a final description of anything, because a description relates what that thing is for someone, and thereby depicts it as seen through someone's previous experiences. Naturally, we have no idea what the thing looks like against the background of experiences nobody has yet had! Furthermore, no one would claim that we can grasp everything at the same time. If we were capable of total experience of situations and phenomena, a sort of panaesthesia, and if we actually made use of this capability all the time, things would look the same for all time and for all of us. Our ways of experiencing things would no longer be driven by specific interests, preferences, wishes, capabilities, or previous experiences. Nothing would be more or less important than anything else; the world would lose structure. All meaning would disappear, as meaning actually derives from the figurally differentiated structure of awareness. When meaning is total we lose it.

Now, the proposition that we can never produce a final description of anything is based on a logical argument. So also is the proposition that if we were capable of being focally aware of all possible aspects of a certain phenomenon simultaneously and if we were indeed focally aware of all possible aspects of that phenomenon, then we would paradoxically lack the capability of experiencing the meaning of the phenomenon in any conceivable sense of the word. Of course, then, we would lack the capability of experiencing that phenomenon differently under different circumstances. In contrast with these logically grounded propositions we would like to argue that the idea that our capability for having focal experience of several aspects of a phenomenon simultaneously is highly constrained, is an empirically derived and empirically verifiable observation.

In fact, to foreshadow the rest of this chapter, it is exactly in terms of our limited capacity for simultaneous focal awareness that we can deal with the paradox that, on the one hand, every phenomenon is experientially inexhaustible, and that, on the other, whatever phenomena people encounter they experience in a limited number of qualitatively different ways, as it was illustrated by the studies used as

---

[5]We do not deal here with the role of aspects present in nonfocal awareness.

examples in chapters 2, 3, and 4. Moreover, it is in terms of the very same limitation that it is possible to make sense of the hierarchical ordering we find in the qualitatively different ways of experiencing something.

We find that in various situations people manage to different degrees to discern and keep all relevant aspects of the phenomenon and of the situation in focal awareness simultaneously. What happens is that single aspects are abstracted or separated out, while others are left undiscerned. Sometimes, and the example that follows indicates this clearly, aspects that should have appeared simultaneously in focal awareness are separated out and placed in a linear sequence, one after the other.

### Example 5.8:  Seeing the Structure of a Text

Let us consider the example of the qualitative differences in reading and understanding the text in Säljö's study, recounted in Example 2.3 (Säljö, 1982). You recall that as far as understanding is concerned there were two distinctly different ways of making sense of the text. In one case the text was read as being about a certain topic (forms of learning) embracing some different ways of looking at learning (classical conditioning, instrumental conditioning, and so on), illustrated by examples (the first by a scene from a prison and an experiment with dogs, and the second by a rat in a Skinner box and other examples, and so on); the text was understood in terms of a hierarchical structure. In the other case the text was read as being about torture and classical conditioning and Pavlov's dogs and instrumental conditioning and Skinner's rats and so on; the text was understood in terms of a linear structure. We illustrated these structures in Figs. 2.7 and 2.8. What is interesting is that the same elements were present in both cases, but they had structurally different positions and functions. If the former understanding better reflects how the text *should be* read—as we argue it does—what it takes to understand the text is a discernment and a simultaneous awareness of the different levels. Therefore, when reading about a particular example, the reader is supposed to be focally aware of the example as such, as an example of a certain form of learning, and of that form of learning in the context of the text dealing with what learning is in a broader sense, and what different forms of it we can find. There is an overarching theme of "forms of learning," and the parts in terms of particular forms of learning and illustrations of them are constantly related in awareness. The linear structure, in contrast, lacks a simultaneous awareness of the parts in relation to one another and to the whole, but has a sequential awareness of the parts one by one. This difference is illustrated in Figs. 5.6 and 5.7.

When "forms of learning" is present as an overarching theme, as illustrated in Fig. 5.6, the reader is aware of it all the time while reading the text, aware of reading about classical conditioning while reading the first and the second example, and aware of reading about instrumental conditioning while reading the third example.

When the text is experienced as a linear sequence of topics, as illustrated in Fig. 5.7, the reader is focally aware of one topic at a time. Wenestam (1978) used the term *horizontalization* to describe this sequential way of reading in connection with a study he conducted in which various texts with a similar structure of principle

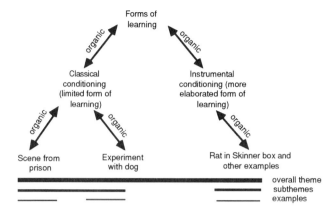

FIG. 5.6. The significance of the imposed structure for awareness of the point of the text as overarching theme and examples.

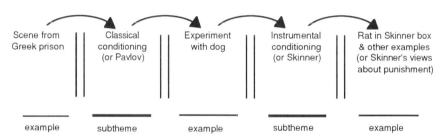

FIG. 5.7. The significance of the imposed structure for awareness of the point of the text as a sequence of items.

and example were read by secondary school students. He arrived at the same sort of qualitative differences as Säljö did in the way that the structure of a text was grasped and remembered. He found that even after 1 week individuals retained—and, surprisingly enough, even in a few cases improved—their initial structural understanding.

## Example 5.9: Being Aware of Numbers

In the example just recounted, of understanding a text, all the elements were present in both ways of experiencing it, in one case simultaneously and in the other not simultaneously but succeeding each other sequentially. If, in the light of this, we return to the ways in which numbers are understood, as described in chapter 4, we find that qualitatively different ways of experiencing numbers reflects whether certain aspects of a complete way of experiencing numbers are focally present in awareness or not.

A complete way of experiencing numbers, as abstract and structured entities such as in *number facts,* involves the discernment and simultaneous awareness of their ordinal aspects, of their cardinal aspects, of the whole, of the parts, and of the singular units. Experiencing numbers as *names,* in contrast, means to be aware of numbers primarily in terms of part–whole relationships and their ordinal, but not their cardinal aspects, whereas experiencing numbers as *extents* means to be aware of numbers in terms of part–whole relationships and their cardinal, but not their ordinal aspects. In the case of *counted numbers* children are aware of both cardinal and ordinal aspects, but they are not experienced simultaneously—they are kept separate.

## Example 5.10:  Being Aware of Learning

Differences in how a text is understood by university students and how numbers are experienced by school children are both differences in the "what" aspect of learning: They are differences in the outcomes of one or more learning tasks. But the perspective of simultaneity can also be applied to differences in the "how" aspect of learning. We have distinguished between a surface approach (the learner focusing on "the sign," in Säljö's case, the text) and a deep approach (the learner focusing on "the signified," in Säljö's case, what the text is about). It is obvious that nobody can bypass the text. To adopt a deep approach means that the learner focuses on the words of the text, the meaning conveyed by the words, and the global meaning of the phenomena being dealt with in the text, simultaneously. In this sense a surface approach is partial in comparison with a deep approach, meaning that less of the whole is being discerned and thematized or focused on, and that in a disjoint manner.

This becomes more obvious if we consider the fact that the dichotomy between the surface and the deep approach is inextricably coupled to another dichotomy between an atomistic and a holistic approach introduced by Svensson (1977). He described them succinctly, respectively, as "merely delimiting and ordering parts of the material interacted with" and "integrating parts by the use of some organizing principle" (Svensson, 1984b, p. 64), which is very close to the difference between the ways in which we have described the two ways of making sense of the text in Example 5.8, earlier. Svensson's dichotomy relates both to the what and the how aspects of learning.

Looking at people's ideas of learning in a more general sense, as we did in chapter 3, we can remind ourselves of a point made by Pramling, Klerfelt, and Williams Graneld (1995) when they argued that the very idea of learning presupposes a simultaneous awareness of something both staying the same and changing. How can a child, for example, see instances of improving a certain skill distributed temporarily and spatially as being instances of improving the very same skill, and thus, by belonging together, constituting learning? They point to the parallel study of Piaget in which he investigated the child's capability of seeing a growing plant as changing and still maintaining its identity: What we see on different occasions and what looks different on the different occasions is nonetheless the very same plant.

The line of reasoning we applied to the difference between surface and deep approaches can also apply to the variation in the object of learning that we described in chapter 3. This variation can be interpreted in terms of the learner having a simultaneous awareness of more and more aspects of the learning situation: the words of the text, the meaning of the text, the meaning of the phenomenon. The learner may have a simultaneous focus on committing to memory and on under-standing (as is the case with many Chinese learners) or on the two as alternatives as is often the case with European learners).

## Example 5.11:   A Ball Moving in a Train

Let us look at a two more examples. Bowden et al. (1992) interviewed first-year university students in physics and final-year (Australian Year 12) high school students about their understanding of particular concepts and principles in kinemat-ics. One of the problems appearing in the interviews read as follows:

> A ball inside a train is rolled towards the back of the train. It travels 2 m along the floor in 3 s, while the train travels forwards at a constant speed of 10 m/s. Discuss the displacement of the ball. (p. 264)

Some of the students participating in the investigation saw the ball's motion in two successive stages: *first* it travels 30 m (at 10 m/s for 3 s) with the train and *then* 2 m in the reverse direction. The displacement of the ball during the 3 s interval was thus 28 m. The interviewers made sure in every such case that the student really meant that there were two *separate* movements.

Although the numerical answer accords with the physics of the problem, the description does not. There are two frames of reference implicit in the problem, from which the movement of the ball can be viewed. For an observer on the train the ball appears moving 2 m in 3 s toward the back of the train. The other, and usually privileged, frame of reference is the ground. How would the movement of the ball appear to an observer standing on the ground if we assume a transparent train? Well, she would see the ball moving in the same direction as the train but with a slightly slower speed. During the 3 s interval the train will have moved 30 m and the ball 28 m. Now the difficulty with this—to all intents and purposes very simple—problem lies in the fact that the movement of the ball as seen from the ground is the resultant of two movements: the movement of the train in relation to the ground, on the one hand, and the movement of the ball in relation to the train, on the other. In order to come up with a satisfactory "discussion of the displacement of the ball in the 3 s interval of time" one has to see how the movement of the ball appears in the frame of reference fixed in the train and in the frame of reference fixed in the ground. To grasp the latter the student must be able to see the two movements, of which the resultant is both separately and simultaneously the move-ment of the ball. Simultaneity in this case refers to simultaneity of the resultant movement and its composite parts, and here lies the difficulty in this seemingly very easy problem. Suggesting that the ball is making two successive movements is one way of dealing with the difficulty: The two component parts are separated and laid after each other, resembling the sequential way of reading the text in Example 5.8 earlier. In two other ways of dealing with the problem either the ground or the train is taken for granted as the frame of reference (although without mentioning the frame of reference explicitly). In the first of these cases the displacement of the ball (2 m) is subtracted from the displacement of the train (30 m). In this case the students do not seem to be focally aware of possible alternative frames of reference, and they probably do not see the *movement* of the ball in relation to the observer on the ground. They simply calculate the displacement of the ball.

The variation between the different ways of seeing the problem can thus be understood as a variation in the extent to which the various aspects of a full understanding of the problem are discerned and simultaneously present in the students' focal awareness. Different ways of understanding a problem are thus partial, and whatismore, they are differentially partial.

### Example 5.12:  Children Drawing Maps

The last example used here to illustrate the constraints on being simultaneously aware of several things in a figural sense concerns children drawing maps. Piaget and Inhelder (1948) distinguished between two different aspects of the relationship between the map as representation and the landscape it represents. On the one hand, there is—or is supposed to be—a *logical* (and mathematical) correspondence between the two, a correspondence in what kind of entities and how many of them are present in the map as compared to the landscape. On the other hand, there is—or is supposed to be—a *spatial* correspondence in how those entities are distributed in relation to each other in space. In an early stage of the development of map-drawing skills, a stage which is fairly frequent among 6-year-olds (Mathews, 1992, p. 106), children seem to focus primarily on logical correspondence. When faced with a landscape to map, typically, a toy landscape, they identify that there are houses and trees there, so when they draw a map they put some trees together on the border of field and they also put some houses together on the border (see Fig. 5.8), favoring

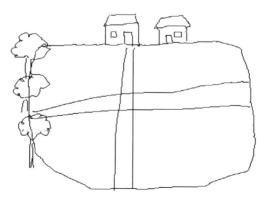

FIG. 5.8. A typical child's map, indicating the presence of houses, roads, and trees without regard to number and spatial correspondence  (adapted from Feldman, 1980).

what Mathews refers to as the logical aspect (what sort of entities have to be present), with a vague sense of the mathematical aspect (how many houses and how many trees), and neglecting spatial correspondence (trees and houses related to each other in space). Thus it appears to be easier for them to *transform* the landscapes in this way than to copy it. The reason is, of course, that when you are unable to focus on two or more aspects simultaneously, you focus on one of them.

The increasingly advanced levels of map-drawing reflect a simultaneous awareness of more and more aspects of the landscape (Feldman, 1980; Mathews, 1992).

## AWARENESS AND THE HIERARCHICAL RELATIONS
## BETWEEN WAYS OF UNDERSTANDING SOMETHING

In this last section on awareness, discernment, and simultaneity we have been trying out our ideas on some examples. The main idea is that the limited number of qualitatively different ways in which something is experienced can be understood in terms of which constituent parts or aspects are discerned and appear simultaneously in people's awareness. A particular way of experiencing something reflects a simultaneous awareness of particular aspects of the phenomenon. Another way of experiencing it reflects a simultaneous awareness of other aspects or more aspects or fewer aspects of the same phenomenon. More advanced ways of experiencing something are, according to this line of reasoning, more complex and more inclusive (or more specific) than less advanced ways of experiencing the same thing, "more inclusive" and "more specific" both implying more simultaneously experienced aspects constituting constraints on how the phenomenon is seen.

Now, such a characterization of the variation between qualitatively different ways of experiencing something cannot rest on an a priori analysis; it is empirically grounded. The way in which we describe the variation reflects our, the researchers', understanding of what differences are critically significant. It also represents our value judgments about what counts as a good, or a better, understanding of a text, of a problem, or whatever. Value judgements cannot be empirically grounded, but they can be argued. We can argue, for instance, that a map that reflects a simultaneous awareness of logical, mathematical, spatial relations is a better map than one which does not do so. It is a better map because it makes it easier for us to find the place we are heading for, which is better than not being able to do so, a value judgement that is not at all hard to defend.

The better experience or understanding of a phenomenon (whether text, problem, principle, or whatever) is thus defined in terms of our, the researchers', analysis of the qualitatively different ways of experiencing or understanding the phenomenon, and less advanced ways of experiencing it are partial in relation to more advanced ways of experiencing it. They reflect a simultaneous awareness of some aspects of the phenomenon reflected by a more advanced way of experiencing it.

## WHAT IS AWARENESS?

In this chapter we have elaborated on the idea of qualitatively different ways of experiencing something in terms of structural and referential aspects and in terms of discernment and simultaneity. In order to experience something *as* something we must be able to discern it from and relate it to a context, and be able to discern its parts and relate them to each other and to the whole. But we discern wholes, parts, and relationships in terms of aspects that define the wholes, the parts, and the relationships. To discern the spatial arrangement of a landscape we have to experience the spatial arrangement as *a* spatial arrangement (among other conceivable spatial arrangements). To experience the cardinality of a set of objects we must experience it as *a* cardinality (among other conceivable cardinalities). To experience a particular situation in terms of general aspects, we have to experience the general aspects. These aspects correspond to *dimensions of variation*. That which we observe in a specific situation we tacitly experience as *values* in those dimensions. A certain way of experiencing something can thus be understood in terms of the dimensions of variation that are discerned and are simultaneously focal in awareness,[6] and in terms of the relationships between the different dimensions of variation. As the different ways of experiencing something are different ways of experiencing the same thing, the variation in ways of experiencing it can be described in terms of a set of dimensions of variation.

If we consider an individual at any instant, he or she is aware of certain things or certain aspects of reality focally while other things have receded to the background. But we are aware of everything all the time, even if not in the same way all the time. The structure of an individual's awareness keeps changing all the time, and the totality of all experience is what we call that individual's awareness. An experience is an internal relationships between the person experiencing and the phenomenon experienced: It reflects the latter as much as the former. If awareness is the totality of all experiences, then awareness is as descriptive of the world as it is of the person. A person's awareness is the world as experienced by the person.

One focus of all the studies described here has been on variation rather than on individuals. Although one way of experiencing something in a particular case has to be seen in relation to the structure of the individual's awareness, we are above all interested in variation. We are justified in calling this chapter "The Anatomy of Awareness" in that it contains a very stripped account of awareness, showing its structure as reflected in the dimensions of variation, in terms of which a certain phenomenon is understood.

If a particular way of experiencing a phenomenon is seen in relation to particular features of an awareness, then the varying ways of experiencing that phenomenon should be seen in relation to particular features of diverse awarenesses. To understand the single experience we have to understand the anatomy of awareness. To

---

[6]To put it slightly differently, a dimension of variation being discerned means that the corresponding aspect *is* in focal awareness.

understand the variation in experience we have to understand the collective anatomy of awareness, or in other words, the different ways in which different phenomena can be experienced, as has earlier been called "the collective mind" (Marton, 1981). This is a shift from individual awareness that varies as to focus and simultaneous awareness of aspects of a phenomenon to a collective awareness in which all such variation can be spied.

# 6

## The Idea of Phenomenography

In chapters 2, 3, and 4 we described the results of a number of empirical studies into aspects of learning in our meaning of the term, "gaining knowledge about the world," as a background to our arguments about the nature of learning, and in particular the nature of the experience of learning. There you have met the variation in several dimensions of learning pertaining both to aspects of the learners' experience of learning at large and to the very phenomena they were engaged in learning. We have presented variations in ways people understand the notion of learning, in students' approaches to their tasks of learning, and in ways they understand the things they have been learning, and we have treated the variation both empirically and more theoretically in terms of experience and awareness. The studies related to different types of learners—school children in Sweden and China, university students of engineering and social sciences, adult learners, and pre-schoolers—and different educational settings. What the studies indubitably have in common is that they all focused on *variation* in ways of experiencing things. To depict variation of experience was indeed one of their prime objects.

A lesser commonality is that most of them can be seen in a framework of the research specialization called *phenomenography*[1]—"lesser" because they often partly extend outside what we today call phenomenography, either in research approach or in time. The early work on approaches to learning actually preceded and gave rise to pheno-

---

[1]Kroksmark (1987) offered the following etymological derivation of the term *phenomenography*: "The word is a compound from two roots: phenomenon and graph. Phenomenon comes from the Greek verb fainesqai (fainesthai) which means *to appear, or to become manifest*, and gives the noun fainemonon (fainemonon) which means *the apparent, or that which manifests itself*. The verb comes from fainw (faino), which means to *bring to light, or to elicit*, the fa- stem implying approximately that which can be revealed and made apparent. The concept phenomenon must therefore be taken to mean that which appears in its own right, or that which is manifest. Phenomenon thus refers to the collected totality of that which is made apparent or manifest.... *Graph* also comes from the Greek, from the verb grafia (graphy), which means *to describe in words or pictures that which designates, for example, an aspect of reality or an experience of reality*. In combination with phenomenon, graphy becomes the act of representing an object of study as qualitatively distinct phenomena" (pp. 226–227; our translation).

menography, whereas studies of number, for instance, arose outside the pheno-menographic framework and approached it as providing a sound conceptual plat-form for continued studies, and in turn contributed to its development.

To cast light on the question, "What is the driving force of phenomenography?" let us carry out a thought experiment. Imagine that there are two students taking an examination, facing the same problem. Let us assume they experience the situation in exactly the same way: They understand the problem in exactly the same way; it is equally important for them to solve the problem; they experience their own capabilities for solving it in exactly the same way; and so on. Their experiences of the problem and the situation are quite simply identical. Can we imagine that one of the two students succeeds with the problem, whereas the other fails? Hardly! We are not able to infer the converse—that two students who succeed with a problem must have understood it in exactly the same way—but we are able to infer that two students dealing with a problem differently must also have experienced it differ-ently. This type of argument gives us grounds to believe that in order to make sense of how people *handle* problems, situations, the world, we have to understand the way in which they *experience* the problems, the situations, the world, that they are handling or in relation to which they are acting. Accordingly, a capability for *acting* in a certain way reflects a capability *experiencing* something in a certain way. The latter does not cause the former, but they are logically intertwined. You cannot act other than in relation to the world as you experience it.

This chapter discusses the whole idea of phenomenography: The unit of phenomenographic research is *a way of experiencing something,* in the sense that the term has been elaborated in earlier chapters of this book, and the object of the research is the *variation* in ways of experiencing phenomena. At the root of phenomenography lies an interest in describing the phenomena in the world as others see them, and in revealing and describing the variation therein, especially in an educational context: "the anatomy of awareness as seen from an educational point of view" (Marton, 1993). This implies an interest in the variation and change in capabilities for experiencing the world, or rather in capabilities for experiencing particular phenomena in the world in certain ways. These capabilities can, as a rule, be hierarchically ordered. Some capabilities can, from a point of view adopted in each case, be seen as more advanced, more complex, or more powerful than other capabilities. Differences between them are educationally critical differences, and changes between them we consider to be the most important kind of learning.

Phenomenography is not a method in itself, although there are methodical elements associated with it, nor is it a theory of experience, although there are theoretical elements to be derived from it. Also, phenomenography is not merely an opportune player that can assume the role needed for the moment. Phenomenog-raphy is rather a way of—an approach to—identifying, formulating, and tackling certain sorts of research questions, a specialization that is particularly aimed at questions of relevance to learning and understanding in an educational setting. In this chapter, its research methods and its research roles are described as subordinate to its nature as a research approach.

This description of phenomenography will take up some of its central features and spread out from those to cover fundamental assumptions, methodological issues, and the way forward.

## THE OBJECT OF RESEARCH

The origin of a research specialization is generally to be found in observations that, having been made, reveal something that seems worthwhile to explore further. In our case the first observations date back to the mid-1970s, some of them already having been referred to in this book, especially in chapter 2. The observation was that when people read a text or listen to a presentation or try to solve a problem or reflect upon a phenomenon, that which they encounter appears to them in a limited number of qualitatively different ways. The different ways in which they experience the text, the presentation, the problem, or the phenomenon are observed to be logically related to each other and to form together a complex that we have called the outcome space. Such observations have been replicated in a very large number of studies that have been carried out during the last 20 years.

What, then, is "a way of experiencing something"? That is exactly the question this book—in particular the third section of the previous chapter—is addressing in its quest for an answer to the question of how we gain knowledge about the world. Let us try to pull together some of the key features scattered in different places in our earlier chapters. "A way of experiencing something" is experiencing something *as* something, experiencing a meaning that is dialectically intertwined with a structure. "A way of experiencing something" is a way of discerning something from, and relating it to, a context. The meaning of something for someone at a particular point in time corresponds to the pattern of parts or aspects that are discerned and are simultaneously objects of focal awareness.

What does it mean that an aspect is discerned and is the object of focal awareness? As we have already pointed out, an aspect that is discerned and held in focus is associated with a dimension of explicit or implicit variation. What *is* the case is explicitly or implicitly seen against the background of what *could be* the case. For instance, discerning and being focally aware of the fact that something is moving implies a dimension of variation with two possible states: rest and motion. Discerning and being focally aware that something is in uniform motion implies an awareness of a dimension of variation with two (or possibly more) states: uniform motion (including rest) and nonuniform motion (acceleration or deceleration). When an aspect is not discerned and not held in focal awareness—say, for instance, that something is at rest and we are not particularly conscious that it is so—we can say either that this aspect is absent altogether or that it is taken for granted and no alternatives are being explicitly considered.

The variation between different ways of experiencing something, then, derives from the fact that different aspects or different parts of the whole may or may not be discerned and be objects of focal awareness simultaneously. As we have illustrated in several examples, as a rule not all the relevant aspects of a phenomenon and of the situation in which it is embedded are discerned and present simultaneously in focal awareness. It is generally the case that some of them are abstracted, separated, isolated. Instead of them being objects of focal awareness simultaneously, they may be separated and experienced one after the other, in sequence. This tells us that certain ways of experiencing something are more complex or fuller than others. They spring from the simultaneous awareness of more parts or more aspects of the whole.

Let us return to the unit of phenomenographic research—a way of experiencing something—which, as we have pointed out several times now, is an internal relationship between the experiencer and the experienced. An internal relationship between A and B implies that neither A nor B would be identically the same without the relationship between them. A marriage is an internal relationship: Man and woman are turned into husband and wife by establishing the relationship between them. How can we picture an internal relationship between person and world? The world, or at least some part of it, is present to the person; the world is experienced by the person. Quite obviously, the person could not be the same person without the world she is experiencing, and if the world is understood in terms of the complex of all possible ways of experiencing it (knowing it, sensing it, being in it), and if the person's biography is unique, and if one's way of experiencing the world reflects one's biography, then the world could not possibly be exactly the same world without the person experiencing it.

This is not to say that if humankind disappeared, then the sun, the Hudson river, and wombats would necessarily disappear as well. The point we wish to make strongly is this: We cannot describe a world that is independent of our descriptions or of us as describers. We cannot separate out the describer from description. Our world is a real world, but it is a described world, a world experienced by humans. Quite obviously, humans did not cause the Big Bang, but the way in which it is conceptualized and described is a human way of conceptualizing and describing it. The implication of this is not necessarily that our way of understanding the Big Bang is flawed or distorted, but that it is partial. Furthermore, the human mind can hardly conceive of what it would take to conceive of the Big Bang through means other than the human mind.

Describing experience and ways of experiencing is entirely different from describing mental representations, short- or long-term memory, retrieval processes, and the rest of the conceptual apparatus of the cognitivists. According to that, thoughts and conceptions are things that go on or are located in one's head, things that are hidden or inferred. We may believe that our speech is preceded by thought, by an ongoing mumbling in the language of thought rapidly translated to a more mundane language such as Swedish or English, and in the same vein we may believe that our acts are guided or caused by conceptions that we bear with us. But if we actually reflect for a moment on how we experience producing speech or acting in some way, we can only conclude that there is no such guidance. When you speak, for instance, you might occasionally reflect or focus in advance on what is to be said, but in general, you experience the words as coming by themselves, without volition. If you say something like "I often think of Piroska," you simply mean that from time to time she, or something of her, is present to you, passes through your awareness, although neither she nor anything of her is present in the flesh. Moreover, when you do something you experience both the situation in which you do it and the relation to whom or what you are acting, but you hardly experience any conceptions guiding your acts. Thus, what is called thinking is something inferred, something assumed, a fiction. There again, a certain kind of experience can be called thinking, mainly the experience of someone or something being not present to our senses but being present to our thoughts. Thinking is thus either a fiction or an experience. We prefer the notion "Cognosco ergo sum" (I experience, therefore I am) to Descartes' original formulation, "Cogito ergo sum" (I think, therefore I am).

In our presentation, and in other phenomenographic studies, terms such as "conceptions," "ways of understanding," "ways of comprehending," and "conceptualizations" have been used as synonyms for "ways of experiencing"; they should all be interpreted in the experiential sense and not in the psychological, cognitivist sense. Obviously, we could not possibly experience anything without having a brain and a nervous system, and we could not possibly have any idea of other people's experiences if they did not talk, write, act, and behave. Describing experience is, however, something other than describing what is happening in the nervous system or describing what a person is doing. It is an autonomous level of description that cannot be reduced to the other levels of description, and it depicts how the world appears to people.

In phenomenography individuals are seen as the bearers of different ways of experiencing a phenomenon, and as the bearers of fragments of differing ways of experiencing that phenomenon.[2] The description we reach is a description of variation, a description on the collective level, and in that sense individual voices are not heard. Moreover, it is a stripped description in which the structure and essential meaning of the differing ways of experiencing the phenomenon are retained, while the specific flavors, the scents, and the colors of the worlds of the individuals have been abandoned.

## PHENOMENOGRAPHY IS NOT PSYCHOLOGY

Now, let us elaborate on a point we alluded to above, and at the same time disavow what has mistakenly been assumed or claimed, that phenomenography has the status of an empirical branch of psychology. In psychology different classes of functions and acts such as learning, remembering, solving problems, making decisions, and thinking make up the system of classification and object of study. In psychology, *what* is learned, or remembered, or thought about is subordinate to this classification. In phenomenography, the system of classification is turned right around: *What* is experienced and *how* it is experienced are in focus, and the

---

[2]For an elaboration of this theme, see the section "Individual and Collective Levels of Description" later.

particular psychological function in which the structural and referential aspects of the experience are embodied is of secondary interest. We are, for instance, interested in the way in which a phenomenon is experienced (structurally and referentially), irrespective of whether it is reflected in the way a problem is solved or in immediate perception or in acting or in remembering. The phenomena of recursion and Newtonian motion, for example, can be experienced in a number of ways that come to light both in reflecting on principles and in nonreflective problem solving. The ways in which children experience number, to take another example that recurs throughout our presentation, can manifest themselves in a multiplicity of problem and play situations. Our description of the qualitatively different ways in which something is experienced is neutral to the psychological functions in which it is revealed. In psychology, learning may be studied, irrespective of whether the learning is about political power or of nonsense syllables. In phenomenography the structural and referential aspects of the experience of political power may be studied, irrespective of whether political power is reflected in political action, in a line of reasoning about the political system in a foreign country, or in the recall of a textbook in political science that has been read.

In phenomenography, then, you can't deal with learning in general, as you can in psychology. That might seem to be a funny thing to say in a book that *is* about learning, but there are at least two ways of addressing this apparent contradiction. For one thing, one can consider a psychological entity such as learning as a legitimate subject for phenomenographic research (i.e., for the exploration of the different ways in which people experience it). This is what chapter 3 is about. The other way is a bit more complex and relates back to the idea of intentionality introduced in chapter 5, that any psychological entity such as learning cannot exist without an object. There is no learning without something learned.

We have by now drawn out some general characteristics of learning—that it is a change in internal relationship between person and world, that it concerns experience, that experience has certain characteristics, and so on—with reference to a number of specific examples. Throughout the book we have drawn on examples of research—and will continue to do so—that retain *what* is learned in the depiction of the *principles* of learning, in the conviction that the *general* can only be revealed through the *specific.* By the end of the book we make a plea, that taking our message as intended means that general ideas and principles need to be developed anew in specific contexts and contents of learning and teaching. In this sense, phenomenography points away from itself.

To take this further, because a way of experiencing something is an internal relationship between the experiencer and the experienced, it reflects the latter as much as the former; in psychology only the experiencer is of interest. Political power, for example, can be seen as a complex of different ways in which political power is experienced. At the same time political power transcends the different ways in which we see it, inasmuch as there are things that can, and in all likelihood will be, discerned about the nature and mechanisms of political power in the future. We reiterate, the set of the different ways of experiencing political power is a subset of all the *possible* ways of experiencing it. There is a part–whole relationship between the different ways identified and the phenomenon itself. The same is true of a particular person's experience of political power, on the one hand, and the set of different ways of experiencing political power described in a particular study that have been found, on the other. Again, there is a part–whole relationship between the two. Here we are making statements on the basis of a consideration of the *experience* of political power, about the *nature* of political power, another indication that our study of experience is essentially nonpsychological.

Moreover, we do not need to restrict ourselves to the words and deeds of particular persons as data for describing ways of experiencing something. For example, the way school systems are organized, schools are built, and how they are run—highly nonpsychological entities—might tell us a great deal about how particular societies, or those in power, conceive of knowledge. A specific way of experiencing something may thus refer to the structural and referential aspects of a person's way of making sense of the phenomenon at a specific point in space and time, but it could equally reflect a feature of a culture in the past or the present.

## IS PHENOMENOGRAPHY PHENOMENOLOGY?

A research specialization, as we spent the second section of this chapter pointing out, should reasonably be defined in terms of its object of research, and phenomenography has human experience as its object, as distinct from human behavior, or mental states, or the nervous system. Now if there were already a well-established science with such an object of research, it would be reasonable to subsume phenomenography under it. The only demand is that this established science would have the object of research as its only defining attribute, and not methods and theories. For example, the field of linguistics has language as its object of research, and any approach to studying language irrespective of methods and theories can be included in the family tree of linguistics. Indeed, there is such a science with experience as its object of research—phenomenology—which is one of the main schools of philosophical thought of this century. Phenomenology does have human experience as its object of research, but with it are inextricably linked a set of methods of going about the study of experience and theories about its nature, which makes its subsumption of phenomenography problematic, to say the least.

From the very beginning phenomenology had the program of developing a single theory of experience by using a particular method, which, befitting a philosophy, is a philosophical method. Philosophers engage in investigating their own experience. Phenomenographers, in contrast, adopt an empirical orientation: they study the experience of others. Thus, although phenomenography and phenomenology both belong to a field of knowledge defined by the criterion of having experience as the subject of study, they differ in the ways they go about that enterprise.

In phenomenology an important dividing line is drawn between the prereflective experience and conceptual thought. Now clearly, phenomenography does not make this distinction: The structure and meaning of a phenomenon as experienced can be found both in prereflective experience and conceptual thought. This is why expressions that might strike the reader as curious, such as "qualitatively different ways of experiencing the second law of thermodynamics," are to be found in phenomenographic writings.

There is a certain similarity between our program of phenomenography and the program of phenomenology as formulated by the founder of modern phenomenology, the German mathematician and philosopher, Edmund Husserl (see, e.g., Spiegelberg, 1982, pp. 69–165). He saw phenomenology as logically preceding the empirical sciences, aimed at clarifying their experiential foundations. Phenomenography is focused on the ways of experiencing different phenomena, ways of seeing them, knowing about them, and having skills related to them. The aim is, however, not to find the singular essence, but the variation and the architecture of this variation in terms of the different aspects that define the phenomena. The simultaneous awareness of all the critical aspects comes close to the phenomenological notion of essence, although in our case it is temporary and transitional. The set of qualitatively different ways of experiencing a phenomenon is finite but not closed; in particular, scientific discoveries frequently introduce new ways of seeing the phenomenon in question.

Phenomenography and phenomenology differ as to purpose. Phenomenology aims to capture the richness of experience, the fullness of all the ways in which a person experiences and describes the phenomenon of interest. Not for the phenomenologist the sparseness of the category of description or the logical hierarchy of the outcome space that the phenomenographer so analytically derives. The phenomenologist wishes to describe the person's lifeworld, the world in which he or she is immersed and which the phenomenological methods bring to light. Whereas the phenomenologist might ask, "How does the person experience her world?" the phenomenographer would ask something more like, "What are the critical aspects of ways of experiencing the world that make people able to handle it in more or less efficient ways?"

Thus, phenomenography and phenomenology share the object of their research, inasmuch as both aim to reveal the nature of human experience and awareness. To the extent that phenomenology is defined through its object of research—human experience and awareness—phenomenography could legitimately be seen as a child of the phenomenology family. To the extent, however, that phenomenology is grounded in a set of particular theories and methods that phenomenography shares only partly, if at all, phenomenography has to be seen as no more than a cousin-by-marriage of phenomenology.

## FIRST-ORDER AND SECOND-ORDER
## PERSPECTIVES AND DESCRIPTIONS

In previous chapters we made statements about the defining aspects of various phenomena in the world, reasoning in terms of the limitations of human awareness, differences, and communication between people. Were we making statements about the world or about people?

What we were doing was making statements about *the world as experienced by people*. Now, in the sciences, as well as in daily life, statements are made about the world, about phenomena, about situations. These statements are made from what we call a first-order perspective. The *ways of experiencing* the world, the phenomena, the situations, are usually taken for granted by the experiencer; they do not see them, they are not aware of them.[3] In phenomenography, where a second-order perspective is taken, it is these underlying ways of experiencing the world, phenomena, and situations that are made the object of research.

Let us introduce the second-order perspective through the problem of the ball in the train, as reported by Bowden et al. (1992), which we described in Example 5.11 of chapter 5. When we described the problem there, we went to some lengths to elaborate on the alternative ways of describing the movement of the ball that arrived at the physically correct answer. The displacement of the ball in that example can satisfactorily be quantified as 28 m in the direction of the train, but qualitatively there are different ways of seeing it, as discussed earlier. The correct answer can be reached by considering sequentially, first the displacement owing to the movement of the train—30 m—and then the displacement owing to the ball rolling along the floor of the train—2 m—which has to be subtracted, giving 28 m. In that way of reasoning, a component of the displacement in each of two frames of reference is implicitly considered, and they are subsequently combined to give the resultant: The displacement is seen as the sum of its parts. Alternatively, the answer can be seen as the result of considering the two frames of reference both explicitly and simultaneously, so that the 30 m which the train moves with respect to the frame of reference fixed in the ground in one direction and the 2 m that the ball moves in the other direction with respect to a frame of reference fixed in the train amount to the ball moving 28 m with respect to the ground.

Now the physicist, or the physics teacher for that matter, is generally looking for correct answers in the sense of the quantity given—correct figures and units. They are considering the problem from a first-order perspective. For them, 30 m–2 m = 28 m is correct and, 2 m, and 30 m are wrong, as is 28 m/s. They are working with first-order descriptions of the situation, checking answers against a predetermined norm, and their students' ways of thinking about, or ways of experiencing relative motion is of marginal interest. (In fact, the ability to analyze the motion into two independent components that can be dealt with separately might be highly desirable, but is not relevant to our current argument.)

If, however, a wrong answer is given—2 m, for example, was an answer seen in some interviews in the study—then the physics teacher might join the phenomenographic researcher in asking: "How did you arrive at that answer? How did you think about the problem? What does the problem mean for you?" This is taking a second-order perspective, and when the answers are analyzed, a second-order

---

[3]This might appear to contradict what was said at the end of the previous chapter, that a way of experiencing something can be understood in terms of what the experiencer is focally aware of. The experiencer, however, is focally aware of the *object* of her experience and not of her *way* of experiencing it.

description of the phenomenon of relative motion is reached. These descriptions are couched in terms of how people understand or experience relative motion and are not in the first place judged to be right or wrong. In the case of the student replying "2 m," the teacher might come to the conclusion that he is taking the perspective of standing in the train, and then go on to investigate other erroneous answers in this light.

The distinction between the first- and second-order perspective is the difference between considering a statement (such as "the displacement of the ball was 2 m during the interval of 3 s") to be a statement about the physical world or about some specified situation and judging it in the light of other statements about the physical world or about the same situation. In particular, it can be compared with the received wisdom of physics, weighed and found, in this case, wrong. Alternatively we can consider the very same statement as reflecting the learner's way of experiencing the problem, making sense of it. We can then take this statement as our point of departure for exploring the learner's understanding of the problem and the phenomenon that it is about.

When we adopt one perspective or the other we may, of course, be perfectly well aware of the alternative, but we have to "bracket"[4] it for the time being. We firmly believe that in good teaching we have to adopt both. On the one hand, we have to find out the extent to which learners have progressed toward the competence that the teaching aims to develop. On the other hand, to be better able to develop that competence through teaching, we have to find out why some learners have been more successful than others in making such progress.

In the research context, the distinction between the first- and second-order perspectives is primarily a distinction between two kinds of objects of research. Admittedly, this gives an outrageously uneven criterion for sorting the objects of research. We have on the one hand, all the scientific research conducted over the centuries that has yielded statements about the world, the physical, the biological, the social, the cultural, which we can all relate to without recourse to a consideration of human experience. On the other hand we have a very, very small number of studies that yield statements about people's experience of the world. Investigations with a phenomenographic orientation belong to this group, along with, for instance, certain branches of anthropology, history, and philosophy of science.

The physicist, the biologist, the sociologist, the archaeologist all want to develop knowledge and make statements about the world, or rather, about aspects of the world she is investigating. She may believe that she is describing the world as it is, or she may believe that she is simply describing the world as she experiences it, but in neither case will her statements be formulated as statements about her experiences, but rather as statements about aspects of the world she is dealing with. Her statements will be judged in the light of other statements about relevant phenomena. They will be judged as to whether or not they seem to be valid, consistent, and useful statements about those phenomena. Her statements will assuredly not be judged as to whether or not they give a truthful or consistent account of her

---

[4]To *bracket* is a term from phenomenology, meaning to suspend judgment.

experiences without regard to what they say about the object of research. Hence, to whatever degree she is conscious of the fact that the reality she is describing is not a reality as such but a reality conceived of and experienced by her, she has to bracket that consciousness.

If we adopt the alternative, second-order perspective, we focus on people's experiences of the world, whether physical, biological, social, cultural, or whatever. Whereas the people whose experiences we are studying are oriented toward the world they are experiencing, we as researchers are oriented toward the various ways in which they experience some aspect of the world. Here, then, is an obvious asymmetry. They can very well experience the world without our studying their experiences, but we can not study their experiences without their experiencing the world. Experiences are reflected in statements about the world, in acts carried out, in artifacts produced. Now, in the light of what we know about the world, such statements can appear more or less valid or consistent or useful, the acts more or less skilled, the artifacts more or less functional. Judgments of this kind belong to the first-order perspective. When adopting a second-order perspective, we have to bracket such judgments. We have to look at the statements, acts, and artifacts to find out what ways of experiencing particular aspects of the world they reflect, regardless of their validity, skillfulness, or functionality. Such a search has to be carried out in the light of other things we know about people's ways of experiencing the world.

Two further points add to the complexity of the relationship between the first- and second-order perspectives. From a first-order perspective the researcher's focus is on the object of research, and her experience (i.e., the constitutive acts of her awareness) is bracketed. But even from a second-order perspective the researcher's focus is on the object of research (other people's ways of experiencing something), and again her experience is bracketed. In one case the world is focused on and experience bracketed. In the other case experience (of others) is focused on and experience (the researcher's own) is bracketed. In the second-order perspective adopted in relation to the object of other people's experiences there is embedded a first-order perspective (in relation to the object of the researcher's experience). In phenomenology, as indicated in the previous section, the researcher's own experience is held in focus while judgments about the object of experience are bracketed. We are habitually oriented toward the objects of our experience (as we discuss further in the section on "The Natural Attitude" in the chapter to follow), researchers in general included. In a phenomenological study the phenomenologist's awareness is withdrawn from the object of experience, and the constitutive acts of awareness are reflexively focused (awareness is bent back as it were, focusing on itself), and it is here that the difference between phenomenology and phenomenography lies. In the former the researcher (the philosopher) is exploring her own experience by reflecting on it. In the latter the researcher is exploring other people's experiences by reflecting on *them*.[5]

---

[5]It could be thought that there is room for phenomenographic investigations to be complemented by phenomenological clarification of the experiential grounds of the researcher's reflection on other people's experiences, as Sandberg (1994) proposed.

The second point we want to raise, and which adds to the complexity of the relationship between the first- and second-order perspectives, concerns the fact that because we consider the experience of the world to be an internal relationship between the experiencer and the experienced, as much is said about the latter as about the former. What can be seen from a first-order perspective could—and, we think, should—be informed by that which can be seen from the second-order perspective.

Phenomenography, when applied to the phenomena dealt with in established disciplines, thus focuses on the meanings on which knowledge about the different phenomena rests, especially in relation to the meanings that those phenomena may have for the learner entering the respective fields of knowledge. The question of the taken-for-granted ways of experiencing phenomena is largely ignored within the research effort in fields that are stable; they are generally characterized by contemporaneous self-evident ways of seeing. Sometimes, however, the very question of how certain phenomena are experienced may turn out to be rather central to the field itself. In chemistry, for instance, it has been shown that the mole, the unit for measuring the amount of substance, is used in an inconsistent way, not only in chemistry education, but also in chemistry as a discipline (Lybeck, Marton, Strömdahl, & Tullberg, 1988; Strömdahl, 1996). In the field of anatomy, by introducing a conceptual apparatus for educational purposes, Eizenberg (1988) revealed the logic inherent in the superrational design of the body. Working in the same spirit, his student Stelmach (1991) treated the major secretory glands of the head and neck holistically as a single integrated unit on the basis of their secretory innervation. By doing so she managed to link coherently structures that, although anatomically closely related, had diverse locations within the standard textbooks. Although the driving force was educational, the outcome was non-trivial for the field of anatomy.

To return to the idea of the second-order perspective in phenomenography, it is the perspective that has to be explicitly adopted when research problems are being posed, when material is being gathered, and when analysis is being done. It means taking the place of the respondent, trying to see the phenomenon and the situation through her eyes, and living her experience vicariously. At every stage of the phenomenographic project the researcher has to step back consciously from her own experience of the phenomenon and use it only to illuminate the ways in which others are talking of it, handling it, experiencing it, and understanding it.

## DESCRIPTION AND EXPERIENCE

Let us summarize how far we have come at this point: the *variation* in ways people experience phenomena in their world is a prime interest for phenomenographic studies, and phenomenographers aim to describe that variation. They seek the totality[6] of ways in which people experience, or are capable of experiencing, the object of interest and interpret it in terms of distinctly different categories that

---

[6]At least, that subset of the totality that is pertinent and accessible for the sort of people being studied.

capture the essence of the variation, a set of categories of description from the second-order perspective.

In other words, the second-order categories of description that are the fundamental results of a phenomenographic investigation describe how the phenomenon in question is experienced. What sorts of things are these descriptions and the experiences they describe? There are three points—two points to what the descriptions are not, and one to what they are—that it is vital to grasp in answer to that question.

First, as we pointed out already, experiences are *not mental* entities: Psychology, in general, in such a context as this would be talking about abstract mental acts and features located within the human being or the human mind. Such a description would not emphasize the nature of the phenomenon, but would rather focus on the psychological acts and structures associated with the experience. From such a perspective, learning by reading a text, for example, is to internalize its syntactic and semantic elements into one sort of mental structure or another that leads to later recall with more or less success.

Second, experiences are *not physical* either: They are not merely a description of the phenomenon or aspect of the world that is at the heart of the phenomenographic investigation. Such a material entity appears in a first-order description. This perspective takes the experiencer for granted, a generalized being of no intrinsic interest, and focuses on the phenomenon as such, as do the materialistic descriptions of classical natural science and the social sciences it has inspired.

The third, and more positive, point is that, being located neither in the subject nor in the world, being neither psychological nor physical, being neither mind nor matter, experiences do comprise an *internal relationship* between the subject and the world, and that is their fundamental characteristic: An experience is of its essence *nondualistic*. Thus, descriptions of experience are not psychological and not physical. They are descriptions of the internal relationship between persons and phenomena: ways in which persons experience a given phenomenon and ways in which a phenomenon is experienced by persons. Learning by reading a text from the phenomenographic perspective is, as many of our examples have shown, as well as our exposition of the anatomy of awareness, a question of discerning and becoming focally and simultaneously aware of all the relevant aspects of the text.

As has been mentioned, the basic principle of phenomenography is that whatever phenomenon we encounter, it is experienced in a limited number of qualitatively different ways. Also, by now we have established "experience" as an internal relationship between person and world (or something in the world).

A person's experience of the world and even her experience of some specific phenomenon, however narrowly discerned it may be, is fundamentally inexhaustible.[7] Let us refer to Andersson's (1978) account of the monumental work by

---

[7]We draw the reader's attention to our earlier claim in chapter 5 that reality is inexhaustible and that phenomena are experientially inexhaustible; here we emphasize that even one person's experience of one particular phenomenon is inexhaustible.

the famous chess player Emanuel Lasker, *Die Philosophie das Unvollendbar,* published in 1919, which Marton has quoted elsewhere:

> Lasker dedicated himself to drawing a line of demarcation between two kinds of entities; none of them exists in the material world, but one has a conceivable limit and the other has not. Nobody has seen "pure silver" for instance, yet we can think of an infinite series of purer and purer silver. Moreover, we can even register a gradual decreasing in the deviance, even if it can never be total. On the other hand, "the thing-in-itself" for example, is not only inaccessible to our senses, but its limit is inconceivable to our minds. We experience a thing in terms of a series of qualifiers, and we cannot impose any order on this series to make it converge towards a quality free from qualifiers. "The thing-in-itself" is "unvollendbar." It is "incompletable." And, of course, what we are talking about is the thing as experienced. Saying that thing is incompletable is tantamount to saying that the experience is incompletable. It can never be fully described. (p. 36)

There is no complete, final description of anything and our descriptions are always driven by our aims.

Because we can never describe experience in its entirety, we are constrained to look for and describe critical differences in people's capabilities for experiencing the phenomena in which we are interested. Now, the totality of our experiences we call awareness, as we discussed at length in the previous chapter, and the critical differences that we are looking for in people's capabilities for experiencing various kinds of phenomena in certain ways can be seen in the light of the nature of awareness.

In this respect, as we have already pointed out, awareness has two most important qualities. One of them is that we cannot be aware of everything at the same time in the same way. If we could, there would not be any differences between individuals as far as their experiences, and hence their acts, are concerned. There would in fact be no world experienced; nothing would be more important than anything else. The other is that we *are* aware of everything at the same time, albeit not in the same way. Awareness is layered. Some things make up the core; they are objects of focal awareness; they are figural. Other things belong to the field, or fields, surrounding the core. Yet others belong to the fringe that extends indefinitely. Although we are not consciously aware of most things, we are aware enough for them to be pulled into the core if the changing here and now were to make them relevant.

Given this fundamental structure of awareness, we can experience something *as* something thanks to the two basic capabilities we are equipped with and the constraints which limit the capabilities: (a) we can discern entities and aspects, and (b) we can be focally aware of a few entities or aspects simultaneously. Learning to experience the various phenomena, which is the most fundamental form of learning in our view, means becoming capable of discerning certain entities or aspects and having the capability to be simultaneously and focally aware of these certain entities or aspects. To grasp this very sentence, for instance, boils down to discerning and being focally and simultaneously aware of its aspect of being an example of the foregoing principle *and* of its aspect of being a part of the characterization of the basic unit of description of phenomenography *and* of its aspect of being a part of an explanation triggered off by a question implicit in this book as a whole *and* of its aspect of being a part of the sixth chapter named "The Idea of Phenomenography" in the book *Learning and Awareness.*

## INDIVIDUAL AND COLLECTIVE LEVELS OF DESCRIPTION

A question that the reader might well have posed when reading phenomenographic studies, and which may have been more or less well answered in context, is; "At what level do the descriptions offered, the ways of experience, apply to the subjects of the respective studies? Do they apply to the individuals or to the group of individuals or to a wider population?" The answer lies in the fact that phenomenography focuses on variation. The objective of a study is to reveal the variation, captured in qualitatively distinct categories, of ways of experiencing the phenomenon in question, regardless of whether the differences are differences between individuals or within individuals. In other words, a description of a way of experiencing might apply in some sense across a group, or, there again, might apply to some aspect of an individual. To the extent that the group represents the variation of individuals in a wider population (or is a theoretical sample of that population), the categories of description can also be said to apply to that wider population.

The variation is, of course, distributed across the group, but to some extent even one single way of experiencing something is distributed. Its different appearances can often have complementary relationships with each other, like having fragments of the same whole spread around, the meaning of one bit derived from the meaning of and lending meaning to the rest. Similar variation might even hold across different cultures, as the results and arguments presented in chapter 3 about cross-cultural ways of experiencing learning show. There, the outcome spaces for two different cultures may hold a partly overlapping and partly complementary relationship to each other. Different fragments of the supracultural outcome space (in the case of the variation found in different cultures being described within a common framework) are found distributed among different cultures (Marton et al., in press). The variation within each culture can thus also be described in terms of this supracultural outcome space, the different parts of which come to the fore more clearly, are more emphasized and appear more frequently, in one culture than in another.

## CATEGORIES OF DESCRIPTION

The way in which a person experiences a phenomenon does not constitute the phenomenon itself. It rather constitutes one facet of the phenomenon, seen from that person's perspective, with that person's biography as background. In contrast, when the researcher describes the differing ways of experiencing a phenomenon, the researcher is describing the phenomenon, again, no more than partially, from the reports or inferences of the subjects, and it is this partial constitution of the phenomenon that is the researcher's description. The complex of categories of description capturing the different ways of experiencing the phenomenon is the outcome space. In earlier chapters we sometimes used the terms *categories of description* synonymously with *ways of experiencing,* constituting a complex called the outcome space. To be more precise, the outcome space is the complex of categories of description comprising distinct groupings of aspects of the phenomenon and the relationships between them.

The qualitatively different ways of experiencing a particular phenomenon, as a rule, form a hierarchy. The hierarchical structure can be defined in terms of increasing complexity, in which the different ways of experiencing the phenomenon in question can be defined as subsets of the component parts and relationships within more inclusive or complex ways of seeing the phenomenon. The different ways of experiencing the phenomenon can even be seen as different layers of individual experiences. People as a rule are not consciously aware of layers of experience of earlier date, but we can assume that they are present as tacit components of more advanced ways of experiencing a phenomenon.[8]

Inasmuch as a phenomenographic study always derives its descriptions from a smallish number of people chosen from a particular population, whether children starting school or computer engineering students, the system of categories presented can never be claimed to form an exhaustive system. But the goal is that they should be complete in the sense that nothing in the collective experience as manifested in the population under investigation is left unspoken. There are certain criteria for the quality of a set of descriptive categories, that can be seen as methodologically grounded or grounded in the anatomy of awareness as expounded earlier.

The first criterion that can be stated is that the individual categories should each stand in clear relation to the phenomenon of the investigation so that each category tells us something distinct about a particular way of experiencing the phenomenon. The second is that the categories have to stand in a logical relationship with one another, a relationship that is frequently hierarchical. Finally, the third criterion is that the system should be parsimonious, which is to say that as few categories should be explicated as is feasible and reasonable, for capturing the critical variation in the data.

Let us elaborate on these criteria. The first reminds us that a category of description is a complex of aspects of the way that the experience of the phenomenon in question has been expressed, and is thereby logically constrained to stand in clear relation to the phenomenon. From the methodological perspective, the criterion reminds us that phenomenography as presented in this book is essentially an educational research specialization, with an interest in learning, and generally learning of some specific content. In that we are generally looking for educationally

---

[8]Curiously enough, this implies that we can understand the anatomy of an individual's awareness by looking at others', less complex, awareness.

critical ways of experiencing things, as discussed at length in chapter 4, an obvious demand of the research effort is that the system of descriptive categories should tell us clear and distinct things about the experience or capability for experiencing those things.

The second criterion is grounded in the argument made earlier, that the categories of description denote a series of increasingly complex subsets of the totality of the diverse ways of experiencing various phenomena. Educationally, it is a reasonable assumption that there is a norm, a particular way of experiencing a phenomenon that is to be preferred over others, and that is what the educational effort is designed to foster. Some ways of experiencing it are more complex, more inclusive, or more specific than others, and they coincide to a greater or lesser extent with those considered to be critical for further educational development. Thus, we seek an identifiably hierarchical structure of increasing complexity, inclusivity, or specificity in the categories, according to which the quality of each one can be weighed against that of the others.

The third criterion of parsimony, apart from being a generally desirable property of research results, relates to the tension between the individual and the group levels, and to the very nature of awareness as we described it in the previous chapter. That the worlds we inhabit are recognizable and communicable at all means that the number of ways of experiencing any phenomenon in the world is limited. As we have said before, if we were subject to panaesthesia (capable of total experience of situations and phenomena) things would look the same for all time and for all of us.

On what principles do these criteria rest? Naturally, given the thrust of this book, they rest in the nature of experience and awareness. The idea of carrying out the thought experiment at the beginning of this chapter was to demonstrate that if people experience a certain situation in the same way, they will deal with it in the same way as well. Differences in how they deal with situations and phenomena imply differences in how they experience them. Moreover, it is certain that we do not all deal with situations and phenomena in the same way. In contrast, if the number of potential aspects, the essential aspects that define the phenomenon, had been infinite, each of us could have experienced every situation and every phenomenon differently, and also could have experienced a particular phenomenon differently each time. We would live in different worlds; we would not be able to communicate; there would be no permanence. Now, we do *not* live in different worlds, and we *are* able to communicate, and we *do* experience the sameness of the world in spite of changes. (In fact changes can only be experienced against the background of permanence.) We have variation and similarity in our way of viewing the world. For this to be the case the number of critical aspects that define the phenomenon must be limited because we learn to experience them by successive differentiations from each other. Oversimplifying things a bit, the different ways of experiencing a phenomenon reflect different combinations of the aspects that we are focally aware of at a particular point in time.

If, for instance, we look once more at the different ways in which children experience number, we find, as was indicated earlier, that different categories of description identified by Neuman, and summarized briefly as the first example in chapter 4, reflect the simultaneous awareness of different aspects of numbers such as ordinality, cardinality, and object–word, part–part, part–whole relationships. Experiencing numbers as abstract and structured entities, on the one hand means to be simultaneously aware of their ordinal aspect, of their cardinal aspect, of the whole, of the parts and of the singular units. On the other hand experiencing numbers as "names," for instance, means to be aware of numbers primarily in terms of part–whole relationships and their ordinal but not their cardinal aspect, while experiencing numbers as "extents" means to be aware of numbers in terms of part–whole relationships and their cardinal but not their ordinal aspect. In the case of "counted numbers" children are aware of both the cardinal and ordinal aspects, but disjointly rather than simultaneously.

One may raise the question, as Säljö (1994) recently did, "Why should the distinction be made between ways of experiencing (or conceptions as we generally used to refer to them) and categories of description?" Indeed, if we look at all the examples in the book and ask if we can find two things, one of which is "a way of experiencing something" and the other "a category of description," we are constrained to reply, "No, we cannot find two things; we can find only one that we refer to by two different names." Why then should we have two names for one thing?

Well, the reason is that what looks as though it is one thing is not so clearly one thing at all. This is indubitably a conclusion we must draw from what has been said in the previous pages. What might be thought of as one thing can appear very different when seen from different perspectives. This is very much what this book is all about. Therefore, when we present a set of different ways of experiencing something, when we refer to this set, and when we make use of it, we can have in mind *that which is described* (ways of experiencing) or *the way in which it is described* (categories of description). We cannot separate them, of course. There is no description without something described, nor can anything be described without a description. But we can "think apart" the two. Yet, why on earth should we do that?

The main reason for making the distinction is that when, in an investigation, we arrive at the conclusion that we have found in a group of learners a number of qualitatively different ways of experiencing a certain phenomenon, we let two kinds of statement collapse into one. One kind of statement pertains to the fact of the qualitatively different ways the particular learners have demonstrated they experience the phenomenon. The other kind of statement is about what we have found to be qualitatively different ways of experiencing the phenomenon in question. Now, even if this seems to be playing with words, it is not.

One way of considering conclusions of this kind is to bring into focus the question of the truthfulness of the ways of experiencing the phenomenon in question in relation to the particular individuals, by asking, "Have we *really* captured how they experience this phenomenon? Does the research method do them justice? Would they have done differently under other circumstances? Can the findings be generalized to other situations at the individual level, or to a population, or to other populations, at the group level?" Intriguing though these questions may seem, they are not necessarily our main questions. The point is that even if one

individual or another may have been misrepresented, even if some of the participants may not have functioned at their very best, even if what we have observed of
one individual or another in the particular situation is not totally typical of them,
and even if the distribution of the different ways of experiencing the phenomenon
in question may not easily be generalized to any population, we can still argue that
we have identified the variation in how the phenomenon in question might be
experienced by people with certain background characteristics. We claim only that
an individual has shown a capability for experiencing something in a certain way,
and we do not say that she is not capable of experiencing it in some other perhaps
more complete or advanced or efficient way. In other words, we may not have
identified the most typical or the most advanced way in which a person can
experience the phenomenon, and we may not have described a generalizable
distribution of the different ways of experiencing it, but we may still very well have
identified the variation in terms of which we can characterize the different ways
the phenomenon appears to the particular person in different situations or different
ways it appears to other similar groups.

In Example 7.7 in the next chapter, for instance, we refer to a study in which
Marton, Asplund-Carlsson, and Halász (1992) found four qualitatively different
ways in which a group of Hungarian and a group of Swedish secondary school
students understood a short story by Franz Kafka. In spite of the fact that there
was a striking difference between the two groups, the variation was identical.
In the same vein, Marton, Asplund-Carlsson, and Halász (1994) found that
while the distribution of ways in which the short story was understood by
Hungarian secondary school students before and after Hungary turned into a
pluralistic democracy in the early 1990s was strikingly different, the variation
in how the story was understood was identical. Therefore, even if the empirical
statements about individuals or groups may not be generalizable, the variation
itself might very well turn out to be so. The point we are trying to make is that
the very identification of the different ways of experiencing a phenomenon and
the variation thereby constituted are a legitimate and worthwhile outcome of a
research undertaking.

When we talk about "a way of experiencing something" we usually do so in
terms of individual awareness. We did so earlier when we discussed what a way of
experiencing something is. And we certainly do so in the two chapters to follow
when discussing the dynamics of learning in the light of the learner's and the
teacher's efforts. When we talk about "categories of description" we usually do so
in terms of qualitatively different ways a phenomenon may appear to people of one
kind or another. Thus, categories of description refer to the collective level. In
consequence, although the described (the ways of experiencing something) and the
description (the categories of description) are inextricably intertwined, the description is never the whole of what it describes, just as a way of experiencing is never
more than part of the phenomenon experienced. The relationship between the way
of experiencing and the category of description resembles, then, the relationship
between Lewis Carroll's grinning cat and the essential grin that is left hanging in
the tree when the cat slowly fades from sight.

## METHODS OF PHENOMENOGRAPHIC
## RESEARCH—CONSTITUTING THE OBJECT
## OF RESEARCH

In a very important sense, the methods of phenomenographic data collection and data analysis are inseparable. For one thing, during the collection of data, whether through interviews or in some other form, analysis is taking place, and early phases of analysis can influence later data collection. But the dialectic relationship is even stronger than that in terms of constituting the object of research. The researcher from the outset delimits the phenomenon that is central to her interest, be it learning as such, or the nature of matter, or whatever. The researcher has a responsibility to contemplate the phenomenon, to discern its structure against the backgrounds of the situations in which it might be experienced, to distinguish its salient features, to look at it with others' eyes, and still be open to further developments. There are various ways of going about this. One way is by considering the phenomenon's treatment in other research traditions: how it appears in literature, in treatises and in textbooks or how it has been handled in the past and in different cultures. If the researcher is to be able to meet the people she is interested in and take part in a discourse that attempts to reach their unreflected experience, then she might herself be aware of many possible starting points they will have, the sorts of situations in which they have met the phenomenon before, and the range of ways in which they might handle it.

### Collecting Data

The studies we have been dealing with in this book have to do specifically with learning, and by now we have elaborated a conceptual framework for learning in terms of the structure of experience and awareness. When we describe the methods of phenomenographic research, we employ the same framework, because we also see research as a learning experience: The researcher is finding something out, and to one extent or another (elaborated on later) the research subjects are also learning. Remember then that in discussing the phenomenographic research effort we are considering a learner (the researcher) learning about a certain phenomenon (how others experience the phenomenon of interest) in a situation (the research situation) that is of her own molding. That molding or structuring, as in other cases of learning, has an effect on the outcome of the learning, both of the researcher (what she is able to bring out of the research effort) and of the people being studied (what they are able to reflect on in the research situation).

In collecting data the researcher wishes to bring to light the ways in which the people being studied experience the phenomenon of interest. This is the phenomenon that the researcher will be learning about in different ways throughout the study. Let us first discuss a single aspect of one sort of data collection, and work outward from that to look at data collection more generally. The kind of data collection is the interview and the particular aspect is that of the interviewee reflecting over his experience in a state of "meta-awareness," being aware of his awareness of something. In chapter 2 we described studies in which the interviewees were asked first to undertake a task (reading a text or solving a problem) and report on it, and then to describe how they had gone about the task. In the first part the researcher had formed a situation, the output of which was of the interviewee's making (a description or a solution), and in the second part the output was a probing of the interviewee's own awareness of producing it. Now it is the second part we wish to discuss first, wherein the researcher or interviewer works together with the interviewee to bring forth his awareness of undertaking the task, a state of meta-awareness, something akin to the newly found insight into her own condition that Helen Keller vividly described, and which we quote in chapter 3. Whereas in the first part, the phenomenon that the interviewee is being asked to handle is already brought to awareness by the interviewer in an open and concrete form, in the second part the interviewee herself has to discern the phenomenon and distinguish it from the situation as whole. The difference might be likened to the difference between experiencing a deer on a sunlit lawn and our earlier deer in the forest at dusk. In the first part the phenomenon is anchored in the interview situation, whereas in the second part it transcends the situation.

Sometimes such reflection occurs spontaneously, and sometimes the interviewer and the interviewee have to persist to reach the required state. But in this sort, or part, of an interview it is important that the researcher is mindful of working toward an articulation of the interviewee's reflections on experience that is as complete as possible. The interviewer is looking forward to the resulting protocol and its viability as data with respect to completeness (Theman, 1983). The interview is now taking place on two levels. On one level there is the situation of interpersonal contact in which the interview resembles a social discourse, in structure if not in content. On the second level, a metalevel, the interview is more like a therapeutic discourse inasmuch as the interviewer is trying to free the interviewee of hitherto unsuspected reflections. Whereas the first level carries with it a relationship that is recognizable in everyday life, the second level is more problematic, and indeed is accompanied by some of the difficulties of a therapeutic situation in which resistance is the most obvious. The second level might be approached through alternative questions, bringing the interviewee repeatedly back to the focus for reflection, or it might be approached through offering interpretations of different things the interviewee has said earlier in the interview. Rejection of such interpretations can occur, when the interviewee sets up a defence structure of denial, reinterpretation, and resistance to further discussion. Such events must be handled carefully, for, as Theman (1983) pointed out, making the interviewee aware of his own thoughts and breaking down or bypassing his defences can be painful, though necessary: "If it is done in the right way, if the interpretation is closely related to explicit or implied statements, then the pain is accepted, even if not at once" (p. 104). In taking the discussion of psychotherapeutic aspects of the interview further, Theman draws lessons from the handling of transference through self-awareness and positioning in the interview situation:

> A conscious subjective control of the relation between the two parties demands a certain self-reflection, good enough to enable [the interviewer] to be conscious of their own questions and interjections as the basis for [the interviewee's] answers and reactions.... Another important factor is to remain aloof, maintaining a certain consciously calculated distance from [the interviewee] while aiming at the same time to get as close as possible. (p. 104, our translation)

Now, the consideration of psychotherapeutic aspects of a phenomenographic interview is very relevant at one extreme of a spectrum of data collection, such as Theman's (1983) study of how the citizens of a city experience political power with reference to a particular political decision. This demanded that interviews be conducted to a large extent at the second level, using the political decision and its field as a concrete reference point (the first level) to reach a deeper consideration of power. At the other extreme lies Lindahl's study, already referred to in chapter 3, in which none of this appears, for the simple reason that the subjects are 1-year-olds who cannot yet speak, let alone reflect over their awareness or actions (Lindahl, 1996). Her films of toddlers during their early months at a day nursery do not allow the researcher to mold the data collection situation at all. Once the researcher and her camera are familiar, it becomes the natural situation.

One dimension in the spectrum of kinds of interview is the degree of reflection demanded of the interviewees, from wholehearted in the adults of Theman's study to nonexistent in Lindahl's toddlers. Another dimension is that of power balance between interviewer and interviewee. As Theman implied earlier, the question of balance in terms of overcoming defenses and the issue of distance versus closeness is ever present in the more reflective parts of an interview, in which the interviewer could easily destroy the relationship by pressing too hard or not hard enough, or by getting too close or not close enough. In contrast, the interviewee always has the power to refuse, to deny the interviewer access to thoughts and reflections, or even to mislead. The interviewer has power of an external kind, being deliberate and calculated, whereas the interviewee has a power that can act from within, being spontaneous and reactive. If the interviewer–interviewee relationship were to break down, then the loss would be to the research effort; avoidance lies in the interviewer's sensitivity to the potential of the relationship and the interviewer's ability to prepare and maintain it.

In phenomenographic studies in general, the researcher forms the interview according to the research question. In the studies related in chapter 2, as already indicated, the interviews had two principal parts, one with a situated theme (What did the author mean? What is meant by X?) and one with a theme that demanded reflection (How did you go about reading? How did it feel?). In the studies of chapter 3, the interviews were of a less structured kind, in which the interviewees were asked to reflect over what learning meant for them, often starting from no more than a direct question. In chapter 4, where studies are described of how pupils and students experience the concepts they meet in educational situations, the two aspects are found in different proportions, with greater reliance on more concrete interviews around specific problems in younger children (with attempts to bring them to reflection) and greater demand for reflection in adults (starting from problems or concrete situations). This draws out differences in the chapters that are central in describing empirical phenomenographic research studies in terms of what characterizes the interviews in which data were collected and reflects the more fundamental difference already taken up in the introduction to chapter 5, concerning whether the primary focus is on experience of the phenomenon or of the situation.

We started this section on phenomenographic data collection by considering one particularly important aspect of an interview, the most common form of data collection, namely the relationship between interviewer and interviewee in bringing the interview to a state of meta-awareness. There are other forms of data collection in which this is less of an issue. The aforementioned study of toddlers is one such, in which long sessions of video filming took place in day nurseries. Other studies have collected written data, such as one in which subjects of varied ages and backgrounds were asked to write on the theme, "When I understood …," later to be complemented by interviews with some of them (Helmstad & Marton, 1992). In principle, there is no impediment to using published documents as data, or even artifacts of other kinds that in some way serve as an expression of the ways in which people experience some part of their worlds.

## Data Analysis

From the outset, then, the researcher has a clear picture of the object of research, which becomes clearer as the situations in which data are to be collected are planned and refined. As the data are collected, a preliminary more or less focused analysis takes place, as a result of which the researcher's picture inevitably gains details, and finds new structure while new perspectives reveal distant unsuspected figures. As the analysis progresses this picture gains depth as particular facets are brought one by one to the fore. These are all phases in the constitution of the object of research. Although the boundaries are laid at the start, the processes of collecting and analyzing data cast light on the boundaries, shift them, fill them in, and turn the whole thing around.

The researcher's question has a phenomenon in focus and is interested in certain aspects of it, maybe with other aspects in the background, or maybe with no interest at all in other aspects. In collecting data, then, an attempt has been made to vary the focus of the subjects' awareness and reflection or meta-awareness around the aspects of interest while taking the rest more or less for granted. For example, in asking students how they understood a particular aspect of a text they have just read, the meaning of the other parts of the text was ignored, and the way they read it was left untouched. When they were being asked about their ways of reading the text, then its meaning was no longer in focus. It was temporarily frozen. Hasselgren (1981) studying the development of student teachers' understanding of children's play, gave them three films to watch on three different occasions. The design of the study, in which different students got different films on different occasions, a Latin square design, effectively prevented the revelation of the aspect of the meaning of what they saw. Because the meaning was varying qualitatively across all the material that he pooled, the analysis was effectively focused on the dimension of variation remaining, namely the structure of what happened in the films. He identified four different "ways of apprehending children at play": *fragmentary* in which a number of isolated sequences were taken up; *partialistic* in which focus was on one part of the film, ignoring the rest; *chronological* in which the sequence of events was retold; and *abstracting* in which the events of the film were described around some abstract idea that was illustrated. The results of the study were thus constrained to revealing the variation in the structural aspect of the students' apprehension of children at play.

Now in the analysis of the data a similar process takes place. Remember that the researcher is a learner, seeking the meaning and structure of her phenomenon (how people experience the phenomenon of the research question). The boundaries of the object of research as it has been and is still being constituted form a divide between, the internal structure that is of primary interest, on the one hand, the ground provisionally taken for granted on the other. The main task, then, for our researcher/learner is to discern the internal structure and the intertwined meaning of the object of research.

All of the material that has been collected forms a pool of meaning. It contains all that the researcher can hope to find, and the researcher's task is simply to find it. This is achieved by applying the principle of focusing on one aspect of the object and seeking its dimension of variation while holding other aspects frozen. The pool contains two sorts of material: that pertaining to individuals and that pertaining to the collective. It is the same stuff, of course, but it can be viewed from two different perspectives to provide different contexts for isolated statements and expressions relevant to aspects of the object of research. The researcher has to establish a perspective with boundaries within which she is maximally open to variation, boundaries derived from her most generous understanding of what might turn out to be relevant to depicting differences in the structure of the pool. The analysis starts by searching for extracts from the data that might be pertinent to the perspective, and inspecting them against the two contexts: now in the context of other extracts drawn from all interviews that touch upon the same and related themes; now in the context of the individual interview.

One particular aspect of the phenomenon can be selected and inspected across all of the subjects, and then another aspect, that to be followed, maybe, by the study of whole interviews to see where these two aspects lie in the pool relative to the other aspects and the background. In a study that involves a number of problems for solution, for instance, the analysis might start by considering just one of the problems as tackled and discussed by all the subjects, and then a selection of whole transcripts that include particularly interesting ways of handling the problem. This process repeated will lead to vaguely spied structure through and across the data that our researcher/learner can develop, sharpen, and return to again and again from first one perspective and then another until there is clarity

As a result of this analysis we identify a number of qualitatively different ways in which one and the same situation or phenomenon has been *experienced* but we also find variation in the different ways in which each of the ways of experiencing are *expressed*. The latter variation is essential if we are to be able to abstract the way of experiencing from the ways of expressing the experience because a number of identically worded statements amount to one single statement, and such indeterminacy would make the discernment of structure and meaning nigh impossible. This points to the general principle: In order that a phenomenon can be discerned from a particular appearance there must be observable variation.

When we work with transcripts (or equivalent data) we experience that there is a sort of play in them: As we read them again and again they keep changing in appearance. The reason is, of course (in line with our own arguments on the nature of awareness), that we cannot be simultaneously aware of everything with the same degree of acuity all the time. The foreground changes repeatedly, and with each shift other things that are present shift to become functions of the current items of figural awareness. The data shimmers in the intense light of our analysis.

In accordance with what we said earlier about not only categories of description but even their fragments being distributed across individuals, the data at the collective level are particularly robust compared with the data relating to individuals. Even if it is difficult or impossible to draw from the data, or even from the phenomenographic enterprise, the ways in which individual subjects experience a phenomenon, the ways in which idealized individuals do so can be abstracted owing to the overlap of the material seen at the collective level. This relates also to the usual practice of selecting a theoretical sample of subjects to cover the group according to a predetermined plan in order to maximize the variation in critical respects (Glaser & Strauss, 1967). Thus, the categories of description derived from the data have a strength that they could not have if individuals were studied. This is an additional reason for distinguishing between "ways of experiencing" and "categories of description," an issue discussed at some length earlier in the chapter.

Another principle now demanded of the researcher is the adoption of the second-order stance described earlier in this chapter. Here we can refer to the hermeneutic principle expounded by Smedslund (1970), that understanding and logic are circularly related. When communicating with another person who expresses something contrary to our view, we can either assume that their understanding of the subject is as ours but their logic is not our logic, or vice versa, that they share our logic but they understand the thing differently. He exhorts us to assume that what people say is logical, given their particular way of seeing the world.

Take the case of Jenny who claimed consistently that she had 5 fingers on one hand and 10 fingers on the other hand in one of Neuman's (1994) studies. It would be very easy to smile at her and dismiss her as untaught (first-order perspective). That expression, however, has the potential to give an enormous insight into children's experience of number when we take the child's place and ponder on what might lead her to say such a thing (second-order perspective).

When that child's apparently illogical, or even wrong, statement is juxtaposed with other similarly misinformed statements involving number, alternative interpretations start to be clarified. In the case of Jenny, she could count the fingers on one hand, and they were called "1," "2," "3," "4," and "5"—she has "5" fingers on that hand. Continuing to the second hand, they were called "6," "7," "8," "9," and "10"—she has "10" fingers on that hand. Jenny understands that the last number she utters refers to these fingers all taken together. In a similar manner, when she was asked how many marbles were in each of the two boxes, as described in chapter 4, she replied "4" and "9," or "2" and "9," or "3" and "9." Now a picture suddenly emerges, that her logic is our logic. She is interpreting the tasks in a consistent way, but her understanding of number is radically different from ours. Jenny sees number as arrayed on a counting line of some sort, on which the position is the name and the name is the number itself. When other children are found to respond similarly, the idea of a category of ways of experiencing "numbers as names" evolves, and when placed alongside other ways of experiencing number, the critical aspects of cardinality and ordinality, parts and wholes, develop to become a conceptual framework for ways of experiencing numbers in a wider sense, all from assuming that the child shares our logic though not our understanding of the phenomenon in question. Having seen that the child's understanding differs from ours, we see that the way forward is to try to reveal their understanding and work toward a shared understanding, as we return to discuss in chapter 8.

Now we have, in the late stages of analysis, our researcher/learner with a sharply structured object of research, with clearly related facets, rich in meaning. She is able to bring into focus now one aspect, now another; she is able to see how they fit together like pieces of a multidimensional jigsaw puzzle; she is able to turn it around and see it against the background of the different situations that it now transcends. All that is left to do is to communicate it to others.

## THE PATH OF PHENOMENOGRAPHY

Phenomenography has been characterized in the beginning of this chapter as a research approach with a strong educational interest. It does indeed originate from an educational interest and it does aspire to serve it as well. Phenomenography offers a way of describing intended or actual outcomes of learning. It aims at depicting competence in the Chomskian sense of the word (Chomsky, 1957). The competence in question is competence to experience various phenomena in certain ways, a competence that reflects changing person–world relations and that evolves as a function of experience. It is thus born out of learning.

It makes sense, of course, that the question of the most fundamental form of learning and questions of hierarchies of capabilities should be dealt with in an educational context. But we should remember that the link is not one of logical inevitability. The issue should be seen more as one of the driving force and of the field of application. Phenomenography should be seen as a kind of basic research with a certain context of origin and with a potential usefulness of a certain kind. Above all it should be defined in terms of its object of research.

The subject of our research, as we have kept emphasizing throughout this book, is the qualitatively different ways in which people are capable of experiencing various phenomena. A way of experiencing something springs from a combination of aspects of the phenomenon being both discerned and presented in focal awareness simultaneously. An aspect is (as opposed to being absent or taken for granted) a dimension of variation. Experiencing something is discerning aspects of it and being focally and simultaneously aware of them. Differences in how something is experienced mean that some aspects are focused on and others or not, or that they are seen in a succession rather than simultaneously. The structure of the variation in how a particular phenomenon is experienced can be seen as inherent in the phenomenon as it is constituted in terms of its various aspects.

Phenomenography aims to reveal the qualitatively different ways of experiencing various phenomena. There are two potential questions to figure out: first, which these ways are, and second, whether or not they appear in a certain case at a certain point in time. The question of phenomenography is the first one. It is about identifying the very ways in which something may be experienced. This is the researcher's way of experiencing how other people's ways of experiencing something vary. It is experience, or rather the nature of experience as seen from a particular perspective. We capture it in a category of description; it is a characterization discerned from that which is characterized. The validity claim is made in relation to the data available. Thus we argue the category of description is a reasonable characterization of a possible way of experiencing something given the data at hand. Whether or not a certain person is really capable of experiencing the phenomenon in question in this particular way, or under what conditions she is capable of doing so, is a question that falls outside phenomenography proper. (Although it is highly reasonable to deal with such questions in conjunction with a phenomenographic study.)

Categories of description depicting the different ways in which a certain phenomenon is experienced and the logical relationships between them constitute the outcome space of that phenomenon. Furthermore, there are logical relationships between different phenomena as they are experienced. We could envisage a complex of categories of description depicting the differing ways in which various phenomena are experienced, which has previously called the collective mind (Marton, 1978) and, earlier in this book, was called the collective anatomy of awareness.

To reveal this collective anatomy of awareness is the path of phenomenography. As we indicated earlier, the rather sparse conceptual and methodological apparatus presented in this book points away from itself. It points to this domain of knowledge, parts of which have been explored by others, but which has not been identified as a field of its own.

# 7

## Learning to Experience

### SOLVING MENO'S PARADOX

We began this book by drawing your attention to a specter that has haunted humankind for more than 2 millennia—Meno's paradox according to which we cannot gain knowledge by searching for it in the world. There are two mutually exclusive possibilities for the relation between the seeker and the knowledge sought: Either the seeker has it, in which case it does not need to be sought, or the seeker does not have it, in which case it cannot be found because it would not be recognized even if it were stumbled upon. The fact remains that we *do* gain knowledge, and therein lies the paradox. Plato's solution was that although we cannot gain knowledge from without, from the raw world, we can gain knowledge from within, from our immortal souls in which all knowledge was deposited many lives ago. But, as we pointed out in chapter 1, it can be shown that in searching inside ourselves for something we do not know, we run into the same logical dilemma as the one we run into when searching outside ourselves for something we do not know. The dilemma prevails. Plato let the genie out of the lamp but failed to get it back.

People may not know the paradox by name but it sometimes can still underpin their way of arguing. For example, some university teachers argue that their students are not able to find knowledge if they do not already have it, but that they simply have to accept the authority of those who know. They imply that students, although they may not be able to search and find, can be told. But this is also plainly wrong. On the contrary, in order to learn about the world from that which one is told by authority, one does have to search for the knowledge that lends meaning. We can only conclude that Plato must have made some assumption when he formulated his paradox that he would have been better off without.

In this book we are promulgating a view that is an alternative to Plato's, as we already indicated in chapter 1. His problem originates from the fundamental Platonian division of reality into an "inner" and an "outer." The "I," "the knower," is conceptually locked into the inner space, into herself, whereas "the knowledge," "the known," is, in the original formulation that Plato refuted, allocated to "the outer." But once the knower and the known, the subject and the object are rent asunder they cannot be reunited.

The solution to Meno's paradox, already to be found in embryo in chapter 1, can now be presented. It lies in not making the distinction between inner and outer in the first place, not seeing the knower and the known, the subject and the object, as separate. What then is meant by "not seeing the knower and the known, the subject and the object," or, we could add, the person and the world, "as separate" ? Quite obviously, we could not imagine the person without her world. Could we imagine her world without her? By definition, that is impossible. *Her* world is hers; it is seen, experienced, by *her;* quite clearly it cannot exist without *her.* But is her world the real world, the world about which she wants to gain knowledge? Obviously the world cannot be identical with the world experienced by a particular person, but the world experienced by a person and the world in general, are not separate. The former is a part of the latter.

Once again, let us think of the world in terms of all the conceivable ways in which it might ever be experienced, known, sensed, imagined, now, in the past, in the future. There is no end to the world thus conceptualized. But beyond it, there is no world at all, not for humans at least. In the course of our lifetime we enter the world and make more and more of it our own. At the same time we contribute to the world. Given that the world is an experienced world and given that our own experienced world is a part of it, the world would not be the same world without any single one of us.

The human–world relation is established at birth, and maybe even before that. From what we can imagine as an initial chaos of sensory impressions the child starts to differentiate and discern certain entities, in all likelihood, starting with mother. As Heinz Werner (1948) described it, development can be seen as continuous differentiation and integration of the experienced world. The former is brought about by separation, the latter by simultaneity. Categories of description corresponding to qualitatively different ways of experiencing phenomena can, as a rule, be ordered in terms of how many simultaneous aspects are objects of focal awareness (as we expounded in chapter 6). More simultaneous aspects define phenomena more narrowly than do fewer simultaneous aspects. The path of development is the opposite to the general ordering principle of outcome spaces from top to bottom, seeming to suggest that learning proceeds from a vague undifferentiated whole to a differentiated and integrated structure of ordered parts.[1]

Whatever we learn or gain knowledge about, our learning takes place as a part of our ongoing exploration of the world, our constituting the world. This means that when we are learning about something specific, we are also aware of the world around us. That which we learn about has to become a part of the world we know.

---

[1]This is in line with the early study mentioned at the start of chapter 2, in which Marton's experimental study of learning indicated that the more that this principle applies in the individual case, the more successful is the learning that occurs (Marton, 1970).

The experience is, moreover, generally a mediated experience: We do not face the phenomenon as such, but the phenomenon as described by others. To an increasing degree we see the world in terms of patterns of a shared culture through a shared language. Our own world becomes increasingly the world of others as well, and the latter world, the world as already experienced, is a constitutive force in learning just as the individual's constitutive acts are. This is an important difference compared with individual constructivism, which sees knowledge as being an individual construction—*within* the individual. We also find a difference if we make a comparison with social constructivism, which sees the social, the cultural, the situational *outside* the individual as the fabric of knowledge. The proposed mechanism of internalization which is supposed to bridge the gap between the inner and the outer cannot give a satisfying account of the individual experience because of its dualism, as discussed earlier.

According to the view we are presenting, learning takes place, knowledge is born, by a change in something in the world as experienced by a person. The new way of experiencing something is constituted in the person–world relationships and involves both. In this way Meno's paradox disappears. We simply do not ask the question: "How do we gain knowledge *from* the world?" Nor do we ask the question: "How do we gain knowledge from the depth of our immortal soul?" Person and world, inner and outer are not separated. We do not have to account for how knowledge travels from one to the other. Instead of trying to account for how the person–world relationship is established, we posit this relationship and study how it changes as time passes.

## THE PATH OF LEARNING

Such changes may be of a more or less fundamental nature. The categories of description corresponding to the qualitatively different ways of experiencing various phenomena, as we elaborated in the previous two chapters, are assumed to capture critical aspects of our way of experiencing the world: differences in the experienced structure and meaning of the phenomenon in question. Changes in this respect are fundamental changes and what we are focusing on is learning in the sense of changes of this kind. But, of course, most learning is not of this kind. Most learning is about developing more detailed knowledge of phenomena that we experience in certain ways, and technically more advanced mastery of skills that we experience in certain ways.

In a way, the view of learning we are advancing is counterintuitive. Is learning not the learning of something *new*? Why are we talking about *changes* in the person–world relationship, which implies preexistent knowledge? Our point is that you can only learn something new about *something,* and by learning *something new* about something, that *something* will change, more or less, which implies that the whole must precede the parts. Moreover, the whole is, according to this line of reasoning, a part of wholes established earlier. One cannot learn mere details without having an idea of what they are details of. Learning is mostly a matter of reconstituting the already constituted world.

It is in this sense that genuine learning always relates to the learner's reality, the world as already experienced. When the whole is missing, learning is very likely to fail. We find an example of such an interpretation of a failure to learn in Sylvia Ashton-Warner's moving book *Teacher* (Ashton-Warner, 1963). She was a teacher of Maori children in New Zealand in the early 1950s and failed to teach them to read and write. But she could not accept that normal, seemingly healthy human beings were incapable of becoming literate. Eventually, she realized that the problem stemmed from the fact that these children did not understand the idea of reading and writing. They grew up in an environment in which the written world was of little importance. They were simply missing the point. This insight turned out to be the key to literacy for these children.

Dahlgren and Olsson (1985) carried out an interview study with nonliterate Swedish preschool children (6 years old) about their understanding of why one might need to learn to read and write, and about how they envisaged reading. A minority of the children turned out to have no idea of the point of reading and writing. When the group was followed up 2 years later after 1 year in school, some of them showed a serious lack of progress in learning to read and write. To a large extent, they were the same children who in preschool 2 years earlier had not understood the point of reading and writing.

On the whole, to return to our previous line of reasoning, we can see in many studies that learners instinctively orient themselves to the more general aspects of situation before focusing on the learning task in a more narrow sense. Kullberg (1991) followed eight children from starting school at the age of 7 years old and through their first 3 years in school, with a special focus on their transition from preliteracy to literacy. She found that before children embark upon learning to read, they direct their attention to the school environment in a general sense, getting adjusted to it. An "initial collision" a few weeks after the start of school marks a shift of interest away from general aspects of school toward the content of school work. In quite a different age range and quite a different time scale, Colaizzi (1973) found that the adult subjects participating in a learning experiment also focused initially on the context rather than on the content of learning.

There are certain aspects of school work that transcend specific knowledge and specific skills, aspects, which, in spite of their tacit nature, are readily picked up by children. Lundgren (1977), for instance, spoke of metalearning, in which students learn something about themselves, such as forming an understanding of whether they are good at solving maths problems or not. The argument has been made several times, that the most important learning that takes place in educational establishments is learning about the fundamentally layered structure of society as it is reflected in the hidden curriculum of the school, and finding out to which group one belongs (Broady, 1981; Gustafsson, Stigebrant, & Ljungvall, 1981).

Investigations into learning in higher education have proven to be fruitful for detecting learning outcomes on this more general level. Dahlgren (1989), for example, showed that an important effect of studies in business administration is that the students become socialized in their field by adopting general patterns of thinking that are common in the culture they are entering. It was manifested in this particular instance of business administration by an initial emphasis on the uneven distribution of economic resources, either from an international or from a national perspective, which was, after 4 years of study, replaced in many cases by a stress on the more efficient utilization of resources or the necessity for more incentives for individual or collective initiatives. Dahlgren showed that at the same time, studying economics at the university level may have a very limited effect in changing students' ways of experiencing economic reality in more specific respects. In particular, former economics students make very little use of the potentially powerful and efficient conceptual tools they encountered during their studies, such as pricing, opportunity cost, and so on. He argues that it is fairly easy to demonstrate that students in higher education pick up the terminology of the field; they develop a way of talking; they pick up facts and information, but it might not last very long (Dahlgren, 1985). It is actually very hard to demonstrate the effects of higher education when it comes to students making use of conceptual and theoretical tools they have encountered in their studies to develop more effective ways of seeing the world and to think about it from the perspective of their studies. Dahlgren's economics students demonstrate this, as does the example concerning Newtonian mechanics that we will take up later in this chapter.

At the global level of values and patterns of thinking, however, the effects of higher education might be very obvious. One example of this is illustrated by Perry's (1970) study of Harvard undergraduates. During their years of studies they appear to change their view of knowledge from an absolutistic one ("knowledge is a collection of right answers") to a relativistic one ("knowledge is simply different ways of seeing reality") and then to the stage of commitment ("although there *are* different ways of seeing reality, I have to take the responsibility for committing myself to a personal view, with an awareness of possible alternative views").

More recently, Perry's result has been extended by Baxter Magolda (1992) in a study of male and female students in a nonelite midwest university. Her findings agree in the main with Perry's, on the development from absolute, to relativist, to personal responsibility in the values attached to knowledge and learning, but project yet a further stage, that of contextual commitment in which certain aspects of knowledge are seen to be relevant in one situation, whereas there might be other aspects justified by another context. Furthermore, differences between male and female stances within each stage of the development have been identified (Perry's students were all male), women tending to relate their knowledge and learning outward toward their peers and teachers, while males tend to look inward with greater emphasis on self.

These studies lend support to the thesis that learners have a primary focus on more global aspects of learning than on the content intended by the instructional setting. We may then ask the question: "What are these global aspects of learning?" Alluding to our discussion in chapter 5, of different constituent thematic fields that surround the theme of awareness, the very situation the learner is a part of provides the immediate context for learning. The sorts of tasks being presented; the nature of the stuff being learned; the expectations of students, peers, and teachers; forms of assessment and future pathways—all these are aspects of this layer of global concern. At a slightly greater distance, in the educational setting the social practice of schooling is often experienced by the learner as the whole within which the specific learning task is only the immediate part. Then again, at least in vocational higher education, the culture that is being inculcated, with its common practices, shared values and ways of thinking, point the way to the learner's whole future world of work. While the phenomena the learning task relates to might make up the theme of awareness, the thematic field that surrounds it is made up of aspects of a wider, more global world, with roots in the current culture and branches that reach out to the learner's future world.

## LEARNING TO EXPERIENCE

As we reminded the reader at the beginning of the previous section, we are focusing on learning that can be described as a change between qualitatively different ways of experiencing something, that is, gaining knowledge about the world. What we have in mind is, of course, the kind of differences that we intend to capture by the categories of description characterized and illustrated in previous chapters, different categories representing more or less complete ways of experiencing the whole, and some coming closer than others to an education-ally critical norm.

The learning in question means that the learner has developed a capability to experience a certain phenomenon when it appears in novel situations in a particular way (which goes beyond the other ways in which she has been capable of experiencing the phenomenon), which in turn means that the relationship between the learner and the phenomenon has changed. The learner has become capable of discerning aspects of the phenomenon other than those she had been capable of discerning before, and she had become capable of being simultaneously and focally aware of other aspects or more aspects of the phenomenon than was previously the case. This is the kind of learning that has earlier been referred to "as a change in the eyes through which we see the world" (Marton, Dahlgren, Svensson, & Säljö, 1977, p. 23, our translation). When this occurs, the learner's awareness of the phenomenon has changed, and it appears different from before. To express the same thing in yet another way, the relationship between the person and the phenomenon has changed.

This does not imply that the person who has undergone such a change will experience the phenomenon in question in exactly the same new way each time it appears. We never experience a phenomenon as such. We experience situations of which a particular phenomenon may be part, transcending it, but still experienced against just that background. The point is that as a fruit of learning the person will be able to experience the phenomenon in a more advanced or more complex way when this way of experiencing the phenomenon is called up by the *relevance structure* of the situation.

## THE RELEVANCE STRUCTURE
## OF THE LEARNING SITUATION

Each situation, whether we consider it a learning situation or a situation in which one is applying something learned, has a certain *relevance structure*: the person's experience of what the situation calls for, what it demands. It is a sense of aim, of direction, in relation to which different aspects of the situation appear more or less relevant. It is the way the learner experiences the situation as a whole, as discussed earlier, that renders the perspective on its component parts.

Several examples of the importance of general aspects of skills and knowledge are in fact examples of the importance of the relevance structure of the learning situations as well. One example that clarifies the idea of the relevance structure of a situation is to be found in Székely's (1950) study from 50 years ago of school students learning some concepts of physics.

The experiment that Székely conducted comprised two phases, that we can call the acquisition and application phases. In the acquisition phase there was variation in the conditions for experimental and control groups of subjects, whereas in the application phases the conditions were the same. The idea was that any difference seen in the application phase could be ascribed to the conditions in the acquisition phase.

This is what happened. The subjects in the experimental group were introduced to a problem at the start of the session, which was administered individually. A torsion pendulum (see Fig. 7.1) was placed before the participant, wound up, and then allowed to unwind, rotating with the two weights hanging on the inner hooks. Then, winding up the pendulum again, the experimenter asked the participant what would happen if the weights were moved to the outer hooks. Some participants thought that moving the weights would make no difference, whereas others believed that the pendulum would unwind more quickly. The experimenter went on to demonstrate that in fact it unwound more slowly. (This was because the moment of inertia was greater, although the experimenter did not say so to the participants.)

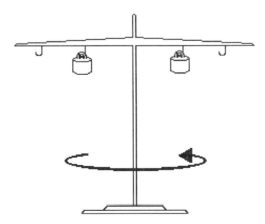

FIG. 7.1. A torsion pendulum, as used in Székely's study, weights suspended from the inner hooks.

To quell their curiosity as to why the result was so, the experimenter gave the participants four pages of explanation in terms of basic mechanics, introducing and explaining concepts such as work, angular momentum, and moment of inertia. The control group, in contrast, were given the explanatory text in advance, asked to read it and try to understand it in preparation for an examination. The same procedure with the demonstration of the torsion pendulum was then followed, but this time as an illustration of the concepts the participants had read about.

The significant difference between the experimental and control groups was the order in which they read and considered the demonstration. The control group read the text in preparation for a test, and in this respect they were in a normal educational situation being told to read in order to learn. They thus read the text with no perspective other than the expectation of being asked to handle what they were reading about. The experimental group, on the other hand, were endowed with a perspective. The puzzling demonstration raised certain questions to which they could find answers in the text. They read it in a certain way—some things were more relevant than others—and thus the task acquired a relevance structure. To use the terms introduced in this section, the control group and the experimental group experienced the task with different relevance structures, and succeeded accordingly.

A few days later, the participants were contacted again without prior notice, and they were invited to take part in another exercise. This time, the conditions were the same for all of them, in which they were asked to solve a problem. First, they were presented with two balls of equal size and mass, although they were told that one was made of a heavy metal and the other of a light metal. Then they were asked to distinguish between them. Most of them realized without difficulty that the one of heavy metal was hollow, whereas the other was solid, and the rest were told so. The solutions that were arrived at involved comparing the balls' rotation in some way, rolling them both either along a horizontal surface or down an inclined plane, in which case the solid ball of lighter metal would roll further because its moment of inertia was less.

The differences in the relevance structures of the situation in the acquisition phase had a profound effect on the way in which the knowledge there acquired was applied in the later phase. Table 7.1 shows the extent of success.

Curiously enough, most of the successful students were unclear as to how they came upon the solution to the problem. They felt a high degree of certainty, but could not say why, so the experiment might be said to have produced an intuitive understanding in some of the participants.

**TABLE 7.1**
The Success Reached by the Experimental and the Control Groups in Székely's Study

|                    | Solved the Task | Failed to Solve the Task |
|--------------------|-----------------|--------------------------|
| Experimental group | 13              | 7                        |
| Control group      | 4               | 16                       |
| Total              | 17              | 23                       |

## VARIATION IN LEARNING

If the relevance structure of the learning situation is the driving force of learning, its chief mechanism is variation. As the title of this chapter suggests, the kind of learning we are dealing with here is one through which the learner becomes capable of experiencing something in a different way from before. This means, as was argued earlier, becoming capable of discerning and separating aspects of a phenomenon the learner has not been able to discern and separate previously, and of being simultaneously and focally aware of aspects she not been able to be simultaneously and focally aware of previously. A change in one's capability of experiencing a phenomenon can only come through a change in one's way of experiencing that phenomenon, so what does it take to change a way of experiencing something? We have just made the point that learning such a change has to be driven by the relevance structure of the situation. It is necessary that something varies, some aspect of the situation that surrounds the person, for change to be experienced, in the least case something changing from one state to another. This change may happen to the learner or be brought about by her. It is through variation that aspects are differentiated within the experience of a phenomenon.

### Example 7.1: Induced Change—Székely's Experiment Reconsidered

In Székely's experiment we can discern the following changes for members of the experimental group:

1.  The weights were moved to extreme ends of the bar.
2.  The question about the angular velocity of the torsion pendulum was raised.
3.  The context of the torsion pendulum shifted to the context of general principles of mechanics.
4.  Those two contexts shifted to the context of rolling balls.

Through these four dimensions of variation, the following were deliberately brought to the fore of the learner's awareness: distribution of mass, inertia as a function of the distribution of mass, and angular velocity as a function of inertia. At least this occurred in the cases where the experiment was successful. Change 1 is a change between two values of the first aspect (distribution of mass); Change 2 is a change between two values of another aspect (angular velocity); Changes 3 and 4 are changes between instances of both aspects.

### Example 7.2: Spontaneous Change—Inventing the Commutative Law of Addition

In Székely's study the changes in the learners' experience, where changes occurred, were brought about by the experimenter. As an example of changes brought about by the learner himself we can take a second look at the case of the little boy solving the problem "2+7= _" in Neuman's (1987) study, as we discussed it in Example 5.2 of chapter 5. While engaged in counting on, "1, 2," a pause, "3, 4, 5, 6, 7," he realized that 7, instead of being some (by now it is unclear which) unit in the second addend, 7 could be the seventh unit, the final unit in the first addend, 7, if the two addends swapped place. He could then say "8, 9" for the two units in the second addend, 2. During the process of counting on, when he arrived at 7, what could have been a taken-for-granted partitioning of the units was addressed by the little boy. He changed the partitioning, by changing the ordinal aspects of all the figures from 3 to 9 and the cardinal aspects of all the units grouped. What triggered off this restructuring and his inventing for himself the commutative law of addition was perhaps the separation in awareness of the ordinal aspect of the 7 from the spoken 7, and the simultaneous awareness of the actual ordinality of the 7 as the fifth, or whatever, unit in 7 (the second addend), and the possible ordinality of the spoken 7 as the seventh unit in what could be made into 7 (the first addend). The separation and simultaneity might have paved the way for a switch between the two ordinalities. The switch logically implies the change for the other units involved, which are probably less close to the core of awareness as 7 was at the instant of the shift.

### Example 7.3:  Spontaneous Change—On Forces

Another similar instance of instantaneous change, and hence learning, is to be found in the study of students' understanding of the forces acting on bodies in linear motion, already described in Example 4.3 of chapter 4 (Johansson et al., 1985) . A student is struggling with the problem: "A car driven at a high constant speed straight forward on a motorway. What forces act on the car?"

> I  So a car is driven straight forward at a high constant speed and you are to draw or tell me what forces act on the car.
> S  Well, it's wind resistance, then.
> I  Ye-es. What is that?
> S  It's the air's particles which …
> E  Ye-es.
> S  … Act on the car in some way.
> I  Ye-es.
> S  And it sort of stands still in relation to the car.
> I  What effect does it have, then?
> S  Against the direction of the car.
> I  I see.
> S  And the engine, or the motive force, then?
> I  Hmhm.
> S  Due to the engine functioning in the car's direction. Then there are different sorts of friction in the car itself which act against, or it can look like it's sideways.
> I  Yes, How is the motive power, how great is it?
> S  *Yes, it's much greater than the others.*
> I  Ye-es. Individually or together?
> S  Together.

I  If you have any more forces here, now you've said—you can write it down, by the way, it would be interesting to see approximately how you …

S  Yes. Then we can say that there's a car here, then …

The discussion proceeds, the student sketching a car with vectors 1, 2, and 3 to represent motive force, wind and friction in bearings etc., respectively, as in Fig. 7.2. The interview continues:

I  Yes. And how were numbers 2 and 3 in relation to number 1?

S  They were clearly smaller.

I  And have you got any more forces that act on the car?

S  We-ell, I'm not sure about that, you know, *maybe they're equally great since the car is moving at a high even speed*, I'm not sure about that.

I  How come you … how did you think when it is equally great … when it's greater?

S  Since the car moves forward.

I  Yes.

S  But since it doesn't increase in speed perhaps it—they're equally great instead.

I  Hmmm.

S  Probably, number 1 is greater only when it's accelerating.

(pp. 240–242, italics added).

In Example 4.3 of chapter 4 we described the two qualitatively different ways of understanding "forces acting on bodies in linear motion" as reflected in the students' ways of dealing with this problem. In the above interview excerpt we can see how the student changes from believing that there must be an excess force acting on the car in the direction of movement, without which it would not move (first italicized statement) to believing that as the car is moving with high constant speed, the forces acting on it must be in balance (second italicized statement). As we pointed out earlier, the former understanding is associated with a focus on the fact that the car is moving (and is not at rest), whereas the latter understanding is associated with a focus on uniform velocity (and not acceleration or retardation). In the first case the student thinks that in order to explain that the car is moving and is not at rest, there must be a force. In the second case, which is in accordance with a Newtonian way of reasoning, the student thinks that a net force would be needed to explain a change in velocity, but there is none. How is the switch between these two ways of experiencing the phenomenon in question brought about?

Our interpretation is that the aspect of the car's movement is separated from the car as such, and the aspect of its movement at a high constant speed is separated from the movement as such. Both these aspects are simultaneously in the student's

FIG. 7.2. The diagram of the car sketched by the subject in Example 7.3.

focal awareness, and a shift in emphasis takes place from "*moving* at a high even speed" to "moving at a high *even speed.*"

## The Natural Attitude

Now, one may ask, why is separation of aspects from that which they are aspects of and simultaneity of aspects in focal awareness necessary conditions for a shift in the experience of the phenomenon to come about?

Habitually, we live in what the phenomenologists call *the natural attitude.* Reality has, as a rule, a taken-for-granted character. We tacitly believe that the world is what we see, the same world that always has and always will be seen, and the same world that others see. Reality and experience of the world are taken to be one. But to change our experience of some aspect of reality we have to break the natural attitude temporarily, thematize the aspect in question (in other words, make it an object of reflection), consider alternatives to what is the case, open our awareness to the possibility that something may be other than we thought. We have to raise to figural that which in the natural attitude remains in the ground. This is what we call separating an aspect from a phenomenon or separating an aspect from that of which it is an aspect, and it can take place instantaneously and without conscious awareness. As far as the example of simultaneity of the two aspects—the movement aspect of the car and the high constant speed aspect of the movement—is concerned, in order to bring about a shift in the figure–ground structure of the two (in this shift high constant speed being elevated to figure while movement recedes to ground), both aspects have to be transitional in focal awareness at the same time.

This way of characterizing a sudden change in a way of experiencing something resembles that which Helmstad and Marton (1992) described of what is common to the different ways in which the act of understanding appears to people. In that study a number of people of widely varying ages were asked to give written accounts of "When I understood something." All the episodes described were about sudden insights, and although these were of different kinds, they were interpreted by the authors as reflecting different conceptions of understanding. Here is a fairly typical account taken from hitherto unpublished data:

When I Understood

The alarm clock rang. I turned it off and turned round. After a while I sat up with a start. The children were playing in the sitting room, why hadn't they woken me! I rushed up and washed, threw my clothes on, ran down to the kitchen and began to prepare breakfast. Typical! When autumn comes I always have problems with getting up. Now I will be late again. The third time this term. I put the cornflakes and milk on the table and called the children, poured coffee for me and Mike. "Mike!" He was still in bed. I ran up the stairs and into the bedroom. "Mike!" I shouted, "we've slept in." He woke and looked around sleepily. It was eight o'clock already and he'd usually worked for an hour by this time. He lay down and sighed, looked at me unsympathetically.

"What day is it today?" he said calmly.

I sat on the edge of the bed. Of course, now I understood, it was Saturday.

You become a bit distracted [as a mature student].

This example illustrates—and it is common to many other accounts obtained in the study—that the natural attitude is broken and restored in the same instant, The fact that we now see things as they are while they looked different before implies that what we thought to be real was only an appearance. In the act of understanding, what is real and what is perceived are retrospectively split and at the same time collapsed into each other again. The natural attitude is suspended and confirmed simultaneously.

## Example 7.4: Spontaneous Change—The Act of Learning

The two examples of spontaneous change discussed so far here ("2+7= –" and "car moving at high constant speed") were about changes in the learner's experience of the "what" aspect of learning. But, we can surely learn about learning as well, our way of experiencing the "how" aspect of learning may change. This can be seen to have happened in Säljö's (1982) study summarized in chapter 2 and elaborated further in chapter 3. In the text read by the participants in the experiment (Fig. 2.6) different forms of learning were described. In the end, the deep and surface approaches to learning were contrasted. One of the participants, Dora, in the interview following her reading of the text and answering questions about it said, repeated from the quote in chapter 3:

> Oh, well, first when I read it I sort of thought like this: right now I'll try to remember as much as possible … and then I went on, and the more I read … when coming to the end of the article I could have burst out laughing cause there they described the type of person I'd been myself at first, those who were trying to learn as much as possible … and then there were certain hints about … that you should try to find the meaning behind it all, so when I read it once again, I tried to make it make sense in quite a different way. (p. 152)

Dora has obviously learned about learning. She seems to have changed her experience of her own learning, and also to have actually changed the way in which she learned during the experiment. She separated the approach aspect of learning in the text and the approach aspect of her own learning. By doing so, a figure–ground reversal was brought about. Reality, in this case her own learning, was elevated to figure while the text receded to ground. This shift left no alternative but to adopt a deep approach.

In terms of the title of this chapter, Dora did learn to experience learning differently. Thanks to her reading of the text in the experiment she now could see learning in terms of contrasting approaches, and this insight was immediately reflected in her way of reading the text.

## Example 7.5: Change in the Context of Repeated Readings—Understanding Kafka

In the three examples of learning as spontaneous change recounted hitherto, variation has meant opening up dimensions, separating aspects, seeing them simultaneously, and letting them be constituent parts in a structural change of how something is experienced. Variation may, however, also mean—and in fact this sense of the word is closer to its common usage—exploring something by more or less systematically looking at it from various perspectives. This is how children explore objects: turning them around, throwing them, tasting them, feeling them. In a metaphorical sense, it also is what researchers do when they explore their objects of research. This is the way in which we gain acquaintance with objects of the mundane world and with the abstract phenomena of scholarship. This is how appresentation develops. This is how we become capable of experiencing the whole when only one of its parts is given. Marton and Wenestam (1988) showed that adopting a deep approach was not a sufficient condition for grasping the conceptual structure underlying an advanced philosophical text, even when it was read as many as five times. Understanding a text of such an advanced nature was seen to be associated with, in addition to a deep approach, the adoption of a perspective within the text. In other words, it had to be looked at it from the point of view of one of its parts. Furthermore, the perspective had to be varied by varying the part from which the rest was observed.

In the Marton, Asplund-Carlsson, and Halász' (1992) study, Franz Kafka's famous parable "Before the Law" was read by Hungarian and Swedish secondary school students three times, with one week between the second and third readings. In outline, the story concerns a man who tries many times to gain admittance to the Law, the door to which is open but fiercely guarded by a man who refuses him entry, saying that he is not allowed in but that he should wait and see. How ever many times and in how ever many ways he tries to get in, he is unsuccessful. As an old man he makes a final attempt, asking the guard why nobody else has ever tried to go through the door, only to be told by the guard that the door was only for him, and now that his life was coming to an end, the door was to be closed.

In a metaphorical sense the group of readers can be thought of as a prism through which the text passed, to be refracted and to exit in distinctly different meanings. Four different ways of understanding the short story were identified, which we do not need to elaborate on here. Let us call them A, B, C, and D. Two of them, D and C, were included in a third one, B, which in its turn was included in a fourth way of understanding, A, which was the most complex of the four. It was found that a number of the students engaged in what was called *reflective variation*. This appeared

within the very same understanding by the very same individual on the very same occasion. A number of students used a form of variation to make sense of what they were reading and we find a certain *movement* in some understandings of the story; they have certain dynamic qualities. These students seem to wish to explore what is meant, what is implied, in the text by trying alternative ways of understanding the whole text or its parts on the one hand and making explicit the implications of their way of understanding the whole text or its parts, on the other. This way of handling the text is strikingly different from that behind the more or less taken-for-granted understanding that most of the students put forward. (Marton, Asplund-Carlsson, & Halász, 1992, p. 10)

There were two different forms of this variation identified. Some students varied the meaning of the whole story, of some of its constituent parts. Hence the label *variation in meaning*. Take for instance, the following extract from one student:

The author constructed this in such a way, I believe, so that everyone should understand it in accordance with his own thoughts, his own personality. Thus it means different things for everyone. The Law could mean absolute knowledge, the laws of nature, our own essence itself, the goal of life or the meaning of life. If the author (or whoever reads it) is religious, you can interpret the door to the law as the gate to Heaven, to which everyone should find his own way. Of course, we can accept the law as it is, law. It would then mean that the law is not equal for all. (Marton, Asplund-Carlsson, & Halász, 1992, pp. 10–11)

In other cases a line of reasoning is developed, the implications of certain details in the story are made explicit, and they lead to yet further implications. This is called *elaborative variation* and is here illustrated by a case in which it yielded a complex understanding of the story, as judged by the authors of the paper:

This is a rather contradictory situation. The man wants to get to the law, but the guard hinders him by the door of the law. Why? This is the first question we ask ourselves. But we do not understand the answer very well. The man will probably never get through the door, law itself stands in his way. If he enters in spite of the prohibition, then he breaks the law, because the law says that he (now or whenever) cannot get in. The man can't take this contradiction since he does not want to break the law. But he must enter at any price and there is no possibility other than to get the guard to reconsider. At first he tries persuasion, but has no success. Then he tries bribery. That is not very 'legal'. This could be important, that is, if the man tries to obtain something, he won't give in at the first difficulty, if there is no straightforward way, he tries the dishonest way, illegally. Nothing is beyond human beings—neither crime nor violence—when they are trying to reach a goal. Most people are like that. But our man feels that as soon as he has entered the door, he will have to answer for his actions, since he has come to 'the law'. Therefore he waits. When he gets old, the guard mentions a kind of solution. The door was OPEN. There are such contradictions which have no solution, it is a paradox. (He can enter, but he cannot!) That is why it is such shocking reading. (Marton, Asplund-Carlsson, & Halász, 1992, pp. 11–12)

The level of understanding of the story was closely correlated with the use of reflective variation, as should be obvious from Table 7.2 where the occurrence of the two most complex forms of understanding is crossed with the use of reflective variation in the course of the different readings.

**TABLE 7.2**
Relationship Between *Best* Understanding Arrived
at and Use of Reflective Variation

|  |  | Use of Reflective Variation on Some Occasion | | |
| --- | --- | --- | --- | --- |
|  |  | No | Yes | Σ |
| Understanding A or B on some occasion | No | 48 | 4 | 52 |
|  | Yes | — | 8 | 8 |
|  | Σ | 48 | 12 | 60 |

*Source.* Marton, Asplund-Carlsson, and Halász (1992, p. 13)

## Example 7.6: The Group as the Vehicle of Variation

In all of the studies described so far, and the results we have put forward as examples of variation as the chief mechanism of learning, the variation has referred to the way in which individuals look on the phenomenon in question. A case of bringing the variation to be found in a group into play in the learning experience is offered by a study of 12-year-olds who grapple with a genuine mathematical problem (Wistedt & Martinsson, 1994). They are given the problem of working out the length of each of three bookends cut from a piece of wood, expressed in some decimal form. They have met halves and quarters expressed in decimal form, and also percentages, but they have not actually met such repeating decimals as 33.333 ... in their mathematics classes. Furthermore, the ideas of errors and inexactitude in mathematics are quite foreign. They do have, however, a long experience of discussing genuine problems in that they have had philosophy on the schedule since they started school. Here, the children provide the variation in that they bring up alternative ways of tackling the problem and freely discuss one another's suggestions.

They work up to the problem of the size of each piece of wood when the whole piece is divided into three equal pieces via the problems of dividing it first into two equal halves, and then into four quarters. Now whether they think of each piece of wood as being 1/3 or 100/3% of the whole, when they try to express the fraction as a decimal they run into the problem that the three parts (in the case of 1/3 first .3+.3+.3, then coming a little closer, .33+.33+.33 and so on) will not add up to 1 or 100. Several children, however, realize that even if you go on adding 3s indefinitely after the decimal point, you will still not get the sum you need: 1 or 100. The error, however, gets smaller and smaller. Although the children fall short of inventing the concept of the limit, the idea of an infinite series of numbers is a significant insight, a new way of experiencing numbers.

The children arrive at this insight through quite an extensive use of variation. In the different groups they vary the content while holding the theoretical problem invariant. They talk about dividing up apples, balls, and cakes, and by doing so they shift from continuous to discrete entities. They iterate between model and reality; they vary the mathematical expression (1/3, 10/3, or 100/3); and they vary the strategy used for solving the problem: following up intuitive interpretations, trial and error, iterating between ideas for solution, testing the ideas and working on successively more precise formulations of the intuitive idea. This study will be referred to again in the next chapter when we look at what it can tell us about the teacher's role in groups.

## Example 7.7:  Changes Over a Year

In all the examples in this section we have discussed learning in terms of sudden restructuring or in terms of processes taking place within comparatively short intervals. But learning is generally more extended in time to days, weeks, or years.

Ekeblad (1994) has studied children between the ages of 7 and 8 learning arithmetic skills during the first year in school in Sweden, as mentioned in chapter 3. She had earlier developed a set of computer games aimed at facilitating the development of a grasp of numerosity in the sense described in the Example 4.1 in chapter 4. Children were invited to use the computer that was placed in the classroom, but their learning had to be seen, of course, against the background of the entirety of their mathematical experiences during the whole school year. Of course, to follow a single child all the time during a whole year is not a feasible plan, much less the three whole classes of children studied here.

One of the children described is a little boy called Erik. At the start of the school year the meaning of numbers for Erik comprises no more than the word sequence for counting. When he is asked to place 9 buttons on a piece of paper he lines them up in a long row. When he is asked to write how many there are, he writes all the numerals: 1 2 3 4 5 6 7 8 9, one next to each button. When, following the same problem we have quoted from other studies, some of the 9 buttons are hidden in one box and the rest of them in another box, and he is asked to give five guesses as to how many there are in the two boxes, Erik makes the following suggestions: 8 and 9, 6 and 7, 1 and 2, 7 and 6, 3 and 2, all pairs of consecutive numbers. After one school year, when faced with the same problem, he comes up with: 8 and 1, 5 and 4, 6 and 3, 0 and 9. At this point, he becomes uncertain of what numbers he has not used, discovers that 2 is a good candidate, and immediately produces the combination 7 and 2. This indicates that by the end of the year Erik has a good sense of numbers, in this instance, "nine," seeming to have the meaning of all its possible decompositions.

A driving force for Erik during the first year is his ambition to appear bright. His relation to numbers is entangled with his relationships to other persons. The moment of his discovery of numerosity and the structural aspects of numbers has not been identified, if indeed such a moment occurred. But after more than 3 months in school, when playing one of the computer games Erik uses finger numbers to find out what 5-and-something might be. But he also counts the numerals on the screen, informed, however, by a sense of reasonable number relations. At the beginning of the year he experienced numbers in their ordinal sense. After some time different understandings of numbers seemed to run in parallel, and by the end of the year different aspects of numbers—ordinality, cardinality, part–whole relationships, and the rest—are simultaneously and focally present in his awareness.

## Example 7.8: Changes Over a Lifetime

Carrying out research that has rewarded the researcher with a Nobel prize can be seen as an extreme form of learning. In December each year the Nobel prizes are awarded in Stockholm, and Swedish television organizes the broadcast of a round-table discussion with the prizewinners in which the question of how they see scientific intuition always comes up and triggers off a lively debate with opinions and personal experiences being recounted. Marton, Fensham, and Chaiklin (1994) have analysed those parts of the transcripts from the annual discussions, covering the years 1970 to 1986.

It was found that two kinds of experience dominated the accounts of instances of scientific intuition. The first one was a strong sense of direction, of a path, of being on the way toward something as yet unknown. The sense was characterized by a feeling of certainty about the choice of path, in spite of the absence of conscious reasons for that choice (reminiscent of the successful students in Székely's study). The second kind of experience referred to was the sudden insight that occurs without any obvious reasons at all, the pieces of the jigsaw puzzle falling into place, the sudden revelation of the solution. Again, there was a feeling of certainty, in this case that the answer has been found, in spite of the absence of supporting evidence. Verification was what remained to be provided. Of these two distinct kinds of experience, the former, the sense of direction, is twice as common as the latter, the sudden revelation.

How can we account for these two kinds of experience such that the underlying mechanisms are made explicit? The prototypical situation is a stage in the research process when some observation, for unknown reasons, is recognized as significant and is followed up in a certain direction. In principle there is always an unlimited number of ways it can be followed. What is it that makes the researcher select one and pursue it for years, sometimes for a lifetime? We can understand it if we think of the particular observation as a part of a greater whole, the answer to the research question, which in no sense exists when the observation is made, but which is nevertheless given in some way, in some form, in the experience of the part.

Appresentation of the whole from a part or aspect of the whole, described in chapter 5, is a conceptual tool for understanding the experiences. Recall the example of the house, one's own home, being appresented in its facade, even its darkened doorway. This vague, tacit experience of the whole guides one's steps:

> And so … as we did our work, I think, we almost felt at times that there was almost a hand guiding us. Because we would go from one step to the next, and somehow we would know which was the right way to go. And I really can't tell how we knew that, how we knew that it was necessary to move ahead. (Michael S Brown, Nobel prize for Medicine, 1985, cited in Marton et al., 1994, pp. 461–462)

When you eventually arrive at the answer, you suddenly see the whole and you know that it is right, you feel the shock of recognition:

> ... you've been thinking about something without willing to for a long time. Then all of a sudden, the problem is opened to you in a flash, and you suddenly see the answer. (Rita Levi-Montalcini, Nobel prize for Medicine, 1986; cited in Marton et al., 1994, p. 462)

In contrast to the appresentation of your home from its darkened doorway, in which the well-known whole is appresent in the part, in the experience of scientific intuition it is a hitherto unknown whole that is suddenly appresent from a well-known part.

In the discussions, a fair number of comments pertained to the issue of explaining scientific intuition in the sense of describing its origin or genesis and giving an account of the necessary conditions for it to appear, with almost half of the laureates in the study remarking on it. Two of the 72 laureates who expressed views on scientific intuition emphasizing a general and, at least partly, innate gift for intuitive thinking while the others stressed the importance of knowledge and experience—far-ranging and intense experience—which, as was underlined by many of the laureates, should be varied. As they expressed it, one should keep looking at a research problem from continually varying perspectives:

> It takes mulling over a problem for a long time from many different aspects. And then sometime, you may be able to put the pieces together and see how things fit. (John Bardeen, Nobel prize for Physics, 1972; cited in Marton et al., 1994, p. 465)

> You just keep asking this question continually, over the years, and change your directions, try, try things here and there. It is not just a single thing, it's a lifetime. (William N. Lipscomb, Nobel prize for Chemistry, 1976; cited in Marton et al., 1994, p. 465)

## Explaining Change and Bringing About Change

We have stated that learning of the kind we are dealing with in this book (i.e., learning that enables the learner to experience a phenomenon in a way she has not been able to experience it previously) comes about by experiencing the phenomenon in some particular way. We have singled out two explanatory constructs that characterize aspects of the experience necessary to bring about the learning in question: The relevance structure of the experience and the variation in the experience. Now, how can we account for the presence of a certain kind of relevance structure and a certain kind of variation? We can, of course, look at individual cases and try to trace the genesis of the nature of experience in terms of the individual's biography. But we cannot explain why people experience a certain kind of relevance structure and a certain form a variation in general terms. From the point of view of an educational knowledge interest, however, we do not have to. It suffices to know that the learner is going to learn to experience that phenomenon in a new way to the extent that we manage to bring those aspects of the learner's experience of a certain phenomenon about.

## THE CONSTITUTION OF THE OBJECT OF LEARNING

### The Realness of the Object of Learning

Learning, as it has been described in this chapter, is an ongoing exploration of the world as experienced. It is never constrained to the learning task in itself, as defined by teachers or researchers. Although the teacher believes that the learners learn about one thing, they might learning about something else. Earlier we mentioned Colaizzi's (1973) study showing that in the initial phase of a learning experiment the participants were focusing on the situation as a whole, on people, and on the material surroundings, rather than on the learning material. Similarly, in Kullberg's (1991) teaching experiment children learned to figure out what it takes to learn in school before they embarked upon learning to read and write. We made the point that learning proceeds from the whole to the parts. But what the whole is by no means is self-evident. We argued in chapter 5 with reference to Gurwitsch (1964) that a theme can be surrounded by different fields of awareness, not only a field pertaining to the object of learning but also fields pertaining to the tasks and settings of the learning, as well as the learner's own role. It appears that learning that has lasting effects is always about *reality,* or about something that is experienced as *real* in some sense. The problem however, is that although the social practice of schooling is experienced as real, it is far from always obvious that the content of schooling is experienced as being about the "real" world—the cultural, social, physical world in which the learner lives.

Maybe this is a lead in the puzzle of why students are found to understand certain aspects of the world in which they live that are explicitly dealt with in their education—such as Newtonian motion and the nature of matter—in ways that differ from the scientific understanding they are taught. Photosynthesis, a cherished topic in science education, is the process by which green plants produce carbohydrate (glucose) and oxygen from carbon dioxide and water by using energy from the sunlight. Expressed in this way, it may not appear self-evident to everyone that photosynthesis is about our own life-world. But what photosynthesis is about can be expressed differently:

> I remember having a very profound experience of suddenly really understanding, when our biology teacher asked us what the most important difference between a pig and a marigold was. And there we sat, all of us soon to be teachers with our academic qualifications, and we had no answer. The teacher had to explain: The marigold makes its own food, the pig has to steal its food! Thus, plants produce their own food and that of others mainly out of sun, air and water. Everything fell into place. But why all those years at school with learning by heart for homework and exams, when this was what it was all about. (Tronström, 1984, p. 28)

Now, students orient themselves to learning differently. In chapter 2 we described different approaches to learning: When learners adopt a deep approach they are trying to see the reality to which the text they are reading refers. In chapter 3 we found ways of experiencing learning that resemble the view that underlies the deep approach. We would thus expect learners who adopt a deep approach to be more likely to change their way of experiencing the phenomena dealt with in their studies.

Prosser and Millar (1989) have been able to show this to be the case. They set out to investigate the relationship between approaches to learning and coming to see the object of learning in a particular way. The study was based on a 6-week course including a topic known to be conceptually difficult for physics students: force and motion. Newton's first law, as already discussed in chapter 4, states that a body remains in its state of rest or uniform motion unless a force is applied to change it, drawing the critical distinction between, rest or uniform motion implying the net absence of force on the one hand, and, change in uniform motion (acceleration or deceleration) implying the net presence of force on the other. Earlier studies, such as that by Johansson, Marton, and Svensson (1985), have shown that whereas students can learn to apply and manipulate the formulas derived from Newton's laws, they tend to retain the qualitative understanding of Aristotle. Qualitative understanding rather than a manipulative facility was emphasized in the course studied by Prosser and Millar. Students were encouraged to discuss their work with one another to reveal the variation in understanding, and laboratory sessions were arranged to favor problem solving over "cookbook" experiments. Students were interviewed some time before and after the course, both to test their understanding of the key concepts and, on the second occasion, to reveal their approaches to learning.

One example used in the pre- and posttest concerns the question already used in illustration in chapters 4 and 5: "A car is driven at a high constant speed along a straight line on a highway. What forces act on the car?" The Newtonian description is of forces in balance (motive force balancing resistance), whereas the Aristotelian description is of a net force in the direction of motion (motive force exceeding resistance). No students indicated the Newtonian understanding in tackling the problem prior to the course, whereas 4 of the 14 participants indicated it afterwards. This is not a very impressive result from the point of view of the teaching (although it is in fact impressive when compared with other reports of the outcome of learning about force and motion).

On the basis of the interviews about the students' experience of their studies, carried out after the course was completed, they were classified as having had a deep or a surface approach to their learning in the course as a whole, rather than on a single occasion. In the context of this topic and this course, the researchers describe students with the surface approach as trying to "categorize and memorize disconnected pieces of material so that they could increase the amount of knowledge they had and meet course requirements" whereas those with the deep approach "abstract meaning from, change their understanding of and develop a personal commitment to the material being studied so that they could explain and better understand reality." Three students were unclear cases, indicating traits of both approaches.

Further analysis reveals that those four students who indicated a more developed conception on that problem in the posttest were, remarkably, the only four who had clearly expressed a deep approach to learning. In Table 7.3 we summarize their

**TABLE 7.3**
Summary of Development of Understanding Broken Down
by Approach to Learning

|                 | Clearly Deep | Approach Unclear | Clearly Surface |
| --------------- | ------------ | ---------------- | --------------- |
| Did develop     | 8            | 6                | 2               |
| Did not develop | 1            | 3                | 21              |

Summarized from Prosser and Millar (1989)

results pooled over four tasks and excluding those students who had the most advanced conception from the start.

This study thus suggests that learning in the sense of changing one's way of experiencing a phenomenon is contingent on one's approach to learning. Prosser (1994) since replicated these findings as to the relationship between approaches and ways of experiencing, which he calls conceptual change, in another field of physics, namely electricity.

Roth and Anderson (1988) also indicated that change in the learner's way of understanding the phenomenon about which she is reading is contingent on her way of going about the reading. In their study something very much like a deep approach was correlated with the ascent of the same kind of understanding of photosynthesis as the one expressed by Tronström, as quoted earlier.

When learning is experienced as being about reality, it concerns the nature of the world we live in and know. As we have pointed out time and again in this book, the world is both a real world and an experienced world. By learning, our experience of the world, or our experienced world, gets more differentiated and more integrated. Our world grows richer, we become more enlightened. What we learn is projected into the world. It is not in our heads but in the world. It appears somewhat different to us thanks to the new knowledge we have gained. Thus knowledge has become a part of ourselves, and it has become a part of the world. It belongs to the increasingly intricate complex we call reality, related to various other aspects and parts of the world.

As we described in chapter 1, some 120 years ago Herman Ebbinghaus wanted to study learning in its purest form by using meaningless syllables, which, as he thought, were not related to anything. Quite obviously, the view we advocate is very different from that of Ebbinghaus; in fact we could hardly imagine getting further away from his ideas than we have. Pure learning according to Ebbinghaus is not learning at all in our view. We believe that learning is something organic: The world we experience changes (that is what we call learning) just as plants and animals and humans grow. They become very different from what they were in the beginning, but still, in a very fundamental sense, they remain the same.

## The Sensuous Experience of the Object of Learning

According to this line of reasoning what we learn is projected into the world, and unless that is so, we are incapable of remembering it. Even seemingly abstract knowledge can be an object of sensuous experience. We can experience it in ways that in certain respects resemble the ways we experience material objects, through our senses. In the case of abstract objects we have sensuous experience of something that can not truly be experienced by any of the senses, which accords with the view of experience we argued for earlier. Experience is seen as transcending the specific psychological modes in which it is apparent. The very same ways of experiencing something can be found in such diverse acts as learning, problem solving or remembering. In relation to the aspects of experience in which we are interested, which we call qualitatively different ways of experiencing something and which are supposed to capture the variation in structure and meaning, the distinction between concrete and abstract is but slight.

University students engaged in intense academic study can serve to illustrate how this apparent dividing line between concrete and abstract is transcended in experience, as seen in Entwistle and Marton's (1994) investigation of students studying for their final examinations. In this small-scale interview study it was found that the students developed tightly integrated bodies of knowledge, which they experienced in a quasi-sensory mode. Experiencing these "knowledge objects" was akin to having a sensory experience, although there was no actual sensory experience at all. A student, focusing on a certain aspect of a knowledge object, say, reported an awareness of its unfocused aspects. These aspects were appresented, again like the legs on the table when the table is seen from above or the rooms that constitute the house when only the facade is seen.

There were qualitatively different kinds of knowledge objects identified in the students' accounts, which we can describe in four distinct categories:

1. Contents of specific books and lectures
2. The logical structuring of a field of knowledge
3. A personal restructuring of a field of knowledge
4. The phenomena to be learned about through knowledge restructuring.

In the first case the knowledge objects reflect primarily the structure of the students' notes. Those expressing this kind of experience seem to believe that they have visual images of pages, the accuracy of which they tend to overestimate. The next two categories refer to experiences of a more transformative nature, the first bringing out the inherent structure of the field of knowledge and the second reshaping it personally. The last category refers to projecting the abstract knowledge into the real world, hence eradicating the dividing line between abstract and concrete:

> S10 [What I visualize] it's the general shape, and once I get that general shape on paper the rest will follow ... [draws] ... At the moment I'm visualising a head there, and that's basically what I see. I know there're muscles in various places, but I'm not going into that sort of detail when I first think of it. I just have the rough shape ... I've learned two dimensional on that plane and two dimensional on that plane, and then I've seen a real skull. So basically I've got these two which are put together....

> I could visualize a square skull in three dimensions by just turning it, and then I'd go to a real skull and see what bones were in the same position, but of course it's a very, very different object. Yet you can sort of, transpose those ideas, so that once you do that and you're given a real skull in the exam it's much easier to go through. So you don't actually have a picture of either a square, non-realistic skull or a real skull, you just know where everything is. (Entwistle & Marton, 1994, p. 168)

The same student captures very nicely the awareness of something (the experience of its presence) that transcends particular modes of experience and is still most vividly experiential:

> S10  I don't perceive it in any particular way, I just know it, I don't actually hear it, see it, write it: it's just present. (Entwistle & Marton, 1994, p. 173)

We offer this as empirical support for the idea that experience can have a strong sensory flavor without actually being a sensory experience. This implies that experience transcends the different sensory modes such as vision, hearing and so on, just as it also transcends the different psychological modes, such as perception, memory, thinking and so on.

We are tempted to call this "pure experience," the experience of the sheer presence of something. The student we quoted captured it very well, but to the extent pure experience exists, people lacking a natural vocabulary to describe it, tend to use words that refer to more familiar forms of experience. It is common to talk of it as if it were visual: "It's like seeing." Marton observed that many of the students participating in a learning experiment of the kind described in chapter 2 reported the experience of seeing the pages, especially those with tables on them, when in the course of a later interview they gave an account of what they had read. When the interviewer inquired about details, it was obvious that they could not actually see anything. Iit was more a feeling of seeing. Marton called this phenomenon "quasi-visual image" (Marton, 1974, pp. 82–85).

A more famous account of an experience for which we lack words, and which may be unique, originates from Wolfgang Amadeus Mozart:

> Thoughts crowd into my mind as easily as you could wish.... Those which please me I keep in my head and I hum them.... Once I have my theme, another melody comes, linking itself with the first one, in accordance with the needs of the composition as a whole: the counterpoint, the part of each instrument and all the melodic fragments at last produce the complete work. Then my soul is on fire with inspiration. The work grows: I keep expanding it, conceiving it more and more clearly until I have the entire composition finished in my head though it may be long. Then my mind seizes it as a glance of my eye a beautiful picture or a handsome youth. It does not come to me successively, with various points worked out in detail, as they will later on, but it is in its entirety [gleich alles zusammen] that my imagination lets me hear. (Penrose, 1989, p. 423)

Now, you cannot see music, and you cannot experience a whole composition simultaneously in any ordinary sense of the word. This is an experience that by definition transcends the senses. Vision is then used as a lived metaphor for capturing the flavor of the experience.

As was described in Example 7.8, one of the characteristics of the research process when regarded from the point of view of scientific intuition is a strong sense of direction toward something which, though not yet evolved, has a strongly felt presence. It is the object of this very advanced form of learning that is being constituted in the bond between researcher and phenomenon, the secrets of which the researcher is trying to reveal. Can this be unique for Nobel laureates? Marton (1992) argued that scientific intuition is just a special case of the intuition that is part of the everyday experience of us mortals, examples of which came to light in the study related earlier of British university students engaged in revision (Entwistle & Marton, 1994). Their experiences of the knowledge objects they were developing were of a quasi-sensory nature akin to the Nobel laureates' experiences of their evolving objects of research.

An account which comes very close to the Nobel laureates' description of the strong sense of direction, of the vivid sensuous experience transcending the known senses, of something that does not yet exist, comes appropriately enough from another Nobel laureate. Albert Einstein, quoted by one of the founders of the Gestalt school of psychology, Max Wertheimer, with whom he had a series of discussions, describes his path toward the formulation of the special theory of relativity:

> During all those years there was a feeling of direction, of going straight toward something concrete. It is, of course, very hard to express that feeling in words; but it was decidedly the case, and clearly to be distinguished from later considerations about the rational form of the solution. Of course, behind such a direction there is always something logical; but I have it in a kind of survey, in a way visually. (Wertheimer, 1945, p. 228)

## WHAT, THEN, IS AN OBJECT OF LEARNING?

The somewhat curious implication of our argument here is that the object of learning is constituted in the course of learning. Or, to sharpen the claim a touch further, learning is the constitution of the object of learning. There are two apparent ambiguities we feel bound to discuss.

First, to readers of this book—or to anyone else—it may seem an odd way of talking, an odd way of thinking, about learning: "The object of learning has to be there to begin with; how otherwise could we learn about it?" This does at first appear to be a highly reasonable objection. We have, however, described learning as a change in the person–world relationship, which implies indeed that the world that the person learns about and the person who learns about the world cannot be described separately from each other. What, then, is implied by the alternative, the received wisdom—first to describe the object of learning in its own right and then to describe what the learner learns about it?

The conventional way of describing learning is, indeed, to start with the researcher's description of the object of learning, whether it be recursion or the nature of matter or Kafka's story "Before the Law." Such a description is intended to depict what the object is really like. Hence no distinction is made between the description and the object described. But can the argument that the description offered is the only conceivable description, capturing what the object of learning is really like, be defended? Can the claim be justified that any other "expert" would describe the same object in the same way? Rarely, if ever, could such a proposition be defended. In that case, what becomes of the argument that the learner is indeed learning about the object of learning as it has been described? If we really want to know what the object of learning is for the learner, we have to find out what it is; describing learning from such a perspective is to a large extent a question of finding out and describing what the object of learning is for the learner. It becomes an empirical question to settle by carrying out an investigation, and not a question to be settled *before* an investigation is embarked upon.

The attentive reader might object, "Have not you, the authors, given in chapter 4 descriptions of recursion, of Newtonian motion, of matter, as objects of learning, descriptions, interpretations, that were merely your own?" In fact, what we tried to do there was not to *define* the objects of learning but to give the reader a *background* which would enable her to make sense of the different objects of learning that were identified. Take a moment to reconsider chapter 4 and you will see that this is so. In fact you should also notice that in introducing the notion of numerosity and arithmetic skills we gave an account of the "object of learning" which, while in accord with the dominant view from the literature, is radically different from that for which we subsequently argued!

There is a second apparent ambiguity in saying "learning is the constitution of the object of learning." It might sound as if we mean that the phenomenon *is* the learner's experience of it. We certainly do not mean that. As we stated earlier, a phenomenon can be seen in terms of the complex of all the ways it may be experienced in the broadest sense of the word, most of them possibly not yet known. One particular learner's way of experiencing the phenomenon relates to this abstract complex of different ways of experiencing it as the part relates to the whole. This part is in all likelihood identical with some other people's way of experiencing the phenomenon. Occasionally, however, the way of experiencing the phenomenon is novel in the absolute sense. A new way of seeing something has been introduced. We have touched upon instances of this kind of learning in Example 7.8, earlier.

Therefore, if we refer to the object of learning on the collective level as the complex of different ways of experiencing the phenomenon to be learned about, instead of saying "learning is the constitution of the object of learning," it would be more correct, if marginally more clumsy, to say "learning is participation in the ongoing and constantly recurrent constitution of the object of learning."

The idea of the object of learning referring to the collective level of description being a complex of possible ways of experiencing the phenomenon to be learned about implies the possibility of a description of the object of learning that is independent of a particular learner or of a particular group of learners. Look at this. We argued first that the object of learning can not be described independently of the learner, yet now we are saying, we can indeed do so! How can we possibly reconcile those two apparently contradictory arguments? Indeed, we cannot describe the object of learning for any particular learner or group of learners independently of that learner or group of learners. We have to *find out* what the object of learning is for her or for them. In contrast, if we have revealed and mapped out the qualitatively different ways in which a certain phenomenon to be learned about is experienced, then we have a description, admittedly partial, of the possible ways in which a phenomenon, the object of learning, can be experienced. This is a description on the collective level, and even if it is independent of particular learners, it is not independent of learners in general. After all, it depicts different person–world relationships. It is a second-order description, a description of the phenomenon *as experienced.* The outcome space of matter, as depicted in Example 4.4, for example, captures what is probably the variation in how most 13- to 16-year-olds in school make sense of matter. Nevertheless, we must always be open to the possibility that another way of experiencing the phenomenon may crop up.

If the object of learning as described on the collective level as a complex of the different ways in which the phenomenon can possibly be experienced is seen from the point of view of individual learning, the latter (i.e., individual learning) can be understood as an appropriation of successively larger and larger regions of the object of learning as described on the collective level. This means that in the course of learning the individual becomes aware of the phenomenon in question in more and more ways, and these ways, we should remind ourselves, are not mental representations of the phenomenon, but relationships between the experiencer and the experienced visible only from a second-order perspective.

We have argued at great length throughout this book for considering ways of experiencing a certain phenomenon as internal relationships between the experiencer and the experienced. These are not in the head of the person but lie between her and the phenomenon, as we have declared again and again. Now we are picturing learning as the appropriation of more different ways of experiencing the phenomenon in question. If you are now moved to ask, *"Where,* then, does the person *have* these capabilities?" the answer we offer is, "in her awareness." Her awareness is the totality of her relatedness to the world. To make sense of all this, it might help to consider once again the alternative that we arguing against, which is the dualistic conception of mind. This is to be found at its most consistent within a cognitive science grounded on the cognitivist dogma, which we can repeat to be "the presumption that all psychological explanation must be framed in terms of internal mental representation, and processes (or rules) by which these representations are manipulated and transformed" (Still & Costall, 1987, p. 2). This implies—and we risk repeating ourselves too often—that there is, on the one hand, an objective, independently constituted (independent of the person) reality out there and, on the other hand, a subjective representation of the outside world in the head of the person. The inner representation is built up by the person receiving sensory information from the outside world. Talking about mind is to talk about a storehouse of representations, and talking about experiencing something is to talk about experiencing its representation.

In our alternative there is no independently constituted reality, and there are certainly not two worlds. Thus, there are no mental representations, either. There is just one world, which is both objective and subjective, an experienced world that we cannot conceptualize in terms that transcend human ways of making sense of the world. But we do conceptualize it as transcending any current understanding of it, which is bound to be partial. In that sense, even if the world is physically independent of us (us meaning humans that live, ever have lived or ever will live), its description is logically not so.

As for our awareness, what we are aware of is exactly this one experienced world. Awareness is not a storehouse of representations. It is an orchestration of all our constitutive acts, such as discernment, relating, focusing, and so on, as we have discussed earlier. Experience is constituted between person and world, reflecting both, and that is why we repeatedly state that it is an *internal* relationship. It cannot exist without both of its constituent parts, nor would the constituent parts remain the same were they not parts of the particular relation.

To the extent that there are acts of constitution and no mental representations, and to the extent that we are aware of everything all of the time, everything has to be constituted all of the time. Awareness should be seen as an immense number of coordinated acts going on all the time, so when we say that someone has appropriated new ways of experiencing a certain phenomenon, it means that she has become involved in some new ongoing constitutive acts, and that she has become capable of being so involved.

It would take far too long to develop this somewhat provocative conjecture here, but it is implied by the logic of the previous line of argument, and goes like this. If awareness is an internal relationship between person and world, if we are aware of everything all the time in some form, if one's world keeps changing all the time, then the whole of our awareness has to change (i.e., is necessarily constituted anew) all the time.

## FIRST- AND SECOND-ORDER PERSPECTIVES REVISITED

As we indicated in the previous chapter, the first- and the second-order perspectives are complementary to each other in the sense that from them you look for and see, different things. Different objects of research are brought into focus. The second-order perspective defines a set of objects of research that can be classified as internal human–world relationships.

In addition to the two perspectives being largely complementary, they also are related in another way. Any first-order perspective statements about any phenomena originate from ways of seeing the phenomena which are usually tacit. We could make the very ways of seeing the phenomena objects of research, in which case we would aim at making second-order perspective statements about them (i.e., statements about the ways in which the phenomena are experienced). This would be true, for instance, for Wertheimer's (1945) study of Einstein's thinking that led to the special theory of relativity, which we mentioned earlier in this chapter.

The validity claims of first-order statements concern under any circumstances the validity of our statements about the world (e.g., to what extent the special theory of relativity offers a consistent and useful description of certain aspects of physical reality). The validity claims of second-order statements concern the validity of our statements about ways of experiencing the world (e.g., to what extent Wertheimer's account offers a consistent and useful description of Einstein's way of seeing certain aspects of physical reality).

The generally complementary relationship between the first- and second-order perspectives does not, however, hold when the phenomenon in question is learning. We have said that for any phenomenon a first-order perspective can be adopted in which statements are made about what it is like while the person–phenomenon relationships are bracketed. Alternatively, a second-order perspective can be adopted in which statements are made about the actual relationship between the person and the phenomenon, and the question of what the phenomenon is like is bracketed. But when it comes to learning in the sense of gaining knowledge about the world, the object of description is the very relationship between the person (the learner) and the phenomenon (that which is to be learned). We could choose, on the one hand, to make statements about the phenomenon, and about the person, and about how the two are related to one another. This is to take a first-order perspective (which we claim will inevitably end in Meno's paradox). On the other hand, we can make statements about the person–phenomenon relationship (how the phenomenon is experienced by the person), how it changes and develops, which is to take a second-order perspective. Quite obviously, we cannot devise a critical experiment that would decide the case between these two perspectives on learning, but we can compare the two rival descriptions as to consistency and fruitfulness.

# 8

# A Pedagogy of Awareness

## THE IDEA OF PEDAGOGY

As men (and women) have reflected on their standing in the universe, they have generally focused on what links them to their gods and what separates them from the lower animals. Is it that we are wise (as gods are, and by implication, the animals are not)—*homo sapiens* as Linné had it—or that we make war—*homo pugnax* (Barnett, 1973)—or artifacts—*homo faber*—again in common with gods but not animals? There is some doubt as to the wisdom of our species with respect to the world in which we live, and other species have been observed to make forms of war and artifacts. But in line with the thrust of our book we would argue, on the evidence offered by Barnett, that humans are remarkable among animals for the way in which they teach their young.

*Homo docens*: This is the concept with which we wish to start exploring the idea of pedagogy before going on to argue for a particular view of teaching that builds on and reflects the view of learning we have developed throughout the book. We have to point out that the word "pedagogy" comes quite naturally to us as a direct anglicization of the word commonly used to refer to teaching in all its aspects in other European languages. Although there are English words sharing the same somewhat obscure Greek roots, in English the meanings of the words are more restricted. Let us clarify what we mean by pedagogy.

First, what makes us say that mankind is the only species with a pedagogical intention, or in other words that actively teaches the young of the species? In what respect are we delimiting the idea of "teaching" here? Or, equally, what do we mean by pedagogy? First, teaching is seen as an activity that deliberately sets out to bring about some sort of change in another member of the same species. Second, the activity directed to bringing about this change is not a casual occurrence. It has to persist until the change is achieved in some measure. Third, and implied by the second criterion if we take it to its logical limit, the teacher has to have grounds for evaluating the behavior, in order to judge if it is satisfactory or not. Then there are aspects of putative teaching that we would wish to exclude, including development according to genetic or cultural patterns, conditioning, imitation of elders or peers, and what could be called accidental learning when imitation leads to an unrelated change of behavior.

Premack (1984), in a fascinating discussion of pedagogy and aesthetics as sources of culture, attempted an analysis from the premise that teaching arises from the need for an older generation to affect a younger one and draws the distinction between genetic solution and the experiential solution. Species that rely on genetics to take care of coming generations simply become adult irrespective of their life experience—members of the insect world are offered as examples—whereas experiential solutions are more complex and varied, involving an intertwining of genetic imprinting, learning, imitation, and pedagogy. Examples have been observed of tribes of animals learning by imitating the serendipitous discovery of one of their members, often a young member, which eventually diffuses through the whole group.

Pedagogy is closely linked to training, and although pedagogy is not seen among animals other than humans, chimpanzees are seen to train other members of the species. In such cases, one chimpanzee is seen to have a goal for the behavior of another, maybe how to walk in pairs or how to reach a piece of fruit, and it intervenes to enable the other to achieve the goal, correcting deviant behavior and repeatedly coming back to the point. Training fulfils the first two criteria for pedagogy: having a deliberate goal for change in another and persisting in intervention until the change occurs. Pedagogy, though, in Premack's definition, also involves the ability to judge or assess the change, and he has found that chimps are actually lacking there. Interest is lost if the trainee resists; there is no personal involvement in the results of the training session; and alternative interventions are not seen. Pedagogy, though, involves *being able to take the part of the other,* being able to judge the success of achievement and being able to adapt the intervention according to a perception of its value to the cause.

Adult humans take the part of the infant other from the moment of birth. It is not only the mother who tries to communicate with baby talk when confronted with a small child, or who uses exaggerated gestures to encourage some sort of behavior! We tend intuitively to make some sort of effort to see the world as the child sees it, empathizing, mimicking, adjusting our speech and behavior. The institutions of education, schools, nurseries, universities, and colleges, have been constructed by society to formalize the human pedagogical project, the effort to transmit one generation's experience, knowledge, and values to the next generation, and teaching is the instrument that has developed to bring it about. A teacher can be seen as one who, as a member of an older generation with a status grounded in an experience of aspects of the world and an experience of transmitting it to members of the younger generation, is accorded the task of transforming ignorant youth into experienced maturity.

This is the phenomenon at the heart of what we mean and encompass by the word "pedagogy." Furthermore, in the traditions of continental Europe, in contrast to Britain and North America for instance, pedagogy is a discipline devoted to scholarship and research in the field of that phenomenon. There are university departments of pedagogy, professors of pedagogy, doctoral theses in pedagogy, and undergraduate majors in pedagogy. Although the discipline is closely related to relevant aspects of what in the alternative traditions are considered to be the foundational disciplines of psychology, sociology, and philosophy, it is centred exactly on the study of the whole field of learning, teaching, bringing up the child, and all related phenomena.

## TRYING TO BRING ABOUT BETTER LEARNING

What might one be able to glean from our book that can contribute to better learning? In chapter 2, we recounted two major studies into how students went about their learning through reading texts, which gave rise to the profound insight into the appearance of and difference between surface and deep approaches to learning. It was seen that most significantly, surface approaches focused on the learning task as such, whereas deep approaches focused on the meaning of the task and the phenomena embodied in it. Furthermore, surface approaches to reading texts go together with inferior understanding of the message and the phenomena, as well as poorer recall performance. The way was seen here to bring about better learning in students: On the basis of the insights into how students who adopted a deep approach tackled the task of reading, texts and tasks could be structured in a better way to induce the same approach in all students. Now, the part of teaching that is most in focus in our book is that of planning learning activities, which is generally known as instructional design, and the message of chapter 2 could be a major insight for planning teachers or instructional designers if it can be built into practice in some way to bring about better learning.

Readers who achieve a better understanding of a text, closer to the author's intention, by adopting a deep approach are known to pause and reflect over how the current passage relates to that which has gone. They try to discern different parts of the text, aim at finding out the main point of each, link the parts to each other and to the whole, and relate the content of the text to their own experience and what they have learned earlier. Why, we can ask, do some students do this whereas others do something else? One possibility is that such differences originate from the perceived demand characteristics of the situation. Students may differ as to whether they believe that they are supposed to understand the text they are reading in the first place or whether they believe that above all else they have to remember the text, being able to recall it subsequently. Thus, studies were conducted in which various manipulations of texts and tasks were tried, that aimed at bringing about traits displayed by students who naturally adopted deep approaches, and then the effects on understanding and recall were examined.

In one such study, 30 students in the economic and political sciences were asked to read the first chapter of a textbook on political science (Marton, 1976). Those in an experimental group were given a text in which each of the five main sections was followed by a set of questions intended to get the students to think in a "deep approach" way, asking, for instance, what main subsections could be discerned, what they were about, how they were related to one another, and how one could summarize the whole section. A control group was given the unadulterated text. Immediately after reading the text, students from both groups were given a test on their understanding of the ideas presented, and a further test was given some 2 months later.

The results were, to say the least, interesting, if not encouraging. The manipulation of the text had a clear effect on how well the students read it, although it was counter to the effect that was anticipated. Surprisingly, the control group, those who had the text in its original form, were able to perform significantly better on the test than the experimental group in both the immediate and the later test.

How can this be interpreted? The attempt to induce a deep approach—discriminating main aspects of a text, seeing their point, relating them to one another and thereby coming to see the overall structure of the text and its meaning—had failed to deliver the performance hoped for. The explanation lies in what the manipulations actually achieved, which was to bring about a radically different demand structure for the experimental group, causing them to focus on the interspersed questions rather than on the meaning of the text itself, so that they became able to mention the contents of various parts of the text in a superficial way without engaging in genuine learning that characterizes the deep approach. The task of reading the text became trivial and mechanical rather than challenging and reflective. Such a text manipulation was dubbed *pointing out* and its effect on learning, *the erosion effect* (Marton, 1976), the whole being a *technification* of learning.

In a parallel study (Dahlgren, 1975), two chapters were given to an experimental group and a control group to read, one after the other. For the experimental group, the first chapter had been manipulated by the insertion of questions directly into the text, not this time aimed at getting the students to tackle the whole text in a particularly structured manner, but rather to address significant aspects of the author's argument. Immediately after reading the first chapter, subjects from both groups were asked questions pertaining to the main arguments and points of the chapter. Then they were directed to read the second chapter, in which no manipulations at all had been made.

Again, it became clear that the experimental insertions did not bring about deep approaches. On the contrary, those in the experimental group performed rather worse in answering questions on the first text they read compared with the control group who were left to their own devices. Furthermore, the experimental group reported finding the first chapter more difficult to read, whereas the control group thought the second chapter was more difficult. Even though the experimental group showed slightly better results in reading the second chapter, which was not manipulated for either group, the overall effect of the manipulation was negative. As in the previous study, students had been focusing on the act of learning rather than on the object of learning.

In yet a third parallel experiment (Säljö, 1975), a different sort of manipulation was attempted, this time attempting to induce alternative approaches in two groups of students. Two groups of 20 first-year students, all female, were given part of Coombs'

(1968) book, earlier referred to in Example 2.1 of chapter 2. The overall intention of this study was to examine a further conjecture about approaches to learning being a function of the perceived demand characteristics of the learning situation.

The two groups were given two chapters with, on the one hand, interspersed questions intended to bring about, respectively, either a deep-type approach related to understanding (questions on the meaning of the text) or a surface-type approach related to memorization (questions of a simple factual nature) and, on the other hand, a final question in common that asked for a summary of the chapter. After reading the third chapter, all the participants were asked to answer the same set of questions, a mix of the sorts of questions to which the two groups had previously been exposed. When the answers to the questions given by the two groups after the third chapter were compared with each other, an effect was clearly seen: The kind of questions they expected, the demands they perceived in the task of reading the text had indeed influenced their ways of reading it.

The most striking effect was, however, that neither of the two groups was better, whatever criterion was used. The effect was that there was a significantly greater variation in outcome in the group which had initially answered the questions supposedly related to understanding. To simplify the results quite a bit, the better half of that group did better, in the sense of having a reasonable grasp of the content of the third chapter, than the better half of the other group, whereas the weaker half did worse than the weaker half of the other group.

A clue for interpreting the unexpected outcome of the experiment is to be found in the accounts offered by some students, which has been characterized as "mentioning." Topics from the text were more or less listed, without very much being said about them. The content simply disappeared. It is suggested that whereas the interspersed questions for both groups had focused on the object of learning (the message of the chapters in one sense or another), the summarizing question had focused on the act of learning, and it was this that had made the greatest impression on the weaker students. Thus, they read the third chapter with the perceived demand structure related to the act of learning, which is associated with a surface approach and a poorer grasp.

A somewhat different attempt to manipulate learning relates to school students reading the allegorical short story written by Franz Kafka, entitled "Before the Law" (Marton et al., 1994), described in Example 7.5 of the previous chapter. After the initial study in which four distinctly different ways of understanding the overall significance of the story were found, a follow-up study compared three groups of students who were given different sets of instructions on how to go about reading the story. One control group was given rather straightforward instructions—to read the text once or preferably several times and then to write down what the text was really about, or what it really meant. The other two groups were given instructions that tried to direct them toward the reflective variation tactics of the more successful students in the earlier study. One group was told to look for several meanings of the law and for several reasons why the man failed to enter the law, and the other group was given a combination of that question as well as the straightforward question posed to the control group.

The result was that when the students were all asked one week later to write down the meaning of the story, what it told the reader, and what the author wanted to say, none of them actually related either of the two more advanced ways of understanding the story. This shows that, at least, the more elaborate instructions failed to bring about the more complex understanding of the story. Furthermore, the more elaborate instructions aimed at *inducing* variation actually had the effect of *reducing* the variation in the ways in which members of the group understood the story in comparison with the variation seen in the control group. Again, the instructions given to certain groups were associated with an effect opposite to that intended. They inhibited rather than enhanced the variation in ways of understanding.

## The Act and Object of Learning

What do these studies tell us? The erosion effect, technification of learning, pointing out, mentioning, reducing the variation in perspective taken—all these are labels of detrimental effects that have been observed when learning tasks are manipulated in an effort to improve learning. We have said that they have the effect of focusing the learner's awareness on the act of learning rather than on the object of learning, and that the demand structure of the learning situation was manipulated along with the text. The students were being guided as to "how" to read the texts and not to the contents of the texts. "How" and "what" were being held apart, and the result was to limit the outcome with respect to "what." In fact it seems as though whereas the researchers tried to guide "the how of learning" as a whole, the students seemed to narrow it even further to the very act of learning, neglecting even the indirect object of learning as we introduced the terms in chapter 5. It can also be noted that only weak support was provided for the notion of pedagogy, "taking the part of the other" being focused entirely on the acts of learning that "the other" might undertake rather than on the object of learning as "the other" might experience it.

Those studies can be contrasted with another (Martin & Ramsden, 1987) in which the results of two programs designed to raise history students' learning skills were compared. One of them used generic material separate from the curriculum content, whereas the other, called "Learning How to Learn," made use of material drawn from the current history curriculum by making it the object of reflection. The students in the latter group were seen to develop more advanced conceptions of learning, in accord with a deep approach, and in addition got better grades on essays and achieved better examination results. Thus, focusing on the object of learning as well as and in conjunction with the way of going about it is found to produce desired approaches and outcomes, whereas separating the what from the how of learning and attempting to train the how without reference to the what is doomed to failure.

## THE TEACHER'S AWARENESS IN TEACHING

If the wish to improve learning is genuine and we have a clear idea of what learning is, based in well-documented and reliable research, and we cannot make manipulative changes to the tasks of learning that appear to be in accord with those results, nor can we train our students in generic study skills that will serve them in many different situations, then what can we do? One point of departure that suggests itself is to look at teachers teaching. What do they do that is identifiably pedagogical? What do they focus on? What dimensions of variation are there in their awareness of the teaching–learning situation? Even if not all learning situations involve a direct teacher, some pedagogical agent must be identifiable in the educational settings we are generally assuming or implying. Let us look at some research into just this issue.

We start by looking at the ways in which teachers' awareness is structured. Alexandersson (1994a, 1994b) posed the question, "What do teachers direct their awareness towards during their teaching?" and to research this, he observed them teaching in their normal classrooms and interviewed them. He filmed 12 teachers teaching a single lesson from their normal teaching duties for 12- to 13-year-old pupils and immediately afterward conducted a lengthy discussion with them in which they were free to comment on whatever aspect of the lesson they wished, with recall stimulated by the film. Subsequently, they were all interviewed using a semi-structured interview, in which matters they had raised in the commenting phase were taken further. Thus in the study the researcher focused, and the participants were encouraged to focus, on their awareness of teaching in the act of teaching.

Alexandersson (1994a, 1994b) identified three ways in which awareness was directed or focused during the teaching activity: toward the activity going on at the moment, toward more general aims, and toward the content that was being taught. A parallel linguistic analysis of the interviews indicated that directedness toward the activity was dominant by far (65% of utterances), whereas directedness toward content focus was least (13%).

Taking this as a starting point, we can elaborate with reference to other studies. For instance, there are studies showing that schoolteachers, in general, focus on their pupils as such, at the expense of the content and the ways in which their pupils understand or experience it. In Alexandersson's terms, this refers to the first two of his categories being more in focus than the third. Take, for example, the study of 36 Swedish schoolteachers reported by Andersson and Lawenius (1983). When they were asked to talk about their work as teachers a distinct lack of mention of content was observed, whether the content of learning or the content of teaching. That was a pilot for a larger study when 53 teachers were interviewed with semistructured interviews around the main topics of concern which by now had been identified. Now, the themes of prime concern for the teachers were found to be classifiable into six areas: aims and goals of teaching, teachers teaching, the frames of teaching, school marks, students with special needs and the school of the future. Once again, there was no mention of content, neither the learning of it nor the teaching of it. As Marton (1994) has pointed out: "We can conclude that out of over one million words uttered by teachers about teaching, not a single one was about the teachers' ways of dealing with some particular content in order to help students develop the mastery of that content" (p. 32).

This result is most baffling. How can teachers so lack focus on what should rightly be at the heart of their work? Baffling or not, they are confirmed by other studies. Annerstedt (1991), for example, found that the majority of the participants of his study—15 each of teacher educators, teachers, and student teachers of physical education—failed to bring up the skills and insights that their subject might be thought to foster in pupils, but focused instead on physical education as an affective aspect of school education or its role in relation to other subjects or more general educational goals.

One third of them did argue that their role was to facilitate their students in developing capacities specific to physical education, both with respect to what they should become capable of doing and in what way they should be able to do it—not only able to jump a certain height, for instance, but also be able to know how to go about it and improve performance. That third, not surprising by now, was predominantly found in the group of teacher educators. Again, when faced with describing the specific professional competence that a physical education teacher should have, compared with, for example, a bank clerk who works voluntarily in a sports club, only 10 of the 45 participants focused on analyzing what their students do or on how to bring about improvement or development. The majority focused rather on the atmosphere they should foster or the management of their activities.

The distinction between focus on content (it is seen as potentially variable) and not on the learners (they are taken for granted) on the one hand and focus on the learners (they are seen as potentially variable) and not on the content (it is taken for granted) was also found by Sundqvist (1993). He gave a text about different theories of political power to each participant in his study comprising two groups of students: student teachers and students of a social science program. In individual interviews they were invited to reflect on the way in which they would teach about its content in school. Although students of both kinds who had newly begun their studies handled the problem very similarly, there was a pronounced difference between those of the two groups who were close to concluding their studies (after 3 to 4 years). The student teachers took the text for granted and focused on the potential variation among pupils, whereas the social science students took the pupils for granted and to a large extent focused on the potential variation in what a text about theories of political power could be like.

Both Annerstedt and Sundquist's results hint at another dimension to the variation between focus on student and focus on content, and that is that the more advanced the level of education, the more the teacher's focus is on content and the less it is on the learner. Now, in the perception that teaching in higher education is not all it should be, there is active development of teaching methods, on which advice is disseminated in an effort to bring teachers' focus on some hitherto unfocused aspect of their teaching, including their students' learning. Trigwell, Prosser, and Taylor (1994), for instance, pointed to the wealth of research into strategies that aim to get university science teachers to go about their teaching tasks so that they pay more attention to individual students and groups of students. Such strategies are based on sets of methods that can be implemented in various situations, and the teacher can apply them to the content of the moment.

Against a background of this research, Trigwell et al. take up the question of what effect such methods and strategies can have in the classroom, or lecture theater, if the underlying intentions of the teachers who employ them are ignored. Their research, based on an interview study of university teachers of first-year physics or chemistry, shows that teachers actually have qualitatively different intentions, whether expressly articulated or not, and they underpin their usage of different teaching strategies. Their intentions and the strategies are logically intertwined. Some apparently student-focused strategies proposed by method developers, such as engaging the students in discussion groups, only effectuate good learning if they are the product of teacher intentions that are directed at least toward their students developing understanding rather than their acquisition of information. The underlying intention of university science teachers, however, is generally focused on the effective transmission of content information, with students coming in only at the receiving end. (In the study referred to, 19 of 24 teachers focused either on the teacher transmitting information or the students acquiring concepts.) The students' learning as such was only peripheral to their teachers, for whom the stuff to be learned was in focus.

This is in keeping with the results of Fensham and Marton (1991), that point to a potential variation in the main thrust of the awareness of content even of teachers with a common discipline, in this case, chemistry. They compared high school and university teachers concerning their views of one central aspect of their discipline, namely theory in chemistry. A feature the groups had in common was that they made a strong distinction between observables and nonobservables, in which, in general terms, the nonobservables count as theory whereas observables have more to do with such aspects as experimentation and observation. Furthermore, the distinction was always made in relation to a person for whom things were either observable or nonobservable. Thus in that respect scientific knowledge was seen as being intimately related to the humans who were involved with it.

The finding that is interesting for our purpose is that a distinct difference was found between the two groups regarding who they considered to be the person for *whom* the observable is observable. The university teachers of chemistry considered themselves to be the observers, whereas the high school teachers considered the observers to be their students. This points to the fact that the university teachers handled their discipline from their own perspective, whereas the high school teachers took more the perspective of their students.

In addition to theory and observation, there was a third kind of entity in the chemistry described in these interviews, namely "basic facts." These basic facts are seen as self-explanatory by both university chemists and high school teachers, although perhaps more clearly so by the former. There seemed to be an idea that words associated with basic facts carry their own meanings, which Fensham and Marton called "the semantic view of knowledge." Thus, seen overall, the results indicate that although the school teachers more readily focused on their students' chemistry than the university teachers did, both groups tended to see the object of learning as self-explanatory.

Now, the whole message of this book hitherto has been one of seeing learning as gaining knowledge about the world or coming to experience some aspects of the world in a particular way. In accordance with this, we are logically constrained to view teaching as a pedagogical effort, that attempts to bring the learners' knowledge about the world to a new pitch, or to bring them to some new way of experiencing aspects of the world. In this aim, the learners and their experience of the world (their knowledge) are inextricably intertwined. It follows that the teacher's awareness (teaching focus and intentions) have to be interwoven equally of the threads of learner and content. This is true of higher education as well as preschool education and all stages in between.

Why are we making so much of this? To return briefly to the work of Alexandersson (1994b), a deeper analysis of the ways he found content to be figural in awareness revealed that it could have two characteristics. Either focus was on the factual content as such (the stuff that the pupils were learning) or it was on the thought content (the ways that pupils were thinking around the stuff they were learning). Alexandersson said of this "That the teacher who carries the structured content in the third main category [i.e., awareness directed towards content (our clarification)] assumes that his or her own thought and that of the pupils comes into contact when a specific content is being communicated" (p. 258).

Here is a powerful idea: the teachers' and the pupils' thoughts coming into contact when a specific content is being communicated. How could that be if the teachers' awareness is never specifically focused on content, as Andersson and Lawenius (1983) found in their schoolteachers? How could it be if awareness is focused on the teacher's own perspective on the content without regard for the students' perspective? How could it be if the chemistry teachers consider chemistry facts to be self-explanatory? A demand for such "thought contact" is that the teacher is aware of the dimensions of variation that refer to content as experienced (how it is understood by the learners) and to the learners as experiencers of the content (how they approach the tasks of learning, how they experience learning itself, how they experience the learning context).

## QUALITATIVE DIFFERENCES IN TEACHING

Just as with learners, there is no doubt that a variation is to be found among teachers in the quality of their teaching. We have all experienced teachers that we felt were good, and just as certainly some that were bad. But what more can we say of such variation than the rather empty good–bad dichotomy? What more can be said about the joint enterprise, the teacher teaching and the learner learning in a more or less coherent collaboration, with the contact between their thoughts that Alexandersson described? What can we identify in the teacher's teaching that might lead to a variation in how students learn what they are intended to learn? Now we are not talking as much about variation that occurs in one and the same class as about the result of the learners approaching the tasks in different ways and achieving different outcomes. We are thinking more of the variation between classes owing to the teaching of different teachers. Inasmuch as teachers have a pretty free hand with what happens in their classrooms, it seems reasonable to expect some sort of difference in what they produce. As we have pointed out, the way in which learners experience and understand what they learn and the ways in which they go about learning it are the most critical aspects of learning. It seems reasonable to expect teachers' ways of experiencing the "what" and "how" of their teaching to be a key aspect, or *the* key aspect, of their teaching.

Patrick's (1992) study goes further than Alexandersson's in that it investigates the different ways in which teachers experience and handle the content of their disciplines. She related ways in which teachers of history and physics to Australian school students in their two final years understand their subjects as the matter of teaching, and how their students correspondingly understand it. She showed that the ways that teachers experience teaching their disciplines, and their disciplines as teaching matter, affect the ways in which they communicate them as well as the ways their students handle them.

She distinguished three broad groups of history teachers, focusing on how they speak of their subject and how they teach it—how they experience it, we could add. One group emphasized the delivery of the material, presentation, and technique. The subject matter and their students' relation to it was unproblematic. Their teaching focused on delivering history, defined by them as the content of the course, to their students, and they spoke of teaching it through words such as "give," "show," "look at," "see," and "do." They wanted their students to get an imaginative grip of the topics they were studying, encouraging excursions to historic sites and seeing films of or about the periods studied. They saw their students' difficulties as arising from laziness or lack of interest in the subject, which they saw as being concrete, perceptible, and knowable.

The second group of history teachers saw their students' learning as having two phases: acquiring and accumulating necessary information and interpreting it to achieve understanding. They expected their students to "look at," "recognize," "come to see," "understand," "see the structure of," and "see points of view in" the history they were tackling. Learning history is seen by teachers in this group as problematic, and the teacher's role is to help the student come to see it. However, the way in which they might see it was taken to be rather unproblematic. The students were simply to share the teacher's understanding because historical knowledge was not problematic in itself. On the contrary, it was something to be acquired and discussed, recognized, and contemplated.

The third group of history teachers that Patrick identified saw learning history as a process of developing interpretations from the outset. For them, historical knowledge was far from unproblematic. The way in which material was approached by the students, the questions they were asking and discussing, and the way they were relating aspects to one another were constantly in these teachers' focus. Particular ways of seeing the ideas being treated might be proposed because they represented some normative way expected by examiners, but they were not treated as privileged. The teacher shared the process of grappling with the content with the students in an attempt to get them to "think," "connect," "change," and "grow."

That the knowledge they were coming to terms with was contingent was implicit in the way they engaged with their students' learning.

Corresponding to these overriding differences in ways of conceptualizing the historical content to be taught and the ways of understanding the students' learning are distinctly different ways for the students to meet the history they were studying. The students were seen to construct[1] an object of study in a mold their teachers formed. When asked in an experimental situation at the end of the two years covered by the study to read an historical passage, and when asked about the content and the arguments it contained, there was a remarkable match between the ways in which the teachers and their students faced it when viewed as an historian's account of some piece of history—whether they saw it as unproblematic or as argumentation with respect to culture, perspective, argument and the role of the historian.

Physics was also described by Patrick as taking on different meanings for different teachers. They establish different curricula at the classroom level and teach accordingly. She described the teachers as constructing objects of study for their students, arguing that teachers actually present their students with different objects of study, which embody different conceptions of what is to be studied. She pointed to one set of physics teachers who understand physics to be a way of understanding the natural world, and who tend to construct objects of study reflecting that, asking their students to observe, formulate hypotheses, and give priority to the meaning of what they are faced with rather than the details such as names and formulae. Questions are posed that lead the students toward the heart of the object of study rather than to its periphery, emphasizing, for instance, the observed relationship between change and force in Newtonian mechanics, and this is done by getting the students themselves to work things out. Another group of teachers see physics as practice, as a set of theories that provide an explanatory system. They focus on enculturating the students into the scientific practices of physics and offer them an object of study comprised of the models of physics and the concepts of physics. A third group of teachers who Patrick classified as seeing physics as calculations, construct an object of study composed, as one might expect, of formulas and equations. Accordingly, the students of three such teachers learn, in the first case to understand phenomena, in the second case to solve problems, and in the third case to recall and apply formulas. As their objects of study have been constructed, so are their objects of knowledge.

This study highlights that teachers teaching exactly the same formal curriculum actually mold it according to their ways of understanding the subject as a whole. Although they might have just the same education and length of service, know exactly the same facts, understand the central concepts in exactly the same way, and so on, they nevertheless form and present their subjects in ways that differ radically. Their students thereby gain access to radically different contents of learning.

The teacher is molding an object of study, and that is what the students direct their awareness to in their learning. The object of study may vary from teacher to

---

[1]Partick used the term *construct* and its derivatives in the way we use the term *constitute*.

teacher within the constraints of a single specified and adhered to curriculum, and that leads to a variation in what students have the opportunity to learn. Then, the ways in which they tackle the act of study, their approaches to the tasks, bring about another dimension of variation, as we have argued in our earlier chapters.

## PEDAGOGY AND LEARNING

Now, pedagogy actually covers a good deal more ground than we are considering in this book. Even the ideas coupled with the word learning extend beyond our limits, which are drawn around learning in an academic (university, school, pre-school) context, and are focused on learning as gaining knowledge about the world, coming to experience aspects of the world in particular ways. Pedagogy as a discipline extends to considerations of the development of health and bodily fitness, social and moral welfare, ethics and aesthetics, as well as to the institutional forms that serve to facilitate society's and the individual's pedagogical aims.

We are modestly but deliberately constraining ourselves to the sort of pedagogical situations in which a student or pupil is engaged in an effort to learn (gain knowledge) about some aspect of his or her world in collaboration with a teacher or instructor, or equivalent substitute. In the rest of this final chapter we look at certain pedagogical aspects of learning. We consider first what it takes to bring about better learning. We observe some efforts that have failed and others that have succeeded. As far as the latter is concerned we in particular examine the pedagogical implications of the relevance structure of the tasks and the nature of variation in learning.

In chapter 1 we discussed Meno's paradox in its several forms, all of which amount to the impossibility of learning anything because the learner either must already know the stuff or is otherwise unable to recognize it when encountered. We mentioned in passing there that Plato had earlier recounted a dialogue between Socrates and Protagoras on the question of the possibility of teaching being able to bring about learning, which was countered, Meno-style, by the argument that the learner cannot know that what the teacher is teaching is true or right unless she already knows it—paradox! Plato's solution to Meno's paradox was his theory of recollections.

By now we have solved that paradox in a much more fundamental way, pointing to the failings of the dualism that was inherent in Plato's epistemology, and which survives today, not only in the popular taken-for-granted views of knowledge and learning, but also to a considerable extent in the scientific approaches of the cognitivists, the individual constructivists, and the social constructivists as well. The nondualistic picture that we have been putting forward throughout this book brings the learner and the phenomenon being learned into one and the same world of experience, thus solving the paradoxical notion of never being able to learn. How can we solve the paradox of teaching?

The solution again lies in questioning the dualism that is assumed. If we see the teacher's knowledge in terms of mental models or images of aspects of reality, then we can reasonably ask what they bring to the learner's task of learning. How do these mental models figure in teaching? How do they pass across to the learners? How do the learners' models relate to the teacher's reality? How can the teacher know whether or not they conform to the teacher's models, the basic demand of pedagogy? We suggest that such questions are unanswerable.

In adopting instead the nondualistic assumption that we have now expounded, we change the form of such questions to focus on meetings of awarenesses, which we see as achieved through the experiences that teachers and learners undertake jointly. This relates also to the notion of pedagogy, in that teachers mold experiences for their students with the aim of bringing about learning, and the essential feature is that the *teacher takes the part of the learner*, sees the experience through the learner's eyes, becomes aware of the experience through the learner's awareness. If we, in accordance with our nondualistic stance, consider the learner to be internally related to the object of learning, and if we consider the teacher to be internally related to the same object of learning, we can see the two, learner and teacher, meet through a shared object of learning. In addition to this, the teacher makes the learner's experience of the object of learning into an object of her own focal awareness: The teacher focuses on the learner's experience of the object of learning. Here we have the "thought contact" that Alexandersson describes, or, as Patrick describes more specifically, the teacher molding an object of study to which the learner directs her awareness.

What does this tell us about successful teaching? What does it take for a teacher to mold an object of study that affords successful learning? How do teacher and learner achieve "thought contact"? Our answer, which we will elaborate in the remaining sections of this chapter through a number of examples, refers back to our nondualistic claim and the principles of learning to experience which we developed in the previous chapter. In order to bring about a meeting of awarenesses, the teacher has to take the part of the learner, and the principles we are espousing are those of building a relevance structure and employing the architecture of variation in forming the object of study.

These two principles correspond to, or are derived from, the two main aspects of learning dealt with, mostly through examples, in the previous chapter. But in spite of having just said that we do not believe that principles of teaching can be derived from principles of learning, we do in fact believe very strongly that such can be done. Are we actually saying "yes" and "no" at the same time?

No, indeed we are not. What we are arguing is that it is possible to specify certain conditions that are necessary for learning of the kind we are interested in having take place. Whatever teaching method one may use, based on whatever so-called principles of teaching, it must address certain features of the learner's experi-ence—a structure of relevance and a pattern of dimensions of variation—if it is to bring about certain qualities in their learning. How something could be taught, how it should be taught, what method of teaching one should use—such prescriptions cannot be derived from any statements about learning. To be sure, there is never one way of teaching something. On the basis of the arguments we have developed about the nature of learning, we are able to specify necessary qualities of learning that teaching should bring about,[2] and within the infinite set of feasible teaching methods satisfying these constraints, we have exemplified reasonable and successful instances of the pedagogy of awareness that we are advocating.

## THE FIRST PRINCIPLE OF TEACHING TO EXPERIENCE: BUILDING THE RELEVANCE STRUCTURE

As was discussed in the last chapter, any learning situation or any situation at all has a structure of relevance for those who experience it, aspects of the situation that indicate what it is aimed at, what it demands, and where it will lead. This is the first principle we wish to analyze as a thread in bringing the teacher's and the learner's awareness into contact.

### Example 8.1: Building a Relevance Structure for Meeting Abstractions

Székely's (1950) experiment, described in the previous chapter casts light on the principle of the relevance structure. You will recall that a demonstration of a torsion pendulum was given to two groups of students accompanied by a short text dealing with the physics concepts involved, which was given to one group after they discussed the demonstration and to the other group in advance of the demonstration. The two groups were subsequently asked to predict behavior which involved just the same physics, and it was found that those who had seen the demonstration first succeeded much better than the others. This indicated that the students whose curiosity was aroused by the somewhat puzzling demonstration had more successfully learned the physics principles described in the text, in that they were able to apply them to a novel situation. The demonstration paved the way for the students to understand the principles involved. It created a relevance structure.

This is an example of our first principle, that the teacher should stage situations for learning in which students meet new abstractions, principles, theories, and explanations through events that create a state of suspense. The events, whether a single demonstration as in Székely's work or a slow buildup as in the work we will come to next, serve to present a shadowy whole, a partial understanding that demands completion and challenges the learner to accomplish it. The whole needs to be made more distinct, and the parts need to be found and then fitted into place, like a jigsaw puzzle that sits on the table half-finished inviting the passerby to discover more of the picture.

---

[2]As we pointed out in the section "Explaining Change and Bringing About Change" in the previous chapter, we do not have to be able to explain the presence of a relevance structure or a pattern of dimensions of variation from the point of view of learning in order to bring about change. To achieve that, it is sufficient to ascertain the presence of the relevance structure and the pattern of dimensions of variation in the learner's experience by pedagogical means.

## Example 8.2:  Building a Relevance Structure
## Using the Children's World

For more than a decade Ingrid Pramling and her research group have been carrying out systematic work in early childhood education very much along the lines advocated in this book. The approach is not based on certain procedures and certain materials, but on the idea that what children should learn in the first place is to experience things in certain ways. To make this happen, the situation must have a relevance structure conducive to such an end. Furthermore, the teacher (or the researcher) has to find the educationally critical aspects of the ways of experiencing something that is to be facilitated and to bring about variation in these usually taken-for-granted aspects.

To a large extent, the teacher is making use of everyday activities in which the children are involved and is thematizing different aspects of them to develop the children's understanding of the social and physical world, numbers, the idea of literacy, and so on. Children's own questions often turn out to be excellent points of departure. Almost by definition, they impose a relevance structure on the situation that is a natural framework for learning.

Let us take one example (Pramling, 1996). While working on the theme "growing new plants," the question was raised by one boy: "Which is larger, the sun or the earth?" The teacher wisely responded "Well, what do you think?" From that point of departure a discussion developed thus:

Marcus:  "The earth because there is air there"
Johanna: "The sun because it can shine so far away."
 Ingrid:  "They are the same, because the sun can shine all over the earth."

The teacher pointed out that the sun cannot be both larger, smaller and the same and asked them how they would go about finding out the answer to the question (p. 578).

Suggestions were put forward, like calling the radio station because they have a space rocket for finding out about weather, and calling the television company because they also study the weather. Stig added that you could go into space yourself and look, whereas Marcus decided to ask Håkan, because "he goes into space sometimes"! Gabi, on the other hand, decided to think about it, and Ingrid decided that her mother could read it for her in a book, which Nanette thought was a good idea too.

At the end of the school day, when the parents fetched their children home, the teacher talked to them and told them what suggestions had been made. The next day they came furnished with some sort of information from the radio station, from books, from their space-traveling friends. On a diagram that the teacher drew in which the sun and earth were depicted with the three alternative relative sizes, the children all chose the one in which the sun was larger. Thus, from a question they posed and took up themselves, they gained knowledge, and they learned about how to go about gaining knowledge from the variation within the group.

## Example 8.3: Building a Relevance Structure
## Appropriate to Learning to Read and Write

A second, rather different example, concerns the school-starters who are about to learn to read, like those we touched on in the previous chapter. In an attempt to empower the group of children who had no idea of why one would want to read and write, and who later showed little progress in learning to read, a program of preparation was embarked on in preschool (Dahlgren, Gustafsson, Mellgren, & Olsson, 1993). It aimed at introducing the children to the culture of written language by trying to stimulate and develop their awareness of it in different ways. The program emphasized, and tried to make it clear to the children, that the written language, through its particular construction—letters, words and sounds and meaning, sentences and pages of text—has a communicative function that has many areas of use for children and adults. It also aimed to involve not only the preschool teachers and the children themselves, but also their parents, so that the children were supported in a coherent way. The authors say:

> The main principle was to immerse the children in a stimulating environment of written language. The immersion took place together with a teacher who gently and responsively helped the children to relate to the written language and its potential. Another important point was that the children should see the tasks undertaken as meaningful, so that plain exercises were avoided and the immersion occurred in connection with, for example, baking, theme work, and genuine communication situations. (p. 93, our translation)

At the beginning and at the end of an 8-week trial, children from two trial classes and two control classes were interviewed about how they understood written language, writing, and reading. To take one aspect of the results we can see how both the trial and control classes fared in seeing the value of being able to read and write. Three categories of response were identified in the totality of interviews. One category comprised answers that amounted to not knowing what use it was to be able to read and write; a second category saw it as being demanded by others; and the third category understood the ability to read and write as necessary for communicative reasons. By the end of the period, 89% of the children in the trial classes understood the communicative use of being able to read and write, compared with 57% at the start, whereas the most significant change in the control classes was that the proportion of children who see the ability as a demand from others increased from 33% to 42%. This indicates clearly that a far smaller proportion of the trial class children entered school bereft of the notion that reading and writing fills a need that transcends the demands of others. Again, a relevance structure had been created in which the children had been put into a situation of readiness for and positive anticipation of the coming tasks of learning to read and write.

Another aspect of the results refers to the way in which the children in the two groups understand, through their actions, what writing is about. There were eight distinct ways identified: mimicking scribble, playing at writing, drawing meaningless letters, copying what another has written, drawing the meaning of what is said, discovery writing using current skills, conventional writing, and writing simple sentences (Dahlgren et al., 1993, pp. 96–98). Most of these names are self-explanatory, and for the purpose of the resulting comparison, it is sufficient to say that starting from no genuine writing at all (mimicking scribble and playing at writing) they come closer and closer to genuine writing (conventional writing and writing simple sentences).

The diagrams in Fig. 8.1 show the progress made by children in the experimental and the control classes. It is clearly seen that the experimental group show a greater change toward more advanced ways of understanding writing than the control group, and also arrive at more advanced understandings, on the whole.

## Example 8.4:  Building a Relevance Structure
## Appropriate to the Development of Arithmetic Skills

With a point of departure in her research into how children experience number, and the observation that some ways of experiencing number fail to lead to arithmetic skills, Neuman (1994; already referred to extensively in earlier chapters) carried out a teaching experiment. One important feature of the teaching approach devised was that it deliberately set out to create in the children the need to deal with numbers in all their forms: ordinal numbers and cardinal numbers, discrete objects and continuous quantities, Arabic number symbols, and Roman numerals as well as tally marks.

The children played a game, set in the land of Long Ago, in which there was no mathematics at all—"no counting, no digits, no measures, no coins, no schools with a subject called maths on the time-table. There was no maths at all" (Neuman, 1994). But the game created situations in which the people living in Long Ago could not act without developing some sort of numbers. For example, finding out if people had been treated fairly, been given equivalent payment for the work they had done in the form of material and oil, for example. These continuous quantities had to be measured, the children decided, and they were able to devise and make use of suitable measures to do so. Thus the concept of measuring and the notion of a unit was developed, because units were the only satisfactory way of ensuring the accuracy of measurements in order to make good comparisons. One example Neuman described was that of checking the amount of oil that had been distributed, which was represented for the children with water. A glass was chosen as the unit and the water/oil was measured glass by glass, which was tipped into a bucket. Then the problem arose that the units disappeared when the glasses were emptied, so it was impossible to check if the two payments had been equal. The need arose for a symbolic representation—number symbols. Raising fingers was one suggested solution; drawing lines on paper was another.

Counting discrete quantities raised other problems. Counting sheep, for instance, led to so many lines that it was impossible to get an overview of them, and to be able to compare them once again. Now something akin to Roman numerals was devised: four strokes, IIII, represented 4 and five strokes could be grouped into

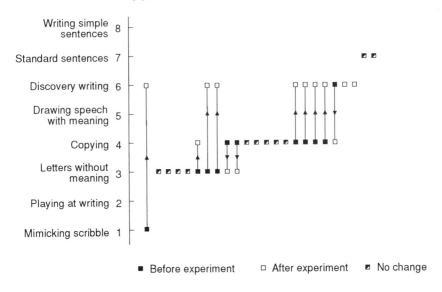

CONTROL GROUP

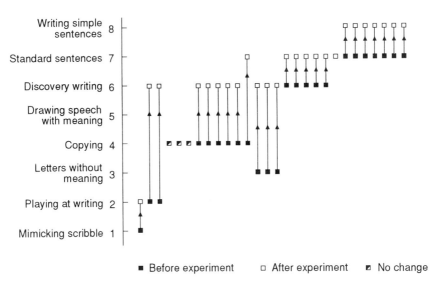

EXPERIMENTAL GROUP

FIG. 8.1. The ways in which reading and writing were understood by the children in the experimental and control groups (from Dahlgren et al., 1993, p. 98, our translation).

a V, whereas ten could form two Vs arranged as an X. The idea behind encouraging Roman numerals was their handlike structure and origin. Eventually, Arabic number symbols were introduced and ordinal and cardinal numbers too, as well as symbols =, <, >, +, and –. Thus the land Long Ago became more and more like the world the children lived in, and the need for the devices of arithmetic was created also there.

We return to this land and its results in Example 8.6 later in this chapter.

## THE SECOND PRINCIPLE OF TEACHING
## TO EXPERIENCE: THE ARCHITECTURE OF VARIATION

The second principle for teaching we wish to promote is that of designing learning situations around the architecture of variation: Whatever the content of instruction is, the object of study which the teacher forms or molds has several faces for the learner to glimpse and mesh into the whole. These faces are partially coincident with the different ways in which learners are found to experience the content, and other faces might be produced by the teacher's own understanding of the wider field from which this particular content comes and into which the learners should link it. There has to be a dimension of variation, which is to say that the variation has to be applied to something that might otherwise be fixed, taken for granted. We now describe some examples of studies in which such dimensions of variation have been introduced.

### Example 8.5. Learning to Learn

In Example 8.2 earlier we talked of Pramling and her research group's work in early childhood education. We emphasized that by taking the point of departure in the children's everyday activities, their own worlds and to a large extent their own questions, the necessary relevance structures of the situation were created. Here we point to the systematic way in which Pramling makes use of the architecture of variation and refer to some of the results reported.

Pramling's (1983) work started with investigating how preschool children think about learning and resulted in three overriding categories which form a developmental progression: *learning by doing* something (a skill, activity or some form of behavior), *learning to know* something (facts or knowledge), and *learning as understanding* something (getting a different meaning, relating things, or drawing conclusions). These are early manifestations of the experiences of learning discussed in chapter 3, and following the arguments there, Pramling saw that the ways the children went about learning and the consequent outcomes of learning sprang from their ways of seeing their own learning. Thus her project became a study to develop the children's conceptions of their own learning.

The study we recount here was an extensive one in which four classes of preschool children took part. It took place in a realistic setting with two of the classes (C and D) pursuing their normal business as control groups and the other two (A and B) incorporating certain principles into their activities designed to promote the children's metacognitive reflection. All the teachers were very experienced and felt by their colleagues to be competent. In most respects, all classes can be said to have been rather similar. In addition, more than half the children in each of the groups, when interviewed at the start of the year, did not know if they would be learning anything in the coming year, but those who did have some expectations of learning thought that they would learn to *do* something.

Pramling (1992) summarized the differences in the classes thus:

> Teachers A and B ... create situations and events where children have to reflect on both the content, the structure and their own learning, as well as on how they think at the different levels. Sometimes it is a question of moving from the specific to the more general and sometimes the reverse.... Teacher C gives the impression of having a view of child development that implies that they should hear about certain facts, which will then be assimilated by the children who are mature enough for them. Teacher D has a more traditional view of learning as something that is transmitted and therefore presents the children with masses of facts. Both C and D's views of knowledge seems to be that the children must be taught facts first and that understanding will then grow out of these. (pp. 51–52)

The general approach used in Classes A and B is to introduce variation and bring about reflection among the children at three levels: the level of content, the level of structure and the level of learning. This is done mainly by the teacher distinguishing and drawing the children's attention to certain features and making them express their own ideas about experiences of and reflections on those aspects. By doing so, the children are made aware of the variation, the dimension of variation, and of the fact that their own view is just one view of several possible views.

An example on the level of content can be found, one among many, in an experimental class in which the teacher wants to teach about signs and symbols. She wants the children to learn that there are different symbols and that they mean different things that we agree on as conventions (Pramling, 1990; Pramling & Mårdsjö, 1994). This example concerns weather symbols. First, the children are told to make up symbols to denote different kinds of weather, and such aspects of weather as high and low pressure, thunder and lightning, storms, sunshine, cold and warm air. They have already talked about these phenomena. Indeed "weather" has been a theme in the class for a while. When the drawings are complete they are hung around the room, and the children are encouraged to talk about one another's ways of depicting the weather phenomena in symbolic forms: Many of the drawings are similar, whereas others differ widely. They compare their own symbols with those used on television, which they find in a book. They talk about why particular symbols have been chosen, why some are easier to understand and others more difficult. As a way of learning about symbols this is radically different from the more traditional approach in which standard symbols are presented and discussed in order for the children to learn just those symbols, as though they were self-evident and given. Here, alternative symbols are drawn out of the children's own experience and used to raise their awareness of symbols to embrace what they mean for others, what the variation of symbolic meaning can be. In this way, from the activities of their own imaginations and experience they reflect on the variation to be found in others' experience and meaning.

Reflection at the second level, that of structure, can be exemplified by class A thinking about getting drinking water into their homes (Pramling, 1990). In a session lasting many days they discuss various aspects of the problem of getting and using water, most of which focus on the structure of processes involved: the piping of water into the homes, the producing of clean water, the cycle of how water gets used, and the rain cycle. Cycles of purification are schematized; a map of the town with its underground pipes and drains is drawn; experiments are performed with steam, and so on, all focusing on the structure of the different processes. Thus, while the children are learning about water (the content), the variation of how water appears in the structure of different cycles (structure) is made focal and the subject of reflection.

For an example of reflection at the third level, over learning itself, we can return to yet another example concerning weather, this time with the teacher asking the children to predict the weather for the next day. After they have come up with a variety of ideas about what might happen, they are told that for the next day they should try to find out how weather forecasting is done. Returning to the question the next day, they tell one another how they thought weather forecasting worked—the observations that can be made and the signs to be found in na-ture—and how they had discovered these. One had asked their mother, another a grandfather, a third had read about it in a book, a fourth seen information about it on television, and so on. The teacher used this as a point of departure for taking up the various ways in which one can learn, find out what one wants to know. Thus the session takes a metacognitive turn, and the children are given the opportunity to reflect on their learning, coming to know, in itself.

For each class two interviews were administered in which the notion of learning was raised, one held at the start of the study and the other after 1 year. Table 8.1 shows the ways in which the children in the classes understood learning on the two occasions. The first result to note is that after a year the children in classes A and

**TABLE 8.1**
How the Children Understand Learning at the Start of Study (1) and After 1 Year (2).

| | Preschool | | | | | | | |
| | A | | B | | C | | D | |
| Occasion | 1 | 2 | 1 | 2 | 1 | 2 | 1 | 2 |
|---|---|---|---|---|---|---|---|---|
| To do | 16 | 4 | 18 | 11 | 17 | 16 | 13 | 10 |
| To know | 2 | 11 | — | 9 | 1 | 1 | 1 | 5 |
| To understand | — | 3 | — | — | — | — | — | — |
| Don't know | 1 | 1 | 2 | — | 2 | 3 | 1 | — |
| Number of children | 19 | 19 | 20 | 20 | 20 | 20 | 15 | 15 |

B had developed their thoughts about learning more than the children had in the control groups, Classes C and D, as Table 8.2 shows.

Now let us look at what happened when these four classes paid a visit to the natural history museum and took part there in a carefully planned experiment. Pramling had conferred in advance with the museum attendant, who knew nothing of the study nor the different classes' backgrounds, and agreed that he should relate to the children in each group when they visited a version of the ecological cycle in which all the details and the structure would be the same. It consisted of first showing a stuffed bird and listening to its song before going on to consider and discuss what happens when such a bird dies. Beetles come and feed on the carcass, digest the matter they eat, excrete it, and that in turn nourishes the soil it falls on, which feeds the trees that produce leaves that fall to the ground and feed worms, which birds eat. Thus the cycle is complete. All the time, the attendant has been displaying the parts of the cycle in a chain on the floor, and he goes through it again, putting arrows from one link to the next, talking about cycles. The presentation was seen to deviate somewhat between groups, the D group going on to discuss what happens if a part of the cycle is missing, and the C group receiving the final and best-structured presentation. For the A group, the attendant deviated most, in that he talked about the food chain and placed the display into a semicircle to illustrate it until teacher A pointed out that there were aspects of the ecological cycle missing.

After the museum visit, the children were interviewed by an outsider, who did not know which children had been in which groups, with one goal (among several) of discovering how the children understood the presentation. She found four overall ways of experiencing the story that was told. The most complete was experiencing *the cycle as a whole*, seeing how all the parts depend on each other for their nutrition. Next came a way of experiencing that focused on the food chain, observing that certain parts supply food for others, but failing to see it as a whole cycle. Third, the story was experienced as being about fragments of the food chain in which certain parts were held in focus or told one by one. Fourth, details of the story were told in the sense that they were named or mentioned without relating them to one another or to the cycle. Table 8.2 shows the distribution of these ways of experiencing the museum story among the different classes.

The evidence for more advanced experience of the visit to the museum and the presentation of the ecological cycle is overwhelmingly in favor of Classes A and B.

**TABLE 8.2**
How the Children Experienced the Story of the Cycle Told in the Museum

|                    | A  | B  | C  | D  |
|--------------------|----|----|----|----|
| The cycle          | 10 | 8  | 1  | 2  |
| The food chain     | 8  | 6  | 1  | 5  |
| Fragments          | 1  | 2  | 6  | 9  |
| Naming parts       | —  | 3  | 10 | 1  |
| Number of answers  | 19 | 19 | 18 | 17 |

Of the four classes, it was Class A that had actually worked with notions associated with cyclic structure during the year, that understood the ecological cycle to the greatest extent. However, they had received the worst presentation at the museum that had confused the ecological cycle with the food chain, whereas Group C had received the best presentation and yet showed the least advanced understanding. All the evidence of this and other experiments during the year was that the overall difference in achievement springs from the different treatments, which aimed at and brought about children's more advanced ways of conceptualizing their own learning.

## Example 8.6:  Teaching Numerosity

In earlier chapters we have made extensive reference to the work of Dagmar Neuman, who investigated how school starters experienced numbers in the range 1 to 10. You recall that there are aspects of their experience that are critical to their development of arithmetic skills, namely a sensuous experience of the numerosity of numbers, including part–whole relationships that unite ordinality and cardinality. In chapter 6 we referred to one child in particular, Jenny, who expressed the understanding that she had 5 fingers on her right hand and 10 fingers on her left hand. This was a case of understanding numbers as names, in which their ordinality was supreme and cardinality did not appear at all.

Neuman took Jenny as a case for further study, and over a period of 2 months from shortly after school started they had one-to-one sessions together (Neuman, 1994). Now, although one cannot pin-point Jenny's learning to one occasion, there is one occasion in which it becomes obvious. First, let us look at the task on which they were working. There was a toy train that had 10 passengers—small wooden dolls who could sit in the train in pairs, two to a bench, one bench behind the other. Jenny stated that there were 5 dolls in one file, 10 in the other, and 10 dolls altogether, consistent with her understanding of the numbers of fingers on her hands.

In the ordinary classroom, Jenny had been working with the other children with Neuman's land of Long Ago, writing the numbers in different ways, including ways in which their ordinal sense was in focus. For example, on one occasion they wrote the Swedish ordering words 1a, 2a, 3e, 4e, ... 10e[3] on pieces of paper and used them as tabards, such as competitive skiers wear, to identify 10 dolls, which they lined up as if to enter a race. At that time, Jenny could not use the cardinal numbers in any form.

Neuman picked out a number of dolls—two in one case—while Jenny looked away, and then, asking her to look at them, she asked Jenny how many there were. "Two" came the reply. Here Neuman made use of Roman numerals, and wrote two strokes, II, one for each doll, and asked Jenny to write it in "our numbers." Jenny

---

[3]These are equivalent to 1st, 2nd, 3rd, 4th ... 10th in English, but are obviously simpler for the school starters to cope with.

wrote "2." When asked which numbers they were wearing, Jenny replied, "a 7" and "a 2." Now Neuman introduced a variation: "The second and the seventh—there're 2 dolls aren't there?" she asked, to which Jenny reluctantly agreed. These 2 dolls and the number 2 now became the objects of activity, in that Jenny drew the dolls and wrote their numbers above them, and they discussed the fact that there are indeed 2 dolls there, just as Jenny and Dagmar (Neuman) were two girls sitting there together.

This, and other activities, continued and Neuman noted that on 18th November, about 3 months after she started school, Jenny showed a new way of experiencing the dolls present. When asked how many dolls there were altogether, she replied 10. In one file she stated immediately, as usual, that there were 5 dolls. Then, when Neuman asked, "And how many in this file?" she paused for a very long time, finally saying, "There are five there and then nearly the same." "Only *nearly?*" asked Neuman, to which Jenny replied, "Yes." "Aren't they exactly the same?" gets a hesitant "Mm?" Neuman intervenes: "Yes, *exactly* five! *Exactly* the same as here!" which appeared to confuse Jenny. Shortly afterward she reverted to replying that on her right hand there are 5 fingers and on her left hand 10.

Four days later, Neuman introduced a new aspect to the play—she wrote an equals sign, which had been used in the general classroom. In the course of working with the dolls and numbers in various ways, the situation arose in which Neuman and Jenny were sharing the dolls between them, not something that came at all naturally to Jenny. They took one each at a time and wrote a stroke to indicate that they had taken it, arranging their strokes on each side of the equals sign. Eventually they had 5 dolls each—a IIIII appeared on each side of the equals sign—and Neuman asked Jenny which dolls she had. Looking at their labels, she stated, "number 7, number 8, and then ... (she has to count) 10 and 2 and 9." Coming up with the number for the doll with the 10e label was an effort, and she dropped the specific form of the label in favor of the counting form, but recovered when saying which dolls Neuman had taken: "number 6 ... number 5, number 3, number 1, number 4." She agreed that they had the same number of dolls, and that IIIII was equal to IIIII, just as was the case with alternative numerals, $V = V$, or $5 = 5$. When now asked how many dolls there were, she counted quietly and said "10," writing "X." "Yes, there are ten dolls" agreed Neuman, "5 dolls and 5 dolls make 10 dolls. Can you write ten using the other numerals?" To this Jenny responded by writing "10."

Now comes the usual question from Neuman: "How many fingers have you got on this hand?" "Five" replies Jenny. "And on this hand?" Let us quote Neuman here:

Now something unforeseen happens. Almost before I have posed the question, Jenny shouts "Five!"—"You know it!" I exclaim, astonished and very happy. The lesson then goes on with other themes, but before it has finished Jenny has put the dolls back in their train. Then I say, just to see Jenny's reaction: "How many are five plus five, then?" To my surprise Jenny immediately begins to count under her breath and answers "ten," in spite of the fact that I used the abstract and general expression "five plus five." To test if my growing hope is to be dashed once more, I pose the same question in a new context: I ask how many toes Jenny has. She takes the shoe and sock off one foot and begins to count: "(mumbling) … four five … I know they, that they're … (mumbling). "—"How many toes in your other sock, then?" I ask. Once again, Jenny immediately shouts "Five!!" happily and with great confidence. Now, however, comes the critical question: "And how many are there on both feet?" Jenny seems to expect this question, beginning her counting even before I have posed it, since again—happily and almost immediately—she exclaims: "Ten!!" (Neuman, 1994, p. 359)

This rather long account is an attempt to catch something of the flavor of Jenny's insight into the mystifying world of number and how it came about. In sharing out the 10 dolls and maintaining an invariance between the shares signified by the equals sign, Jenny discerned the 10 separate objects, each with its own name, that constituted the "tenness" of the dolls in the train. She saw that each of them was part of one share or the other—one set of five or the other—at the same time as being part of the "10." Each of 5 separate objects was seen to constitute a "5" and the two "5s" together were seen to constitute just the same "10" that was the starting point. This insight, transferred to her fingers, and later to her toes, indicated, perhaps for the first time, that the numbers 1 to 10 are not fixed in an ordering, that individual members of the set of 10 can be reordered to make up other numbers, in this case 5. This amounts to an insight into cardinality—that 5 has a fiveness and 10 has a tenness that relates to the numerosity of number—the path to arithmetic skill—and not to the name, which is one way toward arithmetic difficulties. Crucial to bringing about this insight is the separation of the two aspects of number, cardinality and ordinality, through systematically varying one while holding the other constant. The activities are designed to mold the learner's awareness. This is in line with the way in which a way of experiencing is separated from the way it is expressed, by allowing the latter to vary while the former is fixed, as described in chapter 6.

Thus, Neuman's individual work with Jenny, coupled with the principles of the land of Long Ago that the whole class was working with, showed a positive effect. But how did it go across the group as a whole? The teaching experiment was continued over 2 years, and the children who initially showed particular difficulties, especially an inability to do simple sums without keeping track by double-counting, were interviewed at the end of the second year (Neuman, 1987). These 11 children were compared with 13 children who were at the same level when they started school but who were placed in the control classes where instruction was of a traditional type. The basis of the comparison was the approach to and the result of doing the problems in Fig. 8.2.

$$6 + 8 = - \qquad 14 - 6 = - \qquad 82 - 7 = - \qquad 47 = 6 = -$$
$$7 + 5 = - \qquad 13 - 7 = - \qquad 36 - 8 = - \qquad 58 = 6 = -$$
$$8 + 7 = - \qquad 15 - 9 = -$$

FIG. 8.2. Addition and subtraction problems used to compare experimental and control groups after 2 years.

Remember that the aim of the teaching experiment was to induce a sensuous experience of the numerosity of number. One experience that is absolutely not in accord with the aim is that expressed in keeping track by counting and then counting the counting words that are said (double-counting). None of the children, neither experimental nor control groups, had used that method on starting school. Of the children in the experimental class, none used that way to solve any of the problems in the interview after 2 years either, whereas 25% of the problems solved by the control children employed just that method. Furthermore, comparing correct answers achieved, the control group made errors in 43% of the problems, whereas the experimental group made errors in only 4%.

More recently, Neuman's ideas on how to bring about numerosity as a path to arithmetic skills have been implemented in a series of computer programs that can be used with young children (Ekeblad & Lindström, 1995). In one that has been the subject of recent study, a child sits before a computer and on the screen sees a number of objects—between 1 and 10—organized in two moving pattern groups (e.g., 7 organized as a dice-five and a pair, each of which group can move). A special keyboard replaces the usual keyboard, having only 10 keys arranged on which a child's fingers can rest. When the child sees how many objects there are, she depresses the corresponding number of keys, using any combination of fingers. If the answer is correct the child gets as many points as there are objects. The number of objects can increase and they can move with greater speed. Now here are several variations of significance: the number of objects and the number of keys that need to be pressed on the one hand, and the spatial arrangement of the objects, which are arranged in groups of two patterns that move, plus the combinations of fingers that can be used on the other hand. The child's focus is on the number of objects and getting the number of fingers right, but at the same time she is subject to the spatial variation and the different finger patterns that she can achieve. As the child gets more and more correct answers, the number of objects increases up to 10, and the speed increases until everything goes too fast to work with—the game is over, for today at least!

This game was used with an experimental class and a control class, of 21 and 16 preschool children, respectively, aged 6–7, who in Sweden would not have received formal instruction at all (Ekeblad, Lindahl, Lindström, Marton, & Packendorff, 1996). Both classes were given a pretest and a posttest of 17 simple questions administered in individual interviews such as "How many are 5 and 4 added together?" and "You have 3 kronor and want to buy an ice-cream costing 7 kronor. How much more money do you need?" They were also asked to give examples of how many of 9 marbles could be placed in each of two boxes, a task used by Neuman, as mentioned earlier.

An analysis of the ways in which the children tackled the questions showed that for all 17 problems those in the experimental class improved their capability more than those in the control class, with no measures other than using the computer program having been taken. Children who were weakest at the outset improved most, and in spite of some difficulties with language (the majority of the children came from non-Swedish-speaking families) the children in the experimental class became more able to explain how they thought. Children in the control group, in contrast, showed little, if any, improvement between the two test occasions, in spite of the fact that they had been working explicitly with word problems whereas the experimental group had not.

## Example 8.7:  Learning About Inexactitude

In Example 7.6 of chapter 7 we described children working in groups, employing different approaches to an initially intractable problem concerning the inexact decimal representation of the fraction one third. Here we return to that study and use it to illustrate the teacher's role in making use of the variation in approaches to the task exhibited by members of a group. Let us enjoy an extract from one discussion between Alexandra, Karolina, and Lotta, who have just rather easily solved the previous problem, that of the size of each of four equal pieces. Now they turn to the next problem and first try the same result—25%. Lotta is the proposer, Alexandra opposes the idea, and Karolina tries to see if it could be right.

The girls think quietly, drawing their figures:

"See how smart I am" says Alexandra while drawing a figure. "It must be something and a half ... it's something and a half I'm telling you."

"Half?" asks Karolina, and laughs "do you mean something with 5 then?"

"It could be 37 and a half," says Alexandra. "It's a guess. But it's not right actually."

[Alexandra tries some different numbers, as does Karolina]

"I was thinking 32," she says, "but maybe it's 33," she continues enthusiastically. "No, that'd be 99."

"Good grief!" says Alexandra, "then it has to be bigger. No, that can't be right either. Now, I don't get it. It must be more. 'Cause 33 ... 33 and 33 and 34, that's possible."

[Alexandra turns to Lotta] "What do you think?" she wonders. "That's possible: 33 and 33 and 34. Look, that's ... that's 101."

[The observer asks the girls what they have decided and Alexandra answers]

"It's 33 and something"

"Yes, 33 something," agrees Karolina.

"Yes, so it has to be ... one divided by 3. And then you write whatever it is, the little number, there alongside the 33, that's it."

[The observer wonders what little number it might be.]

"33 point 3 ... 33 thirty something," suggests Karolina.

"Yes, but then you've got one over haven't you," says Alexandra.

"Yes, you have," agrees the observer.

"Yes, so you've got to divide it," continues Alexandra.

"How can you do that?" asks the observer.

"Divide it into three parts," says Alexandra.

"What will that be?" wonders the observer.

"It'll be 33 point 33 ..." says Alexandra.

"Is that right?" asks Karolina.

[The observer writes the girls' suggestion on the board. ] "Write a three there," suggests Alexandra. "No, that's wrong. You've got to have one more in any case ... no!" she exclaims.

"Can I get closer?" asks the observer, but Karolina thinks not.

"Yes, carry on," says Alexandra and laughs. "Write some more threes."

[The observer adds another 3 in the next decimal place.]

"No, it's 9 every time," says Karolina.

"Yes, every time," agrees Alexandra.

"And so it gets more and more all the time," says Karolina and laughs again.

"Yes, it's getting closer," adds Alexandra.

The discussion continues like that, the girls trying their suggestions on the board, grappling with the difficulty of always getting a 9 at the end of the sum of the three parts, however many 3s they added in the decimal part.

"But look here," says Alexandra, looking at the drawing they got together with the problem. "How did they do it? Maybe they only drew it so it looked in equal parts. Maybe they didn't work it out."

"But," says Lotta. "I've drawn 100 hearts" and she shows them a piece of paper she has been drawing on. "Can't we divide them up?"

Alexandra and Lotta now turn their attention to the hearts and the task of dividing them into three equal parts. After a while, they tire of trying to count them all, and Alexandra asks for a ruler instead. She wants to measure the diagram they got, and check that the three pieces are indeed equal. During this time, Karolina stands at the board and tries to add 33.4 three times. She gets 100.2, so she adds 33.3 three times and gets 99.9.

"So that's better," she remarks.

"But how far from 100 is it actually?" The observer writes on the board:

$$\begin{array}{r} 99.9 \\ + \ 0.1 \\ \hline 100.0 \end{array}$$

Alexandra looks at the sum on the board: "It works," she shouts.

"Yes, it's the little tenth that's wrong," says the observer.

"Yes, but we can write this, 99 point 9 and then add that little bit," says Alexandra.

They thus come to the realization that 33.3 is an acceptable answer as long as you realize that there is a little error, 0.1, and eventually they improve the answer to 33.33 with an even smaller error, 0.01. They finish off thus:

"Now you're finished. Was it fun?" asks the observer.

"Mmm," answers Karolina.

"Yes," says Alexandra, "great fun."

"Was it difficult?" asks the observer.

"Yes, you really had to think, really!" says Alexandra.
(From Wistedt & Martinsson, 1994, pp. 33–35, our translation)

Thus, the three girls and the observer act together in trying different approaches, adapting an earlier solution first, then looking at the arithmetic, doubting the meaning of the .3, questioning the accuracy of the problem, checking the diagram with a ruler, trying an analogous problem with discrete units instead of lengths, and finally coming to terms with the bit to account for when three equal parts were added together, as an error that can be made smaller.

Look at the role of the observer. The first time she intervenes in this session it is to bring the discussion to a head over how close the 100 could be split up into three equal parts with recourse only to integers when the girls had already come as close as they could. This brings out the insight from Alexandra, with Karolina agreeing, that "It is 33 and something," which is elaborated directly afterwards to "one divided by 3." The observer now focuses their attention on what that "something" or "1 divided by 3" might be. She takes part in the ensuing discussion, but only to keep the girls on their current path of investigating the "something," which is proving rather fruitful. The girls clearly experience the observer as a teacher figure in that they ask if it is right, and she herself assumes that role when she writes their deliberations thus far on the board. "Can I get closer?" she then asks, focusing the girls once more on expressing the "something," rather than on getting it "right." Now she takes a secretary role and writes on the board as she is told. She becomes more passive while the girls take their own paths, measuring the drawing they got and working with 100 hearts. But Karolina persists with her consideration of adding 33.4 three times and 33.3 three times, confirming that the 33.3 is the best they can find. Now the observer once again becomes a participant, serving to focus on the 0.1 error that remains.

What we want to point out here is the role of the observer in this session. Initially, it is she who creates the situation in which the children find themselves, and it is she who molds the group's awareness through now keeping quiet and now intervening. When the variation to be found in the group is roaming free, she holds back and waits for a fruitful instant. Then, she speaks and halts the roaming to bring attention informally to what might be a useful lead. If we were to adhere to the individual constructivist school of thought, we might decry the observer for her insistence on the girls seeing the problem in the same way as she did, forcing them to leave their own construction of knowledge in favor of her preconceived notions. If we were to adhere to the social constructivist school of thought, we might decry her for imposing the problem on the children in the first place. It did not arise from their own world and could therefore not lead to authentic learning. But we do not make either of these objections. We see the observer's role as that of a teacher or pedagogue, effectively bringing the variation to fruition in the form of authentic learning. Remember, these girls had not even met decimals other than .5 and .25 before. Furthermore, they expressed and worked with the very difficult idea (even for much more advanced students) of the error inherent in an inexactly expressed quantity.

## Example 8.8:  Making Use of Expected Variation in the Group

The extract from the work of Wistedt and Martinsson confirms that working in groups is naturally conducive to making use of variation, as Lybeck (1981) demonstrated very convincingly in an earlier study of older school pupils. In Lybeck's study, the variation was deliberately introduced as the material on which teaching was grounded, being the variation in qualitatively different ways in which the students could be expected to understand the concept of density. To go back a step, Lybeck's exploitation of variation in a group was preceded by an interview study in which the ways in which students understood, thought about, and handled the notion of density was thoroughly analysed (Lybeck, 1981). Then in a teaching experiment, an experimental class was taught with a problem-oriented approach, in which the students' own conceptions and ways of thinking about density were transformed into the content of the teaching situation. This meant that in addition to carrying out practical work on the concept of density, they worked in groups in which they were confronted by other students' ways of understanding density. The teacher initiated the process by presenting a problem, that the students experienced in one or another of the already charted ways. He then worked with them to draw out the variation in their ideas, which he raised to focus the learning situation. The variation was exposed to scrutiny. With the help of the teacher, and in the light of the practical work, the different perspectives could be criticized, and a consensus in line with what the teacher saw to be educationally critical could be approached. As Marton (1986, p. 69) commented concerning this study: "The teacher thus functioned as the architect of the pedagogical milieu, the midwife of experience and the sculptor of thought."

## Example 8.9:  Learning to Solve Problems

Ahlberg (1992) conducted a teaching experiment that had some similarities to the previous two examples in that members of groups were exposed to one another's deliberations. She introduced a further form of variation into her teaching—a variation in situation within which certain sorts of learning tasks are met—at the same time introducing a particular relevance structure within the children's own everyday world and world of adventure stories. She introduced 9-year-olds to mathematics problems through a succession of other sorts of problems, early ones which had no mathematical content, then some with a covert mathematical content, and finally conventional mathematical problems to be found in any textbook. Thus the relevance structure of instruction became conducive to solving word problems.

The problems were formulated such that the children could bring reading and writing, storytelling and drawing into the solution process in varying degrees. In this way she integrated the mathematical aspects of problem solving into the world of school as a whole. Furthermore, while some groups of problems were straight-forward, abstract arithmetic problems, and others were word problems, there were also groups in which interpretation of a situation and estimation of a solution were called for, and others that had no tangible mathematical content at all. We see these two aspects of instruction—variation in medium for solution and variation in types of problem, together with the aforementioned variation in situation—as varying what is otherwise taken for granted, namely what a mathematics problem *is*. For most teachers and children there is a stereotypic mathematics problem that has a typical written layout on the page, a typical way of extracting from the words what has to be done mathematically, a typical way of laying out the algorithmic solution, and an absolutely invariable way of stating the answer. The children in the study became able to see mathematics problems as potentially occurrent in a variety of situations, forms, and solutions.

In a way reminiscent of Pramling (described earlier), the children worked in groups and chose from alternative solutions to present to the class, thus revealing and reflecting over the variation of the act and the content of working with the problems. By the end of the term in which the study was conducted, the children proved to do better at solving novel problems of the conventional type than children did in a control group. The children had become quite simply better problem solvers, and it is of special interest to note that it was the poorly achieving girls who made the greatest progress.

Now, according to some situated cognitivists, such word problems are an example of nonauthentic learning of the highest degree (Brown, Collins, & Duguid, 1989). We would argue in the light of this study that although the problems might be nonauthentic for the researchers, they are highly authentic for the children who engage in them. The degree of authenticity, however, might be limited by the extent to which they are relevant to the children (relevance structure) and the extent to which they are subject to variation in dimensions that are otherwise taken for granted (architecture of variation).

## Example 8.10: Variation of the Observer's Viewpoint

Another dimension of variation that has been introduced into the instructional context is that described in the work of Ueno, Arimoto, and Fujita (1990), this time a variation in point of observation. The goal of instruction involved in this study was, once again, Newtonian physics, although from a somewhat different starting point than that which we have considered earlier. This group of researchers hypothesized, on the basis of other research into learning concepts of physics, that students failed to grasp certain aspects of mechanics because they were unable to distance themselves from their earth-bound, their earth-centered, perspective that was taken for granted while the potential for variation was neglected. They automatically gave their own perspective priority and failed to observe situations from other points of view. Ueno et al. set out to change this by means of a computer program, and then sought the effect on their students learning Newtonian mechanics in the traditional way.

The computer program was designed to take a number of questions involving relative motion—the motion of objects relative to one another and that motion relative to the moving earth. A typical question considered in the program is, "How

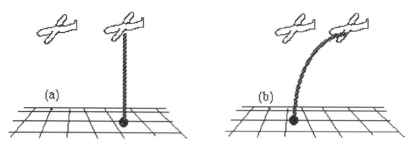

FIG. 8.3. A ball is dropped from a plane flying with uniform motion. It might be seen as falling (a) directly below the normal to the launch or (b) in front of the point of launch, directly below the still moving plane.

is the motion of a ball being dropped from a plane that is moving with uniform velocity to be described?" A common way of predicting the ball's motion is to envisage it falling straight down to land on the ground directly below the point of launch, as in Fig. 8.3a. Now seen from the ground this is an incorrect prediction because on leaving the plane the ball initially has a velocity in the direction of motion, so the ball actually describes a parabolic trajectory and lands somewhat in front of the normal from the point of launch, as in Fig. 8.3b, actually directly under the plane at the same instant. But even this "correct" prediction can be argued with, as it assumes that the earth is still. Seen from a satellite situated high above the plane and the earth's surface, the situation would appear somewhat different in that the rotation of the earth would now be apparent.

The program is designed to allow the user to consider such questions in a variety of frames of reference. As the students progressed through the questions they were asked to account for what they saw, to discuss it, and to compare different situations. In this way, the variation in the frames of reference relevant to each question and the variation of perspective between earth-fixed and outside the earth was made progressively apparent.

Ueno describes two sessions of instruction some four weeks apart. In the first, the motion of various bodies was considered, first with the help of films of genuine situations taken from different points of observation, then with the program giving the students the opportunity to spy the motion from different positions in the system: from the ground, from the plane, or from a satellite high above the earth, in the case of the situation illustrated in Fig. 8.3. In the second session the notions of the inertial system and the equal priority of inertial systems—the relativity principle—were presented. In connection with each of these sessions a pre- and posttest were administered in which a qualitative understanding of motion, relative motion, and, after the second session, force was tested.

The results of the tests showed a convincing improvement in qualitative understanding of basic notions of force and motion, distinguishing now what had previously been a difficulty: appearance and reality. They concluded that learning Newtonian physics involves learning its "metacontext," which specifically involves raising to awareness the variation that is possible in points of observation or frames of reference, which are generally taken for granted as being fixed in the earthbound observer. In this, the computer program acted as an educational device for making the normally taken-for-granted theme of the observer's location and, hence, viewpoint, into an object of variation.

This example points to the incomparable use of the computer to enable the learner to introduce variation to aspects of the object of learning that are not normally capable of being varied. For example, a program described by Diana Laurillard (1995) enables the mass of the earth to be varied, along with other parameters, in a situation of collision of the earth with another object.

## THE ART OF TEACHING ALL THINGS TO ALL MEN[4]

We began this chapter by proposing the somewhat daring thesis that pedagogy is *the* distinguishing feature of the human race, "pedagogy" being used in the sense that one member of a species, by taking the part of the other, engages in acts with the sole purpose of inducing learning in another member of the species.

### The Origin of Pedagogical Practice

Now, if our thesis holds, and humans are indeed distinguished by the pedagogical trait, we would expect them to be capable of exercising pedagogy. As with most human capabilities we would not expect it to be present at birth, but that it would ascend sometime during the individual's lifetime, not too late for the individual to take responsibility for offspring. Ekeblad (1993) might have caught a glimpse of the dawning of this capability in her study of learning elementary math using computer games. In this particular case children in pairs were playing "the gardener game" (in which they were supposed to perceive the numerosity of rapidly changing patterns). The researcher had shown one of the children how the computer was to be handled and explained what the game was about. This child became the "Instructor" who was supposed to assist another child, the "Pupil," with the game. Two distinctively different ways were found in which the Instructors handled the situation.

The Instructor might consider his role to be one of telling the Pupil how to handle the computer game, but it is up to the pupil to find out the numerosity of the pattern. After all, that is what the game is about. For instance (Ekeblad, 1993, p. 3):

---

[4]The first known attempt to establish a science of teaching was made in 1657, when John Amos Comenius published his impressive work *The Great Didactic: The art of teaching all things to all men.* The seemingly sexist subtitle reflects the usage of English at the time when the quoted edition was published and not the attitude of Comenius. In fact he took a firm and explicit non-sexist stance, quite unique for his time. According to its second subtitle, the book was aimed as an "Inducement to found such schools ... that the entire youth of both sexes, none being excepted, shall ... [be] ... instructed in all things necessary for the present and for the future life."

[Task 1—game showing 3 elephants]

> Per    Look at that there now.
>         How many things are there?
> Karin  Three.
> Per    Then you've got to try to get the arrow dow- no, the hand.

In other cases the Instructor tells the Pupil how many things there are and urges her to click on the corresponding figure on the screen with the mouse (Ekeblad, 1993, p. 4):

[Task 1—game showing 4 cars]

> Mats   Now you've got to see how many men come, then go up to the number.
>         Now there're four.
>         Put the arrow on four—with the hand.

The first of these two ways of handling the situation seems to reflect the Instructor's view that his role is to take responsibility for the Pupil's learning. That can only happen if the Pupil is given the opportunity to think for herself, and if the Instructor avoids delivering ready-made answers. It is about showing restraint and letting the Pupil think.

The other way of handling the situation seems to reflect the Instructor's idea that he has to take responsibility for the *Pupil* rather than the Pupil's *learning*, making the Pupil behave in a certain way by telling her exactly what to do.

The distinction between these two ways of handling the task may not appear particularly profound or critical, but whether or not the Instructor tells the Pupil the number she is supposed to find out turns out to indicate a dividing line between two more general patterns of acting. This is how Ekeblad (1993) described these two patterns:

> Asking the Pupil how many things appear seems to imply a willingness on the Instructor's part to assume her capacity to cope with the demands of the game. He does not put the question "How many ..." more than once or twice, but remains in the background, prepared to help with using the mouse if that proves a problem. They mostly follow the game all the same, watching keenly over the Pupil; this is seen clearly if the Pupil takes to saying the number out loud, for then the Instructor happily confirms it. If the Pupil makes a mistake the Instructor steps in and corrects her by giving the right number, and in some cases allowing her to correct the error herself. It sometimes shows that the Instructor recognizes the correctness of not stepping in unnecessarily, as when he happens to say the number but indicates that he should not have done so.
>
> ...
>
> If, on the other hand, the Instructor starts by responding with the numbers there is a tendency for him to carry on doing so, in competition with the Pupil, throughout the game or until she shows herself to be much faster. He also tends to take over the use of the mouse, or put forward particular ideas—where to put the cursor between turns, or how fast it should be. (pp. 4–5; our translation)

Instructors acting in the first of the two ways act in accordance with the idea of pedagogy as it has been developed in this chapter. *They take the part of the other.* Instructors acting in the second way do not do that.

Wertsch, Minick, and Arns (1984) studied how mothers in farm-working families and teachers cooperate with 6-year-old children who have been asked to solve a task. The teachers let the children make their mistakes so they can learn from them, whereas the mothers make the children complete the task without mistakes by telling them what to do. The teachers see instruction, or teaching, as a special kind of activity with the purpose of bringing learning about, whereas for the mothers it is subsumed under a productive activity—mistakes can be expensive in a household. Again, this is the dividing line between the presence and absence of pedagogy.

## Denials of Pedagogy

As should be obvious from our discussion, in this chapter and in the book as a whole, we are committed to the idea of pedagogy. We think it a good thing. But values should not be taken for granted. In a very influential paper, which we could well call "the manifesto of situated cognition," Brown et al. (1989) made a distinction between authentic and nonauthentic activities, as already alluded to in connection with Ahlberg's work on teaching problem solving. Schools are supposed to prepare the pupils for activities outside or beyond the school. There, children should take part in activities of which the long-term aims are to serve other activities. Oversimplifying things a bit, Brown et al. question and criticize this idea. They claim that authentic activities, or authentic practices as they have it, are activities in which learning is not the prime goal, but possibly a by-product. You become capable of carrying out an activity by participating in it, maybe as an apprentice, and not by doing something else. Thus schools, which do have learning as their primary goal, can not easily be places where authentic practice occurs. Not only does this bring into question the practices of the schools of today, which might be seen as less than optimal, but it also questions the very notion of pedagogy. That is a remarkable thing to be able to say about one of the central documents of one of the two orientations that currently dominate educational research. We have referred to this orientation by the umbrella term of social constructivism, and although the diverse kinds of research we lumped together under the label do have certain things in common—an emphasis on cultural, linguistic, social, historical situations of human learning, and cognition—they certainly do not all accept the thesis advocated by Brown et al.

We find another kind of denial of pedagogy in the other dominant orientation in educational research, individual constructivism, at least in its most extreme forms. We accept quite happily the point that learning is contingent on the learner's acts of construction—or constitution, as we would rather say. But going from there to the idea that the learner has to construct all knowledge by herself—which is how the constructivist credo is sometimes interpreted—is taking the argument too far, to say the least. One reason why this kind of constructivism does not work—and never can work—is that it contravenes what we would like to announce as the basic principle of pedagogy: Whenever you fail to get someone to understand something, you have taken something for granted that you should not have taken for granted. Indeed, there are so many built-in taken-for-granted assumptions in the man-made world—the world of ideas such as science, as well as that of a material kind such as instruments, tools, representations—that it is fundamentally impossible for the learner to find out about them on her own. Bergqvist and Säljö (1994) gave a striking illustration of this in the case of the optical bench, a device that enables basic phenomena and principles of optics to be illustrated by providing light sources, prisms, lenses, and so on. When students were encouraged by teachers of a constructivist inclination to see "what things look like," to see "what happens," to "find things out," the "things" being certain basic principles of optics, failure was the outcome. The students did not find anything out, nor did they think it was great fun. The authors' explanation is that "the optical bench itself is a product of a specific theory of optics and … it embodies principles of understanding the world which are discursive in nature and which are not accessible to learners unless they are provided guidance."

An idea central to this book is that there are educationally critical features inherent in capabilities to be exercised in certain classes of situation. A major task of pedagogy, in our view, is to identify such critical features and to focus on them—by building relevance structure, by making use of "the architecture of variation."

In relation to the (individual) constructivist thesis we argue that there are indeed such critical features, and many of them are impossible to discover on one's own because they are theoretically contextual, hidden, taken-for-granted, built in. This is true of the concepts and principles of science, for instance. They transcend the learner's life-world—the world of immediate experience—and fields of consciousness outside it are necessary contexts for understanding these ideas in accordance with what is legitimate within those fields. But left to ourselves we may fail to discover critical features, even of—especially of—entities that are constituent parts of our everyday world, such as numbers, quantities, and texts of quite common kinds. All our examples depict variation in the experience of situations or phenomena in respects that we believe to be critical, and variation between ways in which people experience something implies, to the extent the ways can be hierarchically ordered, that some have better grasp than others. Or to put it more bluntly: Some succeed and others fail. We feel it reasonable to expect pedagogy to bring about more success and less failure.

## Qualitative Differences in Competence in the Workplace

Back to the claims of the social constructivist, or at least of the social constructivist with particular views,[5] that learning boils down to engaging in authentic practices, by which is meant practices in which learning is not the goal itself, but a by-product.

---

[5]As earlier, we delimit our use of the term to those who see learning exclusively as a by-product of authentic practice.

If their thesis were correct, we would expect little or no variation in competence and performance in what they hold up as authentic practices because their claim is that by participating in authentic practices one—everyone—learns. In particular, there should not be much variation in competence and performance acquired through participation in the highly authentic practices of the workplace. Now, it is rather easy to argue that there is at least as much variation in competence and performance in the workplace as there is in schools, or even more, perhaps. We leave it to you, the reader, to judge whether or not it matters which car mechanic works on your car, which chef prepares your food, which surgeon operates on your brain, which economist looks after your money, which violinist performs your favorite concerto.

The point we want to make is that even within one and the same authentic practice there are identifiable differences in competence and performance. It should in principle be possible to uncover the nature of their origins, whatever they might be, and take them as points of departure in enhancing individual levels of functioning. Let us consider an example. At the Volvo factory in the city of Göteborg there is a group of some 50 engineers called engine optimizers, who work on developing the engines for new models of Volvo automobiles. The engines have a number of qualities, such as fuel consumption, durability, exhaust emission, power and so on, and it is the task of the engine optimizer to produce an engine with the best possible combination of properties, subject to a number of legal constraints, by making adjustments to the fuel and ignition systems.

Just as with any other body of professionals, as we pointed out earlier, there is a variation in these engineers' competence. On this there is general agreement, and what is more, the optimizers themselves agree on who is more competent at the job and who is less so. It could be that educational background or years of experience as engine optimizers could account for such difference in competence, but such was found not in fact to be the case. In line with the research approach that this book has been developing, phenomenography, a management scientist investigated this question, seeking insight into the nature of competence (Sandberg, 1994). He studied 20 of the optimizers, selected to cover the range of educational backgrounds and engineering experience, through holding and analyzing phenomenographic interviews that focused on the nature of engine optimization and the nature of the competent engine optimizer, and tried to get them to anchor their general statements in concrete examples of their work. Thus he aimed to make explicit how workers in this category experienced their work, in terms of *what* it is and *how* it is done.

A hierarchical outcome space consisting of three ways of experiencing the work emerged. The least complete of these, I, implying least competence, was one in which competence was seen as accurately optimizing separate qualities of the engine according to requirements, so that the work is organized into a number of separate optimizing steps. At each step one quality is monitored according to a monitoring parameter, and when a satisfactory value has been achieved, the next step is undertaken. This has to be repeated in cycles to take account of interaction between optimizations of the different parameters until all the adjusted qualities combine to make an engine that can be approved. The second way of experiencing the work, II, sees competence as accurately optimizing interacting qualities of the engine in the right order, which is to say that focus has now shifted away from single steps toward working in steps that have a relationship to one other and to the whole engine. Thus, whereas I was an additive view of optimization, II is more of an integrated and interactive view in that the aim of the optimizer is now to optimize a single quality such that it interacts with the other qualities to lead to an approved engine. The third way of experiencing the work, III, as well as focusing on the single adjustments to qualities of the engine in such a way that they lead in interaction to an efficient engine, also focused on the relationship between the approved engine and the putative user. Now, when an optimization is being carried out, the optimizer asks himself how the driver would experience the finished product.

The hierarchical set of ways of seeing the work of the optimizer introduces at each stage a new factor into the optimization consideration. To the individual qualities of the engine, I, is added the integration and interaction of qualities, II, and then the engine is turned round and seen from the driver's perspective, III. Now, these are different ways in which the engine optimizers experience their work and competence at their work, but what does it say about competence in any other way? The most interesting thing is that those engineers who were found to voice the most advanced ideas of competence (III) were actually those who were judged to be most competent by their fellow engine optimizers. Furthermore, competence is seen to depend less on education and years at work than on the way in which the work is viewed.

What we want to illustrate with this example is that within the practice of one branch of engineering there is a range of competence and performance that can be identified as varying with a dimension of the way of experiencing the actual work undertaken.

## The Philosopher's Stone

We have questioned the two currently dominant orientations in educational research: individual constructivism and social constructivism. One earlier point of criticism was that although in a sense they are mirror images of each other, both have a dualistic psychology as their ground. Hence Meno's paradox applies to both: They cannot account for learning. The criticism raised in this section concerns what we called "the denial of pedagogy," which obviously does not apply to all, perhaps not even to the majority, of research brought together under the two umbrella terms. There are, admittedly, educational practices derived from these research orientations that are not easily distinguished from educational practices derived from the research orientation we have advocated throughout this book. Most of our examples of building a relevance structures of situations conducive to learning come very close to trying to constitute an authentic practice (in a wide sense of the word). This is particularly true of Dahlgren and Olsson's (1985) study described in Example 8.3 in this chapter. In Ekeblad's (1993) study, discussed earlier, learners were encouraged to learn from their own acts in accordance with what one could consider to be the epitome of the practice of pedagogy as we have described it, and that could undoubtedly be embraced by constructivists as well as by us.

Our criticism here concerns research and educational practices less than certain ideas associated with certain practices. What we have called "the denial of pedagogy" is the inverted version of what has been—and to a large extent at least outside educational research circles is—the everyday way of thinking about pedagogy: The search for the philosopher's stone, for a method that can be applied generally and that would yield learning in an efficient and impressive way. This is the commonly held idea of what "The art of teaching all things to all men" might be.

To the individual constructivist, there are no such methods. The only way to learn is to learn by oneself. This is supposed to be universally true. Hence in a sense there is a universal method by which learning is brought about. To the social constructivists, there are no such methods. The only way to learn is by participating in authentic practices. This is supposed to be universally true. Hence in a sense they too have their universal method for bringing learning about.

We say there *is* no universal method by which learning is brought about. In this book we spelled out a view of learning that is in itself rather general: We argued that the way in which we experience acts, situations, and phenomena is the most fundamental aspect of learning. We also described some general properties of human experience and human awareness and pointed out some of the ways in which those properties can be used as points of departure for bringing about changes in experience and awareness, or in other words, in bringing about learning. Moreover, that learning is to be brought about by means of pedagogy. Furthermore, we argued that the ways in which we experience and are aware of particular phenomena or particular classes of phenomena are of crucial importance. They are the keys of learning in our meaning of the word. But there is not *one* key, there are as many keys as there are capabilities. There are indeed general mechanisms and general principles—we have tried to make them explicit in this book—but they exist and have to be found again and again as aspects of concrete abilities, definable as particular skills, particular insights, and particular complexes of knowledge. This is to be seen in the mere fact that we have used so many examples, not only to illustrate, but to communicate, the general mechanisms and general principles.

We did not advocate certain methods of teaching. We argued that certain kinds of learning are more fundamental than other kinds of learning. We depicted such kinds of learning in quite a large number of cases. We argued that certain things must happen for certain kinds of learning to come about. There is never *one* answer to the question of how we can make these things happen, but what answers are possible are a function of—and vary with and within—what particular kinds of learning we wish to bring about.

The art of teaching all things to all men springs from the realization that there is no art of teaching all things to all men.

# Epilogue

In the prologue to this book we expressed the hope that our readers would study the whole book to find out about our view of learning and experience, that is, to seek the structure in what we say, to see the parts against the background of the whole, to trace threads from one part of the book to another, to follow lines of thought as they develop from a passing mention to an object in focus, to empathize with the empirical research, and to reflect critically over our conclusions. Thereby, we expressed the hope, that you would learn about learning, become capable of experiencing learning in a more powerful way. Here in the epilogue we wish to come back to the whole, bring some of our ideas together, and focus once again on the main arguments of the book.

We argued again and again that experience forms the individual's awareness of the world around her, an experience being an internal relationship between the person and the world. We also argued again and again for experience as an object of empirical research, grounded in our observations that there is only a limited number of distinctly different ways in which people are capable of experiencing any of the things they meet.

To provide an analytical framework we characterized a "way of experiencing something"—which is the unit of our research—as comprising a structural and a referential aspect, the former being further analyzable into internal and external horizons. The variation in the different ways that people experience something can be understood in terms of the limited human capacity to discern and to be aware of diverse aspects of situations and phenomena at the same time. A particular way of experiencing something represents a combination of related aspects that are simultaneously present in a person's focal awareness.

Every experience is an experience of a situation and of one or more phenomena, the situation being the here and now of the experience and the phenomena transcending the particular experience. A situation can be experienced only in terms of the phenomena that transcend it and, vice versa, a phenomenon can be experienced only in terms of concrete situations.

Our prime interest is the *variation* in the ways in which people are capable of experiencing various situations or phenomena. This variation reflects *differences* in what aspects of the situation or phenomenon are discerned and simultaneously focal in awareness. By *aspect* we mean a dimension of variation—that which, once set in focus and no longer taken for granted, becomes potentially open to variation in awareness. If you become aware that something *is* in a certain way, then you also become aware that it *could be* in some other way. If a person has led such a sheltered life that he has never come across a language other than his native language, say English, then he could hardly be aware that his language is of a particular kind. He takes it for granted. It would take contact with another kind of language—Urdu, Japanese, Xhosa, or Finnish—to bring the person's own language into focus, to make that aspect or dimension of variation of his experience of language open to variation in awareness. That which is taken for granted is not capable of variation; that which is focal in awareness is.

The researcher may choose to study the variation in ways of experiencing a situation (or a kind of situation) or the variation in ways of experiencing phenomena. In either case, the variation found will reflect the variation in what is discerned and what is simultaneously focal in awareness. After all, the experience of situation and phenomenon is one experience, and it is the researcher who takes a stand to focus on one or the other.

The researcher defines her object of research by taking certain aspects of the whole experience for granted and letting others vary. A participant in a study is asked a question that focuses on the aspect of the phenomenon in which we are interested, and a number of transient features are introduced. If the answer falls outside the realm of our interest, we continue by directing the questioning back to its focus. When a child in a study we have taken up in this book was asked, "You have two kronor and an ice cream costs 9 kronor, so how many more kronor do you need?" it was his way of dealing with "$2 + \_ = 9$" that was of interest, and not the price of ice cream or choice of flavor or methods of paying. If he had answered "I'd rather buy some sweets," the interviewer simply would have recouched the problem in terms of sweets. The numerical aspect of the experience would remain the same, but the props would be allowed to vary. Thus we place constraints that are not negotiable. We define our object of research.

Having done that we try to be as open as possible to what might possibly relate to that object of research, constantly—if not consciously—questioning our own understanding of it. If a child answers the question with "9," we look askance at the answer to start with, but in the light of the variation we find in how other children reply we can see the problem from more and more perspectives until the answer "9" can be assigned a certain logic from that child's understanding of number. We look for variation in how subjects respond to or handle the questions we put; we look for all that could conceivably be relevant to our object of research; we look for ways in which our object of research could be experienced by our subjects that would enable them to respond in the ways they do. Again, the example on number that appears in several places in the book offers concrete examples of that.

Whether carrying out interviews or analyzing data, the object of research is central, but around it there is a constant variation and play. The perspectives that appear, the interpretations that come to mind, the inconsistencies that arise and later get resolved, all serve to make the object of research take on different appearances, because we are unable to be simultaneously aware of everything with the same degree of acuity. In other words, the researcher's awareness of the object of research time and again switches focus. The foreground keeps changing and one aspect becomes focal as a function of what other aspects are simultaneously in focal awareness. The focus changes, the boundaries shift, the object of research shimmers in the light of the study.

Thus the researcher's experience of conducting research is entirely in line with our view of human experience and human awareness, which is only to be expected in that the research we describe into learning is in itself a form of learning. We have described experience as an internal relationship between the person and the world, whether the child and the math problem, or the researcher and the object of research. Our experienced world is not in the head—that way Meno lies—but rather everywhere we are. Our experience projects itself into the world. The totality of our experience is our awareness, and that is constituted repeatedly in our neverending experiencing. The structure of awareness changes all the time, and so does our experienced world.

## WHY ARE SOME BETTER THAN OTHERS?

We opened up this book by pointing to the fact that people do things differently. Mostly they have learned to do them differently—some better, some worse—or they have learned differently—some better, some worse—to do them. That statement implies that we have criteria for judging the quality of what is being done, and learning is what can be said to have taken place if an individual improves performance relative to those criteria.

Can we make people better learners by finding out what it takes to learn? In the second paragraph of the book we declared that we believe we can. Eight chapters later, can we substantiate that claim: Have we found out what it takes to learn and can we use it to improve learning? We would like to argue that we have and that we can. Learning, as anything else, can be seen in a number of distinctively different ways. We suggest that an interesting and useful way of seeing it is as a change in someone's capability for experiencing something in certain ways. What we can do with something, what we can possibly know about something is contingent on what this something *is* for us, what *meaning* it has for us, how we can *experience* it. On such grounds we claim that the capability for experiencing X in a certain way—or in certain ways—is more fundamental than the capability for knowing something about X or the capability for doing something with X.

Experience, capability for experiencing, differences in capability for experiencing, finding out about differences in capability for experiencing were described in terms of systems of variation throughout the book. We pointed to different kinds of variation, ranging from dimensions of variation being aspects of the individual's experience of something to variation between persons on the same occasion and within persons on different occasions. Now, variation of this latter kind can be accounted for in terms of variation of the former kind because variation in how a phenomenon is experienced reflects the simultaneous presence of different aspects of the phenomenon in focal awareness. Again, the presence of a certain aspect implies that there is a dimension of variation corresponding to that aspect  as opposed to its being taken for granted. For an aspect of a phenomenon to be present in awareness it has to be *discerned* as an aspect, which implies awareness of potential variation, and it has to be seen as being *simultaneous* with other aspects of the phenomenon. Therefore, the capability for experiencing a phenomenon in a certain way can be understood in terms of discernment of aspects, simultaneity of discerned aspects, and potential for variation (as contrasted with taken-for-grant-edness) in discerned aspects of the phenomenon in question. The variation in how a certain phenomenon is experienced, between or within individuals, can thus be understood in terms of the different ways of experiencing it being different complexes of dimensions of variation.

Being aware of an aspect of a phenomenon is thus not being aware of an independent, free-floating aspect as such, but being aware of the phenomenon *in terms of* this aspect, possibly, probably, alongside other aspects. Awareness of the phenomenon of a body in motion can imply an awareness of such aspects as force, velocity, acceleration, equilibrium, frame of reference and so on. Being aware of frame of reference, for example, as an aspect of the phenomenon implies a potential for *varying* the frame of reference—shifting away from the otherwise taken-for-granted ground and considering the body from some other perspective. Discerning it as an aspect opens—and springs from—the potential for variation, and integrating it into the phenomenon simultaneously with other aspects gives the way in which it is experienced.

Sometimes an aspect of a phenomenon that should have been discerned is taken for granted, as we have illustrated in the case of frames of reference (Examples 5.11 and 8.10). The ground—that which is at rest—is such a self-evident frame of reference that it is neglected as such. The qualitatively different ways of experiencing a phenomenon originate in the set of aspects that are discerned.

Sometimes different aspects of a phenomenon are discerned but can not be handled simultaneously. Then they become separated due to the split in awareness. They are dealt with one at a time instead of simultaneously. This may be the case with the logical–mathematical and spatial features of maps drawn by young children (Example 5.12) or with the reading of hierarchically organized texts (Example 5.8). The different levels that are aspects of each other may appear as separate topics: first one, then another, then a third.

The aspects present in focal awareness and the relationships that pertain between them correspond to the structural aspect of an experience. The referential aspect—the global meaning of the phenomenon—derives from the structural aspect, and vice versa. By accounting for differences between different ways of experiencing a phenomenon in terms of the underlying[1] complex of aspects in awareness, we can understand why some *learn* better than others, why some *are* better than others—in certain situations, in relation to certain criteria. Thus we satisfy the first part of our claim: we have found out what it takes to learn.

Can we make use of it to bring about better learning? In chapter 8 we pointed to some of the ways in which we can make use of systems of variation in the name of pedagogy: By introducing or withholding variation in different combinations of dimensions, aspects may be discerned, become objects of focal awareness, separated, fused. Paying attention to the relevance structure of the learning situation and the way in which variation is designed, the teacher can be instrumental to the constitution of the learner's awareness of the phenomena being addressed.

The central theme of this book is that the way in which we experience a certain phenomenon, the specific meaning it has for us, is the most fundamental aspect of learning. Learning is learning to experience. Being good at something is to be capable of experiencing or understanding it in a certain way. The topic of this book, the phenomenon dealt with, is learning itself. To learn about it is, in accordance with what we argued on some 200 pages, to be capable of experiencing it in a certain way, and it is exactly the capability of experiencing learning in *this* particular way that we hope we have brought about.

ANGLO-EUROPEAN COLLEGE OF CHIROPRACTIC

---

[1]"Underlying," as used here, does not refer to another level of description than that of experience, neither to the subconscious, nor to the chemistry of the brain, for instance. It denotes layers of experience, less easily accessible to reflection, whether the learner's or the researcher's reflection.

# References

Ahlberg, A. (1992). *Att möta matematiska problem. En belysning av barns lärande* [Meeting mathematical problems. An illumination of children's learning]. Göteborg: Acta Universitatis Gothoburgensis.

Ahlberg, A., & Csocsán, E. (1994). Grasping numerosity among blind children. *Report from Department of Education and Educational Research,* Göteborg University, 4.

Alexandersson, M. (1994a). Focusing teacher consciousness: What do teachers direct their consciousness towards during their teaching? In I. Carlgren, G. Handal, & S. Vaage (Eds.), *Teachers' minds and actions: Research on teachers' thinking and practice* (pp. 139–149). London: Falmer Press.

Alexandersson, M. (1994b). *Metod och medvetande* [Method and consciousness]. Göteborg: Acta Universitatis Gothoburgensis.

Anderson, J. R., Pirolli, P., & Farrell, R. (1988). Learning to program recursive functions. In M. T. H. Chi, R. Glaser, & M. J. Farr (Eds.), *The nature of expertise* (pp. 153–183). Hillsdale, NJ: Lawrence Erlbaum Associates.

Andersson, B., & Renström, L. (1979). Temperatur och värme: Kokning [Temperature and heat: Boiling]. *Reports from Department of Teacher Education, 3,* Göteborg University

Andersson, E. (1978). *Bokstav i kunskapens hjärta.* [Letter in the heart of knowledge. Report from the project experiential learning and cognitive development]. *Rapport från projektet Upplevelseinlärning och kognitiv utveckling,* Department of Education, Göteborg University, 19.

Andersson, E., & Lawenius, M. (1983). *Lärares uppfattning av undervisning* [Teachers' conceptions of teaching]. Göteborg: Acta Universitatis Gothoburgensis.

Annerstedt, C. (1991). *Idrottslärarna och idrottsämnet* [Physical education and teachers in physical education].Göteborg: Acta Universitatis Gothoburgensis.

Ashton-Warner, S. (1963). *Teacher.* New York: Simon & Schuster.

Barnett, S. A. (1973). Homo docens. *Journal of Biosocial Science, 5,* 393–403.

Baxter Magolda, M. B. (1992). *Knowing and reasoning in college: Gender-related patterns in students' intellectual development.* San Francisco: Jossey-Bass.

Beaty, E. (1987). Understanding concepts in social science: Towards an effective strategy. *Instructional Science, 15,* 341–359.

Bereiter, C. (1985). Toward a solution of the learning paradox. *Review of Educational Research, 55,* 201–226.

Bergqvist, K., & Säljö, R. (1994). Conceptually blindfolded in the optics laboratory. Dilemmas of inductive learning. *European Journal of Psychology of Education, 2,* 149–158.

Biggs, J. B. (1979). Individual differences in study process and the quality of learning outcomes. *Higher Education, 8,* 381–394.

211

Biggs, J. B. (1990). *Approaches to learning in secondary and tertiary students in Hong Kong: Some comparative studies.* Paper presented at the seventh annual conference of the Hong Kong Educational Research Association, University of Hong Kong.

Booth, S. A. (1992a). *Learning to program: A phenomenographic perspective.* Göteborg: Acta Universitatis Gothoburgensis.

Booth, S. A. (1992b). The experience of learning to program. Example: Recursion. In F. Détienne (Ed.), 5 ème workshop sur la psychologie de la programmation, (pp. 122–145) Paris: INRIA.

Bowden, J., Dall'Alba, G., Martin, E., Masters, G., Laurillard, D., Marton, F., Ramsden, P., & Stephanou, A. (1992). Displacement, velocity, and frames of reference: Phenomenographic studies of students' understanding and some implications for teaching and assessment. *American Journal of Physics, 60,* 262–268.

Broady, D. (1981). *Den dolda läroplanen* [The hidden curriculum]. Stockholm: Symposion.

Brown, J. S., Collins, A., & Duguid, P. (1989). Situated cognition and the culture of learning. *Educational Researcher, 18,* 32–42.

Chaiklin, S., & Lave, J. (1993). *Understanding practice. Perspectives on activity and context.* Cambridge: Cambridge University Press.

Chomsky, N. (1957). *Syntactic structures.* The Hague: Mouton & Co.

Chomsky, N. (1959). Review of B. F. Skinner's "Verbal Behavior." *Language, 35,* 26–58.

Clancey, W. J. (1992, June). "Situated" Means coordinating without deliberation. Presented at the McDonell Foundation Conference "The Science of Cognition", Sante Fe, New Mexico.

Cobb, P. (1994). Where is the mind? Constructivist and socio-cultural perspectives on mathematics development. *Educational Researcher, 23,* 13–20.

Colaizzi, P. (1973). *Reflection and research in psychology: A phenomenological study of learning.* Duquesne: Kendall/Hunt.

Coombs, C. H. (1968). *The world educational crisis: A systems analysis.* New York: Oxford University Press.

Coombs, C. H. (1971). *Utbildningens världskris* [The world educational crisis: A systems analysis]. Stockholm: Bonniers.

Csocsán, E. (1988, July). Blind children's model of basic mathematical concepts. Paper presented at the ICME Conference, Budapest.

Dahlgren, G., Gustafsson, K., Mellgren, E., & Olsson, L.-E. (1993). *Barn upptäcker skriftspråket* [Children discover written language]. Stockholm: Liber Utbildning.

Dahlgren, G., & Olsson, L.-E. (1985). *Läsning i barnperspektiv.* Göteborg: Acta Universitatis Gothoburgensis. (The child's conception of reading)

Dahlgren, L. O. (1975). *Qualitative differences in learning as a function of content-oriented guidance.* Göteborg: Acta Universitatis Gothoburgensis.

Dahlgren, L. O. (1985). Higher education: Impact on students. In T. Husén & T. N. Postlethwaite (Eds.), *The International Encyclopedia of Education,* (pp. 2223–2226). Oxford: Pergamon Press.

Dahlgren, L. O. (1989). Fragments of an economic habitus. Conceptions of economic phenomena in freshmen and seniors. *European Journal of Psychology of Education, 4,* 547–558.

Day, J. M., (1994), Introduction. In J. M. Day (Ed.) *Plato's Meno in focus* (pp. 1–34). London: Routledge.

diSessa, A. A. (1993). Between brain and behavior: Response to Marton. *Cognition and Instruction, 10,* 261–280.

Driver, R. Asoko. H., Leach, J, Mortimer, E., & Scott, P. (1994). Constructing scientific knowledge in the classroom. *Educational Researcher, 23,* 5–12.

Ebbinghaus, H. (1964). Memory. A contributuion to experimental psychology. New York: Dover. (Original work published, 1885).

Eizenberg, N. (1988). Approaches to learning anatomy: Developing a programme for preclinical medical students. In P. Ramsden (Ed.), *Improving learning. New perspectives* (pp.. 178–198). London: Kogan Page.

Ekeblad, E. (1993). *Barn som pedagoger. Två sätt som sjuåringar använder för att lära en kamrat spela ett mattespel* [Children as pedagogues, Two ways that seven year olds teach a friend to play a maths game]. *Rapporter från Institutionen för pedagogik,* Göteborgs Universitet, *15.*

Ekeblad, E. (1994, March). *What's in a case? Conceptions of number in context.* Paper presented at the 22nd congress of the NFPF, Vasa.

Ekeblad, E. (1995, March). *First-grader's conceptions of "How you learn maths"*. Paper presented at the 23rd congress of the NFPF, Aarhus.

Ekeblad, E., Lindahl, M., Lindström, B., Marton, F., & Packendorff, M. (1996). *The development of number-sense in a computerized learning environment*. Unpublished manuscript, Institutionen för pedagogik, Göteborgs Universitet.

Ekeblad, E., & Lindström, B. (1995, August). *The role of phenomenographic research in the design of instructional computer applications for number concepts*. Paper presented at the 6th European Conference for Research on Learning and Instruction, Nijmegen, The Netherlands.

Entwistle, N. (1976). The verb "to learn" takes the accusative. Editorial introduction to symposium: Learning processes and strategies—I. *British Journal of Educational Psychology, 46*, 1–3

Entwistle, N. (1984). Contrasting perspectives on learning. In F. Marton, D. Hounsell, & N. Entwistle (Eds.), *The experience of learning* (pp. 1–18). Edinburgh: Scottish Academic Press.

Entwistle, N., & Marton, F. (1994). Knowledge objects: Understandings constituted through intensive academic study. *British Journal of Educational Psychology, 64*, 161–178.

Eriksson, R., & Neuman, D. (1981). *Räknesvaga elevers matematikundervisning under de sex första skolåren*. [Mathematics teaching for children weak in maths during the first six school years]. Unpublished manuscript, Department of Education, Göteborg University.

Feldman, D. H. (1980). *Beyond universals in cognitive development*. Norwood, NJ: Ablex.

Fensham, P., & Marton, F. (1991). *High-school teachers' and university chemists' differing conceptualizations of the personal activity in constituting knowledge in chemistry*. Department of Education and Educational Research, Göteborg University, 1.

Feynman, R. P., Leighton, R. B., & Sands, M. (1963). *The Feynman lectures on physics. Vol 1*. Reading, MA: Addison-Wesley.

Gardner, H. (1987). *The mind's new science*. New York: Basic Books.

Gibbs, G., Morgan, A., & Taylor, E. (1984). The world of the learner. In F. Marton, D. Hounsell, & N. Entwistle (Eds.), *The experience of learning* (pp.. 165–188). Edinburgh: Scottish Academic Press.

Giorgi, A. (1986). *A phenomenological analysis of descriptions of concepts of learning obtained from a phenomenographic perspective*. Publikationer från institutionen för pedagogik, Göteborgs universitet, 18.

Glaser, B., & Strauss, A. (1967). *The discovery of grounded theory*. Chicago, IL: Aldine.

Gurwitsch, A. (1964). *The field of consciousness*. Pittsburgh: Duquesne University Press.

Gustafsson, B., Stigebrant, E., & Ljungvall, R. (1981). *Den dolda läroplanen* [The hidden curriculum]. Stockholm: Liber.

Halldén, O. (1994). On the paradox of understanding history in an educational setting. In G. Leinhardt, I. L. Beck, & C. Stainton (Eds.), *Teaching and learning in history* (pp. 27–46). Hillsdale, NJ: Lawrence Erlbaum Associates.

Hashisaki, J. (1985). Set theory. In *The New Encyclopedia Britannica* (15th ed., Vol 27, pp. 238–244). Chicago: Encyclopedia Britannica Inc.

Hasselgren, B. (1981). *Ways of apprehending children at play: A study of pre-school student teachers' development*. Göteborg: Acta Universitatis Gothoburgensis.

Helmstad, G., & Marton, F. (1992, April). *Conceptions of understanding*. Paper presented at the annual meeting of the American Educational Research Association, San Francisco, Ca.

Henderson, P. B., & Romero, F. J. (1989). *Teaching recursion as a problem-solving tool using Standard ML*. Paper presented at 20th SIGCSE Technical Symposium on Computer Science Education, Louisville, KY.

Hofstadter, D. R. (1979). *Gödel, Escher, Bach: An eternal golden braid*. London: The Harvester Press

Hounsell, D. (1984). Learning and essay-writing. In F. Marton, D. Hounsell, & N. Entwistle (Eds.), *The experience of learning* (pp. 103–123). Edinburgh: Scottish Academic Press.

Hutchins, E. (1995). *Cognition in the wild*. Cambridge, MA: MIT Press.

Johansson, B. (1975). *Aritmetikundervisning: En rapport om en datainsamling*. [The teaching of arithmetic]. Reports from Pump-project, Department of Education, Göteborg University, 9.

Johansson, B., Marton, F., & Svensson, L. (1985). An approach to describing learning as a change between qualitatively different conceptions. In A. L. Pines & T. H. West (Eds.), *Cognitive structure and conceptual change* (pp. 233–257). New York: Academic Press.

Jönsson, L., Linell, P., & Säljö, R. (1991). Formulating the past: Remembering in the police interrogation. *Activity Theory, 9/10*, 5–11.

Katona, G. (1940). *Organizing and memorizing.* New York: Columbia University Press.

Keller, H. (1908). *The story of my life.* New York: Doubleday.

Kember, D., & Gow, L. (1991). A challenge to the anecdotal stereotype of the Asian learner. *Studies in Higher Education, 16,* 117–128.

Korovessis, P. (1970). *Metoden.* [The method]. Stockholm: Rabén & Sjögren.

Kroksmark, T. (1987). *Fenomenografisk didaktik* [Phenomenographic didactics]. Göteborg: Acta Universitatis Gothoburgensis.

Kullberg, B. (1991). *Learning to learn to read.* Göteborg: Acta Universitatis Gothoburgensis.

Laurillard, D. (1995, May). *Understanding representations.* Paper presented at the symposium Understanding Understanding II, University of Edinburgh.

Lave, J. (1988). *Cognition in practice.* Cambridge, UK: Cambridge University Press.

Lindahl, M. (1996). *Inlärning och Erfarande. Ettåringars möte med förskolans värld* [Learning and Experiencing. One-year-olds' encounters with the world of preschool]. Göteborg: Acta Universitatis Gothoburgensis.

Lundgren, U. P. (1977). Model analysis of pedagogical processes. *Studies in education and psychology, 2.* Stockholm: Institute of Education.

Luria, A. R. (1979). *The making of mind: A personal account of Soviet psychology.* Cambridge, MA: Harvard University Press.

Lybeck, L. (1981). *Arkimedes i klassen. En ämnespedagogisk berättelse* [Archimedes in the class-room]. Göteborg: Acta Universitatis Gothoburgensis.

Lybeck, L., Marton, F., Strömdahl, H., & Tullberg, A. (1988). The phenomenography of "the mole concept" in chemistry. In P. Ramsden (Ed.), *Improving learning: New perspectives* (pp. 81–108). London: Kogan Page.

Martin, E., & Ramsden, P. (1987). Learning skills, or skill in learning. In I. T. E. Richardsson, M. W. Eysenck, & D. W. Piper (Eds.), *Student learning* (pp. 155–167). Milton Keynes: Open University Press.

Marton, F. (1970). *Structural dynamics of learning.* Stockholm: Almqvist & Wiksell.

Marton, F. (1974). *Inlärning och studiefärdighet* [Study skills and learning]. *Rapporter från Pedagogiska institutionen.* Göteborgs Universitet, nr 121.

Marton, F. (1976). On non-verbatim learning. IV: Some theoretical and methodological notes. *Scandinavian Journal of Psychology, 17,* 125–128.

Marton, F. (1978). *Describing conceptions of the world around us. Reports from the Institute of Education.* Göteborg University, no 66

Marton, F. (1981). Phenomenography—describing conceptions of the world around us. *Instructional Science, 10,* 177–200.

Marton, F. (1986). Vad är fackdidaktik? [What is pedagogical content knowledge?]. In F. Marton (Ed.), *Fackdidaktik I* (pp. 15–78). Lund: Studentlitteratur.

Marton, F. (1992). Phenomenography and "the art of teaching all things to all men." *International Journal of Qualitative Studies in Education, 5,* 253–267.

Marton, F. (1993). Phenomenography. In T. Husén & T. N. Postlethwaite (Eds.) *The International Encyclopedia of Education* (2nd ed. pp. 4424–4429). Oxford: Pergamon Press.

Marton, F. (1994). On the structure of teachers' awareness. In I. Carlgren, G. Handal, & S. Vaage (Eds.), *Teachers' minds and actions: Research on teachers' thinking and practice* (pp.. 28–42). London: Falmer Press.

Marton, F., Asplund-Carlsson, M., & Halász, L. (1992). Differences in understanding and the use of reflective variation in reading. *British Journal of Educational Psychology, 62,* 1–16.

Marton, F., Asplund-Carlsson, M., & Halász, L. (1994). The reverse effect of an attempt to shape reader awareness. *Scandinavian Journal of Educational Research, 38,* 291–298.

Marton, F., Dealy, E., & Dall'Alba, G. (1993). Conceptions of learning. *International Journal of Educational Research, 19,* 277–300.

Marton, F., Dahlgren, L. O., Svensson, L., & Säljö, R. (1977). *Inlärning och omvärldsuppfattning* [Learning and conceptions of reality]. Stockholm: Almqvist & Wiksell.

Marton, F., Dall'Alba, G., & Tse, L. K. (1992, January). *Solving the paradox of the Asian learner.* Paper presented at the fourth Asian Regional Congress of Cross-Cultural Psychology, Kathmandu, Nepal.

Marton, F., Fensham, P., & Chaiklin, S. (1994). A Nobel's eye view of scientific intution: Discussions with the Nobel prize-winners in Physics, Chemistry, and Medicine (1970–1986). *International Journal of Science Education, 16*, 457–473.

Marton, F., & Säljö, R. (1976a). On qualitative differences in learning I—Outcome and process. *British Journal of Educational Psychology, 46*, 4–11.

Marton, F., & Säljö, R. (1976b). On qualitative differences in learning II—Outcome as a function of the learner's conception of the task. *British Journal of Educational Psychology, 46*, 115–127.

Marton, F., & Säljö, R. (1976c). Utveckling är inlärning är utveckling [Development is learning is development]. *Forskning om utbildning, 3*, 6–14

Marton, F., Watkins, D., & Tang, C. (in press). Discontinuities and continuities in the experience of learning: An interview study of high-school students in Hong Kong. *Learning and Instruction,*.

Marton, F., Wen, Q., & Nagle A. (in press). Views on learning in different cultures. Comparing patterns in China and Uruguay. *Anales de Psicologia.*

Marton, F., & Wenestam, C.-G. (1988). Qualitative differences in retention when a text is read several times. In M. M. Gruneberg, P. E. Morris, & R. N. Sykes (Eds.), *Practical aspects of memory: Current research and issues* (Vol. 2, pp. 370–376) Chichester: Wiley.

Mathews, M. H. (1992). *Making sense of place: Children's understanding of large-scale environments.* Hemel Hempstead: Harvester Wheatsheaf.

Mugler, F., & Landbeck, R. (1994, November). Student learning at the University of the South Pacific: A pilot study. In R. Ballantyne, & C. Bruce (Eds.), *Proceedings Phenomenography, Philosophy & Practice Conference* Brisbane.

Nagle, A., & Marton, F. (1993, August-September). *Learning, knowing and understanding. Qualitative changes in student teachers' views of the relationship between some educational phenomena during the first term of pre-school teacher education in Uruguay.* Paper presented at the fifth European Association for Research on Learning and Instruction Conference in Aix en Provence.

Neuman, D. (1987). *The origin of arithmetic skills: A phenomenographic approach.* Göteborg: Acta Universitatis Gothoburgensis.

Neuman, D. (1989). *Räknefärdighetens rötter* [The roots of arithmetic skills]. Stockholm: Utbildningsförlaget.

Neuman, D. (1994, July-August). *Five fingers on one hand and ten on the other: A case study in learning through interaction.* Proceeding of the 18th PME Conference. Lissabon, Portugal.

Newton, I. (1686). Principia (Philosophiae Naturalis Principia Mathematica). London, UK: Royal Society.

Patrick, K. (1992, November). *Teachers and curriculum at year 12: Constructing an object of study.* Paper presented at the joint conference of the Australian Association for Research in Education and the New Zealand Association for Research in Education, Deaking University, Geelong, Victoria.

Pavlov, I. P. (1927). *Conditioned reflexes* (G. V. Anrep, Trans.). London: Oxford University Press.

Penrose, R. (1989). *The emperor's new mind: Concerning computers, minds and the laws of physics.* Oxford: Oxford University Press.

Perry, W. G. (1970). *Forms of intellectual and ethical development in the college years: A scheme.* New York: Holt, Rinehart & Winston.

Petrie, H. G. (1981). *The dilemma of enquiry and learning.* Chicago: The University of Chicago Press.

Piaget, J. (1907). Un moineau albinos [An albino sparrow] *Organe du Club Jurassien, 41*, 36.

Piaget, J., & Garcia, R. (1991). *Toward a logic of meanings.* Hillsdale, NJ: Lawrence Erlbaum Associates.

Piaget, J., & Inhelder, B. (1948). *The child's conception of number.* London: Routledge & Kegan Paul.

Pramling, I. (1983). *The child's conception of learning.* Göteborg: Acta Universitatis Gothoburgensis.

Pramling, I. (1986). The origin of the child's idea of learning through practice. *European Journal of Education, 3*, 31–46.

Pramling, I. (1990). *Learning to learn.* New York: Springer Verlag.

Pramling, I. (1994). *Kunnandets grunder* [The foundations of knowing]. Göteborg: Acta Universitatis Gothoburgensis.

Pramling, I. (1996). Understanding and empowering the child. In D. Olson, & N. Torrance (Eds.), *Handbook of education and human development: New models of learning, teaching and schooling.* Oxford: Blackwell.

Pramling, I., Klerfelt, A., & Williams Graneld, P. (1995). Först var det roligt, sen' blev det tråkigt och sen' vande man sig ... : Barns möte med skolans värld [It's fun at first, then it gets boring, and then you get used to it ... : Children meet the world of school]. *Rapporter från Institutionen för metodik i lärarutbildningen, Göteborgs universitet, 9.*

Pramling, I., & Mårdsjö, A-C. (1994). *Att utveckla kunnandets grunder* [Developing the foundations of knowing]. *Rapporter från Institutionen för metodik i lärarutbildningen, Göteborgs universitet, 7.*

Premack, D. (1984). Pedagogy and aesthetics as sources of culture. In M. S. Gazzaniga (Ed.), *Handbook of cognitive neuroscience* (pp. 15–35). New York: Plenum Press.

Prosser, M. (1994). Some experiences of using phenomenographic research methodology in the context of research in teaching and learning. In J. A. Bowden, & E. Walsh (Eds.), *Phenomenographic research: Variations in Method. The Warburton Symposium* (pp.. 31–43). Melbourne: RMIT.

Prosser, M., & Millar, R. (1989). The "How" and the "What" of learning physics. *European Journal of Psychology of Education, 4,* 513–528.

Renström, L. (1988). *Conceptions of matter: A phenomenographic approach.* Göteborg: Acta Universitatis Gothoburgensis.

Renström, L., Andersson, B., & Marton, F., (1990). Students' conceptions of matter. *Journal of Educational Psychology, 82,* 555–569.

Roche, J. (1988). Newton's *Principia.* In J. Fauvel, R. Flood, M. Shortland, & R. Wilson, (Eds.), *Let Newton be! A new perspective on his life and works* (pp. 43–61). Oxford: Oxford University Press.

Rogoff, B. (1990). *Apprenticeship in thinking. Cognitive development in social contexts.* New York: Oxford University Press.

Roth, K. J., & Anderson, C. W. (1988). Promoting conceptual change learning from science textbooks. In P. Ramsden (Ed.), *Improving learning: New perspectives* (pp. 109–141). London: Kogan Page.

Russell, R., & Ginsburg, H. P. (1984). Cognitive analysis of children's mathematical difficulties. *Cognition and Instruction, 1,* 217–244.

Ryle, G. (1949). *The concept of mind.* London: Hutchinson.

Säljö, R. (1975). *Qualitative differences in learning as a function of the learner's conception of the task.* Göteborg: Acta Universitatis Gothoburgensis.

Säljö, R. (1979). Learning in the learner's perspective. I. Some common-sense conceptions. *Reports from the Department of Education,* Göteborg University, No. 76.

Säljö, R. (1982). *Learning and understanding: A study of differences in constructing meaning from a text.* Göteborg: Acta Universitatis Gothoburgensis.

Säljö, R. (1994). Minding action. Conceiving the world versus participating in cultural practices. *Nordisk Pedagogik, 14,* 71–80.

Sandberg, J. (1994). *Human competence at work. An interpretative approach.* Göteborg: BAS

Seuss, Dr. (1966). *Cat in the hat.* New York: Beginner Press.

Skinner, B. F. (1953). *Science and human behavior.* New York: Macmillan.

Skinner, B. F. (1957). *Verbal behavior.* Englewood Cliffs, NJ: Prentice-Hall.

Smedslund, J. (1970). Circular relation between understanding and logic. *Scandinavian Journal of Psychology, 11,* 217–219.

Spiegelberg, H. (1982). *The phenomenological movement: A historical introduction* (3rd ed.). The Hague: Martinus Nijhoff.

Steffe, L. P. (1991). The learning paradox: A plausible counterexample. In L. P. Steffe (Ed.), *Epistemological foundations of mathematical experience* (pp. 26–44). New York: Springer.

Stelmach, M. Z. (1991, July). An application of student learning research in medical education. Paper presented at the annual conference of the Australian and New Zeeland Association for Medical Education, The University of Melbourne, Carlton, Victoria.

Still, A., & Costall, A. (1987). Introduction: In place of cognitivism. In A. Costall & A. Still (Eds.), *Cognitive psychology in question* (pp. 1–16). Brighton: Harvester Press.

Strömdahl, H. (1996). *On mole and amount of substance: A study of the dynamics of concept formation and concept attainment.* Göteborg: Acta Universitatis Gothoburgensis.

Sundqvist, R. (1993). *Didaktiskt tänkande: En studie om uppfattningar av undervisning* [Pedagogical thinking. A study of conceptions of teaching]. Unpublished licentiate thesis, Åbo Akademi, Vasa, Finland.

Svensson, L. (1976). *Study skill and learning.* Göteborg: Acta Universitatis Gothoburgensis.

Svensson, L. (1977). On qualitative differences in learning: III. Study skill and learning. *British Journal of Educational Psychology, 47,* 233–243.

Svensson, L. (1984a). *Människobilden i INOM-gruppens forskning: Den lärande människan* {The image of man in the research of the INOM-group: Man as learner]. *Reports from the Department of Education and Educational Research, Göteborg University, 3.*

Svensson, L. (1984b). Skill in learning. In F. Marton, D. Hounsell, & N. J. Entwistle (Eds.), *The experience of learning* (pp. 56–70). Edinburgh: Scottish Academic Press.

Svensson, L. (1989). The conceptualization of cases of physical motion. *European Journal of Psychology of Education, 4,* 529–545.

Székely, L. (1950). Productive processes in learning and thinking. *Acta Psychologica, 7,* 379–407.

Taylor, E., & Morgan, A. R. (1986, April). *Developing skill in learning.* Paper presented at AERA annual conference, San Francisco.

Theman, J. (1983). *Uppfattningar av politisk makt* [Conceptions of political power]. Göteborg: Acta Universitatis Gothoburgensis.

Torney-Purta, J. (1990). International comparative research in education: Its role in educational improvement in the US. *Educational Researcher, 19,* 32–35.

Trigwell, K., Prosser, M., & Taylor, P. (1994). A phenomenographic study of adademics' conceptions of science learning and teaching. *Learning and Instruction, 4,* 217–232.

Tronström, G. (1984). Efter tio år började jag förstå ... [After ten years I started to understand... ]. *KRUT, 2,* 28–30.

Ueno, N., Arimoto, N., & Fujita, G. (1990, April*). Conceptual models and points of view: Learning via making a new stage.* Paper presented at the annual conference AERA, Boston.

van Rossum, E. J., & Schenk, S. M. (1984). The relationship between learning conception, study strategy and learning outcome. *British Journal of Educational Psychology, 54,* 73–83.

Vera, A. H., & Simon, H. A. (1993). Situated action: A symbolic interpretation. *Cognitive Science, 17,* 7–48.

von Glasersfeld, E. (1990). Environment and communication. In L.Steffe & T. Wood (Eds.), *Transforming children's mathematics education: International perspectives* (pp. 30–38). Hillsdale, NJ: Lawrence Erlbaum Associates.

Watson, J. B. (1924). *Behaviorism.* New York: Norton.

Wenestam, C.-G. (1978). *Horisontalisering: Ett sätt att missuppfatta det man läser* [Horizontalization. A way of misunderstanding a text]. Reports from the Department of Education, Göteborg university, 157.

Werner, H. (1948). *Comparative psychology of mental development.* New York: International Universies Press.

Wertheimer, M. (1945). *Productive thinking.* New York: Harper & Row.

Wertsch. J. V. (1985). *Vygotsky and the Social Formation of Mind.* Cambridge, MA: Harvard University Press.

Wertsch, J. V., Minick, N., & Arns, F. J. (1984). The creation of context in joint problem solving. In B. Rogoff & J. Lave (Eds.), *Everyday cognition, Its development in social change contexts* (pp.. 151–171). Cambridge, MA: Harvard University Press.

White, N. D. (1994). Inquiry. In J. M. Day (Ed.), *Plato's Meno in focus* (pp. 152–171). London: Routledge.

Wikström, Å. (1987). *Functional programming using Standard ML.* Hemel Hempstead: Prentice-Hall.

Wistedt, I. & Martinsson, M. (1994). *Kvaliteter i elevers tänkande över en oändlig decimalutveckling* [Qualities in how children think about an endlessly repeating decimal]. Rapporter från Stockholms universitet, Pedagogiska institutionen.

# Author Index

# Subject Index